Boxer

Boxer

The Life of a Cumbria Great

Mike Gardner

The authorised biography of
Arnold 'Boxer' Walker

Scrum-half:
Kells, Workington Town, Whitehaven,
Cumbria, England and Great Britain

YOUCAXTON PUBLICATIONS
OXFORD & SHREWSBURY

ISBN 978-1-911175-58-2

Cover design: *Jolly Good Design, Cheltenham*
Marketing: Mike and Lesley Gardner.

Page design: YouCaxton Publications
enquiries@youcaxton.co.uk

This book is dedicated to my
brother-in-law Les,
who did so much to make
me the player I was
and the person I am.

Arnold 'Boxer' Walker

Arnold 'Boxer' Walker played 274 professional games for Workington Town, Whitehaven, Cumbria, England and Great Britain. He skippered Cumbria to two county championships and a rare 9-3 win over New Zealand in 1980. In the background is his great friend Ralph Calvin.

Contents

What They Said

Boxer is Mike Gardner's second book about a rugby league player. His first on Willie Horne was a master-piece. I have had the pleasure and privilege of proof-reading both books. As players Arnie Walker and Willie Horne had plenty in common but as personalities, they could not have been more different – and Mike's books are completely different from other rugby league books, thank goodness. It's not the tries or the goals or the matches that matter most for Mike. It's the honest portrayal of the person – the good, the bad and the plain ugly; the sunshine and the darkness.

*Robert Gate – historian and author of
more than 25 books on rugby league*

As someone who has read countless books about rugby league and its players, both for research and purely for pleasure, I can say without hesitation this biography is right up there with the very best. Anyone who read the author's wonderful tribute to the legendary Willie Horne will not be disappointed with this hugely entertaining story of another far north western folk hero.

Steve Andrews – Barrow Rugby League Club historian and author

Arnold 'Boxer' Walker is one of the most outstanding players, and colourful characters, that Cumbrian rugby league has ever produced.

During those glory years, and the times after the limelight subsides, there is a riveting story waiting to be told, capturing all the emotions in a way, I believe, that could only have been captured by Mike Gardner.

The result is a book that goes well beyond the achievements of one of our greatest rugby league players. It is a reflection of the game during this era, and a personal insight into the highs and the lows that fame can produce.

Quite simply it's a must read, if only to find out what happened on the infamous trip to Benidorm after Town's Lancashire Cup victory.

Dave Bowden – Former Workington Town chairman

Mention the name Boxer in West Cumbria, especially in sporting circles, and it is instantly synonymous with only one person – Arnold Walker, a superb rugby league player and an almost equally, if that's possible, wonderful one-off character. The story of his life on and off the rugby field was dying to be told, so well done to Mike Gardner for telling it in such illuminating and at times stark detail – truly warts and all.

What makes this book so appealing (not just the rugby) was the way in which it is so deeply evocative of what life was really like in Whitehaven, Arnold's home town, where times could be hard but the community spirit high, especially at Kells, the mining village where he grew up and which helped forge that gritty and often mischievous character.

I often referred to him as the Little Big Man for his ferocious spirit, so *Boxer, The Life of a Rugby Great*, will stand tall on my own book shelves. A special book about a very special player.

Alan Irving – *former sports editor, Whitehaven News*

It is quite simple, as soon as I saw him, within two minutes I knew he had IT, and I want to emphasise the capital letters. I know that is very brief but it sums Arnold up perfectly. He was a genius and a tough kid

Even at 19, he had everything. I think of him as a George Best – how can you improve someone like him. You couldn't tell George how to play and that's how I will always think of Boxer.

Harry Whitaker – *scrum half, Hawick, Workington Town and York*

The abiding memory is of a sudden roar from the terraces as yet another grudge match between Barrow and Workington detonates just in front of the Craven Park popular side and at the heart of the melee stands a blond, slight figure in a Town jersey swinging punches like Rocky Marciano in a title fight.

The hardest field game in the world has spawned more than its share of colourful characters, but there will only ever be one Boxer Walker.

Now the life and times of this revered west Cumbrian mighty atom have been crafted into a top-notch page-turner by prizewinning author Mike Gardner and I cannot recommend this book highly enough.

Frank Cassidy – *Former North West Evening Mail Sports Editor*

I have known Boxer since we first played primary school football against each other on Kells Welfare – he was a tough competitor even then and instantly recognisable with his mop of blond hair. As he grew up into one of the best scrum-halves in rugby league, his charisma shone through. I always remembered him as the little lad on the Welfare, and nobody could know how delighted I was to choose him as the number one scrum-half in the first World Ratings, and how proud of him I was when he finally got to play for Great Britain and England. Boxer's story became one of great sporting drama, followed by no little human drama as he battled the impact of his career-ending injury. That story has been told so well by author Mike Gardner in this book, a moving story that reminds us vividly of a different age in a vastly different world, as lads like Boxer spent their weeks working down the pit and emerged on the weekend as local heroes on the rugby field. All had dreams of being a star, but few shone as brightly as Boxer.

Harry Edgar – Rugby League publisher

Boxer has a wonderful tale to tell, and Mike Gardner is the perfect writer to tell it. One of a select band of a greats, equally respected at Workington and rivals Whitehaven, Boxer's compelling story transports the reader back to the glory days of West Cumbria Rugby League. Just like Boxer himself, this book is a knockout.

Martin Morgan – Former Sports Editor, Whitehaven News

Boxer had a heart as big as a lion and he is right up there with the greatest scrum halves ever. What a tackler he was – it was like having another forward on the field. I loved playing with him because you know he would never let you down, even if the rest of us were having an off day, he would always give 100 per cent.

Jim Mills – prop forward, Widnes, Bradford Northern, Halifax, Workington Town, Wales and Great Britain

Boxer was a player with great style and he was a pleasure to coach. He never gave me any trouble at all. We had a bit of banter which was expected and I enjoyed that too. He never gave me a single problem, not once. Boxer was in the thick of everything all the time. We have always respected each other. When he first came to Haven everything I wanted he did and I loved working with him.

Phil Kitchin – *stand-off, Whitehaven, Workington,*
Cumbria and Great Britain

Boxer is one of the best scrum halves in the history of the game. He was an unbelievable player and if I was picking a team he would be the first name down. He was so fearless and such a good tackler. The best thing about Boxer is what a great person he is. After every game we played against each other, when I went to the bar, he was always there waiting to buy me a pint.

Reg Bowden – *scrum half, Widnes, Fulham,*
Warrington and Lancashire

Paul Charlton, who scored 227 career tries as a world-class full back for Workington Town, Salford, Blackpool, Cumbria, England and Great Britain. 'If Boxer was playing in the Super League today, he would be the best scrum half in Great Britain and one of the best in the world,' says Paul.

Foreword

By Paul Charlton
Full Back – Workington Town, Salford, Blackpool Borough, Cumberland,
England and Great Britain

I am honoured to say a few words about my special friend Boxer Walker – what a player and what a man. I want to start by telling you a story about the only time I was sent off in my career – and remember, I played more than 700 games in 20 years.

I was playing for Workington Town at Widnes and the story involves their hooker, Keith Elwell, who had played for England. I remember it quite clearly - it happened on the halfway line. Boxer had the ball and he ended up getting elbowed from the side by Elwell. He just cleaned Boxer out - he levelled him. Boxer was on the floor and I had seen everything.

I just flew in and belted Elwell - I was just going to hit him again and I could feel this big arm on my shoulder. I looked around and it was Big Jim Mills and he was saying: "Paul, don't do it," in his Welsh voice, I think the referee was Peter Geraghty. We had a bit of a scuffle on the floor and the referee came in and said: "Come here, Paul. You're off."

Boxer has always been a special mate. I know he would have done the same for me. He would have backed me up. We have known each other for a long time. He was a fantastic player and he would admit himself that he could be a nasty player. He was a cocky little bugger. Yet, he is very humble about what he has achieved in the game.

We go way back to when I was playing full back for Kells. I remember well, Boxer's father Duncan, he was just like Boxer, a character but a good man. Duncan did a lot for Kells, alongside Jim and Madge Kitchin. They were at every game. Boxer was on the football field one day - I think he was around 10-years-old – and I was practising kicking goals, although I was never very good at it.

He would run and pick the balls up for me and I would say to him: 'Get behind the sticks, little fella.' That is how I first got to know him. And then he started coming through the ranks as a Kells player.

I had been transferred to Salford when Boxer signed for Town and we played against each other a few times early in his career. I remember thinking right away to myself: 'This kid's got something. He looked the part and he wasn't out of place.' I was at my prime then. It was obvious that he could be a bit of a terrier in those games and though his football skills had to develop, I knew he had great potential and I wasn't surprised when Boxer went on to achieve great things.

I knew he would - you could see it, even at that age. Mind you, the international selectors weren't fair to Boxer. He was so good he should have played a lot more times for Great Britain and he would definitely have done a great job for the side. That was a shock, him not getting picked more, and it has always been a disappointment to me.

When I came back to Workington, Boxer was the lynchpin of the team. He would stick his nose into anybody's business and just get on with the job. Any team in the league would have loved to have had Boxer in their side. He always gave 100 per cent and would never take a backward step. He was very, very skilful. And what a defensive player. He just had a special knack of knocking down those big men. He just seemed to grab hold of a shirt and a shoulder. Looking back, I still can't figure out how he did it. He had his own way and it worked every time. A few times I thought a player had got past Boxer but then he seemed to always end up on the ground. No one ever got past him, no matter how big they were. And another thing that made him so important to Town was the fact that Boxer hardly ever missed a game, he was never injured.

He was such a good player that he could play off the cuff – no one knew what he was going to do. Yet he always played for the team and if I called a set play he would follow everything perfectly, if that was what I had wanted. He was easy to play with. I remember he had a great sidestep and off either foot so he was really good at making breaks. And in that great Town team we had plenty of speed outside, we had a lot of guys with lots of pace to finish his break off, like Ian Wright, who was a cracking player and very quick. They would all follow Boxer knowing they would get the ball at just the right time. He never let me down, never, not once. He would play until he dropped and he often played with an injury, that's just the sort of guy he was and that's one of the big things he brought to Workington Town, that great team spirit we always had and he was a central part of that.

Before a match, Boxer was always very jovial - until around 20 minutes before the kick-off and then, all of a sudden, he would change and put his game head on. Not every player can do that. Some of the lads could worry for a week before the game but guys like Arnold would go out the night before and turn up and give you a good game.

Boxer was a very consistent scrum-half. I don't think I can ever remember him having a bad game. He was a very steady player and as a coach that's what you always want. When I came back to Town from Salford as player-coach, Eddie Bowman and Les Gorley, two of the club's senior players, came to me and told me that they had a very important message for me from the entire team. They said they were representing all the players and that everyone wanted me to know that they were all happy that I was there and everyone was going to play their guts out for me. Later that year we won the Lancashire Cup for the first time.

Some of the Super League teams from today wouldn't have lived with that Town side. I am certain about that. We wouldn't have played a structured game - we would have thrown the ball around. Today's game can get boring. If Boxer was playing in the Super League he would be the best scrum half in Great Britain and one of the best in the world. He was a character - he had something about him, something magical and unpredictable. He would never give in, no matter what the score was - he'd just keep going right up until the final whistle. It was so good to have him in the Town team.

If Boxer had ever left Workington for a bigger club he would have been a big success but I guess his heart was always in Cumbria.

I remember when he got his serious back injury - I was at that game and I was really frightened for him. Yet he was never bitter. Players get injured and sometimes very badly and Boxer just accepted it as part of the game. He was always someone who enjoyed a joke. I remember one day I was training at Town and I said to the lads that I fancied a curly perm. Boxer and Derek McMillan, who were great mates, said that I would never do it. Well, the next week I got the perm and my hair was a disgrace. When I walked into the changing rooms, Boxer just burst out laughing along with the whole team. They started calling me Shirley Temple. I felt like an idiot and I got it all cut off the following week. It was just before a cup final if I remember correctly.

Apart from his ability on the field, I want to tell you how important our friendship has been. I am delighted to have known and played with Boxer and I know he feels the same way about me. We have had a lot of fun and played a few jokes on each other over the years - that's one of the ways we bonded so tightly together.

There were two sides to him. He was a winner and he was so aggressive. He didn't back down for anyone. Never. I remember in the Lancashire Cup Final that we won, one of their players head-butted him. Boxer just got up off the floor, stared at him and all it did was fire him up. He would talk to opposing players to get in their heads but no one could get through to him. He was too strong and too determined. All the Town players we played with were like that. We had a mean streak in us and Arnold, as the scrum-half, was right in the thick of it all the time. He was a big star for Workington.

To think we go back to when Boxer was just 10-years-old and picking the ball up for me when I was training at Kells. There's always been something special between us, something locked in there. I know he enjoyed helping me on the field at Kells when he was just a kid. It just happened. I can't put it into words – there was a bond between us.

The best way to describe it is to say that we would fight for each other and always be there for each other. If we had to go to war, me and Boxer would be there, standing together first in the line. We would die for each other. That's the bond we have and not only with each other but with the odd other special person and family. That's how much Arnold means to me. You couldn't wish to meet a nicer person.

Boxer would have been a revelation if ever he had played in Australia. It would have improved him and it would have been great for him to experience another culture. Let's face it - he's never really been out of Whitehaven, has he? He has lived there all his life.

Looking back on my time in rugby league, our Lancashire Cup win in 1977 is right up there as one of the highlights of my career. Every

one of us gave 100 per cent - there were no show ponies in that team
- everyone worked and the whole team wanted to do well. A lot of us
grew up together and that was a big part of it. No one gave us a chance
of beating Wigan. The guys were special and it was an amazing day.
For me to be skipper of these lads was such an honour. And, of course,
Boxer was a big part of that win.

Boxer, it was an honour to play with you – you were a great player
and you will always be a very special friend.

Introduction

By Mike Gardner

Arnold 'Boxer' Walker and his teams of rugby league heroes lit up the stadiums of northern England 40 years ago. You are about to join him on a bumpy journey, sharing his memories of an amazing life. You will learn about a forgotten world, when he first began playing rugby as a small child in the streets of Kells, a poor working class district, high up on the cliffs, where, long, long ago, a cable railway connected the pits at the top of the steep incline to the main line in Whitehaven and its beautiful harbour and imposing 17th century villas.

You will join him down the coal mines that stretched deep below the Irish Sea, where death threatened every day and you will learn about the remarkable players who played with and against him, the highs and the lows, from Cup Final victories to when he was lying in a hospital bed unable to move, his neck broken as doctors look at x-rays and shake their heads thinking Boxer might never walk again.

None of this will make any sense without the context of his young life in Kells, and the role Cumberland and its mines and steelworks and insular community played producing men like Arnold Walker. His influences are most emphatically displayed by the exploits of Douglas Clark, who was born near Maryport in 1891 and could carry a hundred-weight (51 kilos) bag of coal under each arm when he was just 14. He went on to play almost 500 games for Huddersfield and was inaugurated into Rugby League's Hall of Fame in 2005.

Clark's life reads like a film script and not long after signing for the Yorkshire side for £15, he was fighting in the trenches of Passchendale and earning the Military Medal after being gassed and wounded in 18 places by shrapnel. He was discharged in a wheelchair but was back on the front line within four months.

At the end of the Great War he was rated 95% disabled but returned home and continued his rugby career, and the only word that comes close to describing his recovery is miraculous. Clark played on two Australian tours for Great Britain, won 18 international caps and made 31 appearances for Cumberland.

He was the All-in Wrestling Champion of the World, winning the Championship Belt outright after beating two successive challengers, and touring Australia in 1934 and 1936. At the age of 45 he was undefeated in 19 contests, continuing until the age of 50 when he retired from the ring. People who witnessed him in action swore he was the 'strongest man on the planet.'

Clark's astonishing life gives a unique example of the bloodline coursing through Boxer's veins. The economic boom in the late 40s and 50s, which was mirrored in the success of Workington Town, was already in decline when Boxer signed for the club at the age of 19. He received £750 for scribbling his signature on the back of a cigarette packet in a car park at Grasslot, close to Maryport, with his mentor, friend and occasional disciplinarian, Tom Mitchell, grinning with satisfaction after finally landing a player he had been chasing for more than two years.

It is difficult to find any relevant video footage of Boxer and his Cumbrian heroes that might enable their genius to leap from these two dimensional pages and into your hearts and minds in the way that is impossible with the written word. There are two clips on *YouTube* which you will find fascinating and they will give you an inkling of the true dimension of Boxer's qualities.

The first is a four-minute review of the 1977 Lancashire Cup Final, when Town overcame a star-studded Wigan side at Wilderspool, Warrington. The footage begins with two Town forwards driving into Wigan's red and white defensive wall, probing for weaknesses. Eddie Waring's chaotic voice is providing a distracting background to the footage. Second row Les Gorley breaks through the line, drawing in three opponents, before presenting the ball gently and so perfectly to supporting centre Ian Wright as one might hand a tray full of drinks to a friend in a packed pub and he touches down behind the posts.

Wright leaps up in celebration before being surrounded by Town supporters who can't control their excitement, and we are given a reminder that all this took place 40 years ago by the long hair, flares and moustaches, popular with television programmes at that time such as *Starsky and Hutch* and *The Dukes of Hazzard*.

"Three points to nil," says Waring. "What a delightful and delighted crowd this is."

One of the fans is wearing a white cap in Town colours, of the kind one might expect to find in a Popeye cartoon and the view pans away to show Boxer with his arm around the try scorer, and they are trotting back to the halfway line together, determination etched on their faces.

Town have possession again and Boxer is collecting the ball at acting half back. He dummies left before sidestepping and swerving around three players who are left holding onto nothing more than empty Lancashire air and a gap has appeared, just for a moment and Peter Gorley is in the clear now but desperate red arms drag him down and the chance has gone. But no. Peter flicks out another perfect pass and stand-off Ray Wilkins is behind the posts for another try.

"That was one out of the blue," says Waring. "A very good one by Les Gorley," he adds incorrectly but nobody is listening as the camera closes in on Walker. "With that little lad making it very well indeed." And Boxer is punching the air in celebration before Great Britain full back Paul Charlton puts an affectionate arm around the scrum half and they are walking towards their own half before the film flickers and now we are shown the cup on the podium adorned with blue and white ribbon in front of dignitaries, and fireworks begin to explode in the background.

We are watching captain Charlton pacing the steps, a huge grin on his face while his team lines up obediently behind him awaiting a signal that the presentation can begin. Fans are leaning over the balcony, embracing the players. Charlton is shaking hands, a blue and white scarf around his shoulders. They are on the move. Ray Wilkins is close behind his captain, and backs are being slapped and then you see Charlton holding the cup high above his shoulders, punching the air while camera bulbs light up the scene as the early evening twilight falls across the stadium. Wilkins, right arm raised, is struggling to cope with the weight of the base which is the size of a large anvil. Charlton recognises a familiar face and he leans into the crowd with the cup in his right hand, stretching out to share the moment with Harry Walker, the Town director.

"And even the officials of Workington are having a kiss," says Waring. "So there it is from Wilderspool, Warrington, the score Workington 16 Wigan 13, hope you have enjoyed it. Good-bye."

Boxer's second appearance on the Internet involves a leading role in a gloomy look at the demise of professional rugby league and how it has mirrored economic hardship in Cumbria. The documentary, which was first transmitted on Border TV in 1978, is narrated by Eric Robson, author, film maker and sheep farmer, best known for his role as chairman of *Gardeners' Question Time,* which was first broadcast on Radio 4 in 1947, and his friendship and collaborations with Alfred Wainwright, the Lakeland fellwalker and guidebook author.

The film begins with a panoramic view from a high point somewhere in Workington town centre and could have been taken from a Lowry painting. You are seeing cranes, pylons, gasometers, rows of terraced houses and tall chimneys billowing white smoke and in the distance, the beautiful Lakeland peaks of Blencathra and Skiddaw.

It was posted on *Youtube* by Ian Thompson, who was an outstanding centre for Town in the 70s and 80s. It was probably recorded on a VHS video when it was originally shown. The picture is jerky and blurred and this lack of clarity, combined with the fact that it is filmed in black and white, gives the appearance of great age, perhaps 80 years or more, so much so, you would not be surprised to see carts and horses trotting across your television screen, perhaps even someone in a peaked cap riding along on a Penny Farthing bike.

"Sunday afternoon in Workington, Cumberland, another part of the north west where mining and Methodism put down roots together," says Robson, the dismal feeling of desperation and hopelessness heightened as the images flick across the screen. "But here, it is different – there is a rival religion – rugby league."

More terraced streets are filling the screen, with Ford Anglias and Vauxhall Vivas parked neatly in long lines, this time framed by the steelworks and you are transported into the middle of a rugby league game, the crowd blasting out, 'Town, Town, Town.'

"Its band of supporters may have dwindled since its heyday in the 40s and 50s but their fervour is not diminished," we are told as the camera focuses on Town's bohemian chairman Tom Mitchell, looking suitably eccentric, wearing a large hat of the kind one might expect to find on John Wayne, sun glasses and sporting a long, white beard like a character in *Treasure Island*.

The action changes again and now we are watching an amateur game on a muddy field in Ellenborough, a suburb of Maryport, with a post office, a school and two small churches and not much else. Two Cumbrian players with formidable careers are being interviewed. The first is Ike Southward, Town's Ashes-winning winger from the 50s, who still holds many club records, including top try scorer at 274, and who was sold to Oldham for a world record fee of £10,650 in 1959 - the equivalent of £250,000 today. The second is the club's assistant coach Andy Key, a powerful prop forward who played twice for Cumberland, and for Town, in the 1955 and 1958 Challenge Cup finals at Wembley stadium. They are, as they say around here, good marras, and it is easy to sense the closeness of their friendship as they chat warmly together, while large men thunder up and down on the pitch behind them.

"There were four lads out of this village who played at Wembley," says Andy. "From one street, not threequarters of a mile long."

"Aye, we signed for Workington too young," says Ike, puffing away at his cigar. "We were just 17, eh."

And two still photographs are shown, one of Ike, perhaps four stone lighter and wearing his 1956 England cap and shirt, and one of Andy, shaking hands with the Duke of Edinburgh at Wembley, looking incredibly youthful, no more than 17-years-old, alongside triple Town tourist Brian Edgar.

"Ike was very fast," says Andy. "And I was big, about 13½ stone when I was 14, you know, I think it was my size that got me on a bit."

And the two friends begin laughing together as they relive forgotten days.

"We progressed from a tin to a pig's bladder and then Ike got this ball and we were that proud of it, we used to take it to school with us," says Andy. "And we were walking up from Maryport to Ellenborough and the ball went over into the River Ellen just over there. It went about a mile downstream and we got it out of the harbour at the finish. We would have drowned for that ball."

Ike finishes the story, affection flowing between them, large smiles on their faces. "Well I finished up jumping in the muck-midden didn't I, up to the waist. We were both crying cos we didn't want to lose that ball."

The documentary keeps switching scenes and viewpoints without warning, but it is no less an experience for that and now Arnold 'Boxer' Walker, is shown in action for Town tackling a Warrington forward to the background of the narrator making a common mistake for the origin of Boxer's nickname.

"Workington's current scrum half, Arnold Walker, Boxer to Town's supporters because of his tendency to transform hand-offs into punches, is a younger product of this same village tradition."

He is a handsome young man with long blonde hair and an impressive moustache of the style popularised by movie star Burt Reynolds.

"I was a mascot at Kells Rugby League Club," he says, with his pure, broad Cumberland accent unhindered by the camera. "I used to follow them and Paul Charlton, my captain of Workington now, well, I was his mascot when he played for Kells. It's unbelievable how we should be playing together now. I was only six or seven and it just developed from there.

"My mind's in sport but there isn't enough money, see. If they were getting gates like football, well, but when you are only getting 5,000, that is why we are only semi-professionals."

The image of Boxer fades away and you are watching a scene from the terraces of Derwent Park, and then he is shown loading a wheelbarrow, wearing a Town shirt and the narrator uses the link to explain the scum half's switch from mining to manual work at the nuclear power plant at Sellafield.

"There were a lot of young lads leaving when I left the pits," says Boxer. "Especially single lads who were fed up of the pits and they wanted up into the fresh air. That's the main reason they want to leave."

A group of miners is shown walking away from a claustrophobic cage above the pit shaft on the surface at Beckermet, one the country's few remaining iron ore mines, located seven miles south of Whitehaven. They are wearing donkey jackets and safety helmets with the lights still blinking in the darkness.

"Third generation, like," says Town's county hooker, Alan Banks. "My other grandfather worked at the mines, so it's in the family. Hope this place stays open a bit longer." But inevitably, the balance sheet proves more powerful than a plea from a good man for work and the mine closed the following year.

Once again the camera shows more scenes from the industrial landscape, the large cooling towers of Sellafield far away in the distance and in the foreground a train is moving slowly, its carriages full of industrial waste and Eric Robson is telling us: "Old, decaying industries like this have never topped the wages league, but once the rugby pitch offered something more useful than a pocket money bonus.

"Now Windscale, and the general rise in working class living standards, together with a decline in rugby league gates, have brought the game's rewards to the level of a handy extra. Players get a minimum of £15 appearance money, up to £30 for a home win and £40 for an away victory."

Banks has returned and he is explaining that a generation before, rugby league players could earn more in 80 minutes than seven days down the pit. And how it is more rewarding to work weekends, he says, and get £60 rather than £12 for a reserve game. But Banks is not a reserve player. He is a talented county forward. And he is now shown in Town's defensive line alongside Boxer and looking a much bigger man, his shirt hanging loosely over his shorts.

The narration is taken over by Andy Key who confirms Banks' arithmetic with even more powerful evidence. "My first pay for Workington Town, as a kid of just 17 was £24 and my father, who was working at the gasworks at Maryport, well, he would be working seven days a week for about seven or eight pounds. One and a half hour's pleasure and you were making the money."

Another Town legend and present coach Sol Roper, who played in the 1955 and 1958 Challenge Cup Finals, and is employed as a crane driver, is shown discussing the merits of Workington's pack with former Town and Haven forward Dennis Martin before the viewer is transported to a moonlit training session and Sol is barking out orders while large, anonymous men obey him dutifully, and he finds time to put his arm around Boxer, and you are left with the impression that he is treating the little man with great reverence, someone who is special, a star, before Roper moves towards the forwards.

"Come on Gary, what's up with you," he shouts. "Come on lads, let's move it. Davy you should be down now. Let's go. Come on. Pick it up a bit. That's better. Come on Arthur, you can do it."

Over the next few minutes, the documentary switches focus abruptly, without warning, and we are watching a hound trail, a unique Cumbrian sport in which dogs with amazing speed and stamina sprint nine miles in less than 35 minutes, over 12-foot walls and rumbling rivers and thick bushes, rocks and forests and large boulders and barbed wire fences and up mountains so high it would take an Olympic athlete all day to climb. Sol is shown walking among the considerable crowd, and in the background are rows of bookmakers shouting odds and scribbling numbers on large black boards.

"Now then Arthur, what do you fancy?" he asks and the dogs are shown sprinting off into the distance with the Cumbrian fells ahead of them, howling with excitement as they track an aniseed trail. "I've backed the favourite, Glendale, and if it wins, I get paid out and if it loses, I'll get nowt," Sol says, feeling good about his chances of a winning bet. "I used to have a dog but not now. They are too much work and there's not enough time."

We are back at floodlit Derwent Park and you are struggling to make out the players who are shown running through huge pools of water while the rain is crashing down in great sheets around them and Sol is suddenly making an unlikely comparison. "If you train the lads well, they are just like dogs. They want to win."

The race is nearing completion and owners and trainers are waving flags, blowing whistles and shouting encouragement as the leading dogs break through the mist. The crowd is shown peering through the gloom, many with the assistance of large binoculars and suddenly the dogs are among them and the camera closes in on the action as the winners flash over a large white tape stretching across the field.

Sol nods his approval and the crowds are suddenly gone and there's no one about. A lone dog is trotting towards the finish, and he's looking exhausted as if he has been pulling a sack of potatoes behind him around the fells and Sol can't hold back his admiration. "They still carry on because they love the sport. Look at this one coming here," he says. "This dog will be lucky if it finishes. It will probably never win one."

The mountains and lakes move slowly out of focus, and you are looking at old footage, from the 50s, of Ike Southward and his incomparable team of internationals, running along the Golden Sands beach, close to Whitehaven harbour, a large white lighthouse behind them. The film is badly out of focus and there is no commentary to describe the ghostly figures who are passing the ball expertly from side to side. Then you see Brian Edgar, Syd Lowdon and Harry Archer posing for the camera.

The film is being displayed on a wall somewhere deep inside Derwent Park, the projector clicking away in the background and former coach Jim Brough, captain of the 1936 Great Britain Tour to Australia and coach to the 1958 Ashes winning side, is teasing Andy and Ike about his time coaching Town and the jokes are flowing... "But the only trouble was, Jim, you wouldn't part with money," laughs Ike. "Aye, you kept knocking it off us. All those half a crowns."

"But what about all those extra bonuses for the more points you scored?" pleads Jim, but the players are having none of it.

"But you started to handicap us," says Ike, a mischievous grin on his face. "We were on five bob a point and we started knocking a few 40s up so you knocked it down."

Everyone is laughing now and Jim has the presence of mind to quiz Ike sarcastically: "You never asked for a transfer, did you?"

"No, I didn't," he answers sheepishly. The conversation switches to life growing up in post-war Cumberland. "You had to wait for the first pan of chips in them days in the family. You had to run home."

Unbelievably, now we are seeing small boys, perhaps 10-years-old, ballroom dancing unconvincingly to a tuneless piano, wearing tuxedos and bow-ties and the teacher is telling them... "Now remember at Blackpool, you will only have one chance," she says with great enthusiasm and you are left with no doubt that it is all spectacularly important to her. "No prize for being the best individual dancer in formation dancing. It's teamwork. Think about each other." And now they are in a field, with large grins on their faces playing rugby erratically and acting for the camera.

The viewer is whisked away again, and we are in the Town boardroom watching Rene Anderson pouring cups of tea and dispensing cakes and cucumber sandwiches among older men wearing suits and striped ties. Rene has already appeared as the benevolent dance teacher and now she is centre stage again displaying her talents as organiser, cook, waitress and teamaker. In today's corporate world she would be probably be known as the club's Public Relations Officer.

And now you are in Town's changing room, among these brave men preparing to go to war against Warrington. Boxer's back is being violently rubbed by an unknown physio as the time drifts inexorably towards kick-off just a few minutes away.

"Let's play as a pack and not as individuals," orders coach Sol Roper, but no one is paying much attention, the players mingling in the background, chattering among themselves.

"Hey, let's have some backing up. Get right up in his bloody behind now. We must have these two points. Get a grip of their pack right away and let's have quick play-the-balls."

The angle switches to a shower cubicle where Boxer is shown being violently sick before walking past the cameraman, wiping his mouth, uttering expletives. Assistant coach Andy Key smiles warmly and pulls the scrum-half towards him whispering advice, and director George Graham is already in full flow in one last attempt to inspire the team, banging his fists to emphasise the importance of the occasion.

"Right, men, you've heard what your coaches have had to say. It's vital today that we win," shouts the director, who was known affectionately among the players as Gorgeous George on account of his fondness for flamboyant clothing. "£50 quid clear to win. Now get out there and do it."

The players gather around the treatment table and obediently listen to Paul Charlton, blasting out encouragement. He is the captain and one of the greatest full backs in the history of the sport. Paul has his back to the camera and he is not in a very good mood on account of his recent acquisition of a not very complimentary nickname following a severe perm – Shirley Temple. You know the documentary is ending as church organ music begins playing in the background, drowning out the words as he grabs a ball and hits the table violently. "Now come on, let's get out there and beat the bastards," says Paul. "We're the boys that make the noise."

Everyone is shouting together in perfect unison... "hey, hey, hey," before heading out to the field, in front of 5,000 fans waiting expectantly.

The volume of the music increases and you are shown a few moments of slow motion action from the game, including a particularly violent tackle from Town's powerful forward Ian Hartley. He throws the player to the ground using a stranglehold familiar to Hulk Hogan and you wouldn't be surprised to find out that the unnamed Warrington forward is knocked out before eventually coming to in the dressing room, rubbing his head and wondering where he is, as if he had been hit on the head by a sledgehammer. A loud hooter sounds and the players are trudging off, heads bowed, to the commentary of Radio Cumbria's Ron Morgan... "This is Town's fourth consecutive defeat and not a very impressive showing."

And the final word is left to Andy Key, putting on a brave face, struggling to hide his disappointment. "You only get out of life what you put in," he says. "If you are not prepared to put it in, you won't get it out. That's it. You've got to go down fighting - we'll just have to pick ourselves up off the floor again."

The credits start to roll over a picturesque view of the Derwent estuary, small boats in the foreground, seagulls flying across the landscape and the imposing belltower of St Michael's, the town's beautiful 18th century church, rising up into the grey sky.

More terraced houses, pylons and industrial chimneys fill the screen, and the early evening light fades away with one last artistic image of the rugby posts at Derwent Park, one last reminder of how sport and an unknown economic future affect the lives of this unique, remote outpost of the game, forgotten and far away from the heartlands of Lancashire and Yorkshire and even further from the Houses of Parliament where Margaret Thatcher, who would be elected Prime Minister the following year, would begin her ruthless destruction of the country's mining communities.

Within seven years of the first broadcasting of the film, Haig Pit became the final colliery to close in Cumbria, bringing an end to an industry that began in the 16th century and at its height employed thousands of workers in 13 pits across the county.

Update: In the early part of the 20th century, there were more than 1,300 pits across the United Kingdom, employing 1.2 million miners. Not long after the Miners' Strike in 1984, when the Conservative Party changed trade union legislation, suspended welfare payments to the families of miners and mobilised the police force, the industry was all but finished. In 2013, the mining industry employed less than 4,000 workers across the country. On Saturday, December 19, 2015, the UK's last deep coal mine was closed at Kellingley colliery. People lined the streets of nearby Knottingley in West Yorkshire to watch as the pitmen walked the mile from the town hall to a miners' social club. Crowds cheered and applauded as the procession passed by, led by Knottingley Silver band

and someone wearing an impressive Grim Reaper costume, completed by an appropriate scythe.

Most people attending the rally, alongside children and dogs, carried flags and were wearing yellow National Union of Mineworkers' stickers with the slogan *Coal Not Dole*. When the march reached the Knottingley miners' welfare reform social club, miners could be seen wiping tears from their eyes as the band played a number of songs, including *Danny Boy*.

§

Boxer was a very easy player to dislike when you are supporting an opposing team. He was so good, you see. Boxer was the captain of almost every team he played for, and before that, if he wasn't the skipper, it would likely be because a coach might believe he was too small, too arrogant, too inexperienced, too unpredictable, too volatile and extremely unlikely to follow plans that had been carefully predetermined as most likely to bring victory. Boxer admits himself he was all these things. But they didn't trouble him, not for a second.

He liked to win, that was always his motivation. And he didn't care how. Town and Haven had fine teams but the big names of the game such as Wigan, Leeds and Widnes, had more expensively assembled sides and attracted much larger attendances. But Boxer had a spectacular capacity to ignore what most impartial observers might refer to as 'overwhelming odds.' He had an astonishing contempt for reputations and a heartfelt faith in the ability and courage of his team-mates. His capacity to inspire them and to manufacture confidence was so powerful it was as if he was passing on super powers like characters in a Marvel comic.

They enjoyed playing for him and with him and Boxer was fortunate to line up alongside some of the greatest of all time – Paul Charlton, Les Gorley, Jim Mills, Peter Gorley and Eddie Bowman, all full internationals – and that was just with Town and does not include Haven, Cumbria, England and Great Britain.

I saw Boxer play perhaps a dozen times, mainly for Town, and my recollections as a Barrow fan, are not a pleasant experience.

The intervening years have dimmed my memory at the edges but this is what I see, when I look back, in my mind's eye. It will be at Craven Park,

Barrow, perhaps an early round of the Lancashire Cup. There is a big crowd, around 6,000, and the game is tight and perhaps we are one point ahead. Town have the ball as the minutes slip by and they are looking dangerous and Boxer is everywhere, at first receiver and spraying passes out to huge forwards, probing left and right, and Barrow's blue line is struggling to cope.

Then he gets the ball, throws a dummy perhaps, or misses out two men with a long pass, or sidesteps - it could be anything, but somehow, one thing is always constant in my memory – and the result is always the same – a late and unexpected Town comeback that defeats my team, my heroes, my town and it's always the responsibility of this tiny man with long blonde hair and a fondness for late tackles and the dark arts of professional sport that would become known many years later as sledging.

So I admired him as a player but I didn't think much of Boxer as a person in the way we all hold our own views of public figures, perhaps unfairly and based only on their behaviour on the field of confrontation.

Fast forward 15 years and I am sitting in the *News & Star* editorial offices situated in Dalston Road, Carlisle, as the newly-appointed Sports Editor and my telephone rings.

"Is that Mr Gardner?" the caller asks. "I want to congratulate you for writing the life story of Willie Horne, who was my hero and I want you to write my life story, please. I'm Tom Mitchell. Come to my house at 7pm on Wednesday night and we can sort everything out."

Tom was a fascinating character. He was a Cumbrian farmer, who also worked for the Ministry of Agriculture, and was a very successful businessman and a dominant figure in the rise of Workington Town, with a fondness for acquiring rugby union internationals. Journalists could not prevent themselves from describing him as charismatic, colourful, legendary, eccentric, larger than life and enigmatic - all these words and many more. They are all accurate and go along just fine with his appearance which includes wearing large hats and the cultivation of a white beard which make him look like an Old Testament character in a biblical movie.

So now I am sitting in a large living room in Tom's imposing farmhouse, on the outskirts of the town, close to the River Derwent, and the old man, who is now 84, is holding court and giving me explicit instructions on his exact requirements, how he wants his book writing and who I should interview. It is evident that he has a powerful personality.

We reach a compromise and arrange further meetings when I would dispense advice on publishing, where he might get the book printed and the importance of photographs of which he has several thousand. Tom writes the book himself, with the assistance of his family.

His autobiography, which was entitled *The Memoirs and Sporting Life of Tom Mitchell,* was published shortly before his death to critical acclaim and beautifully summed up in the intro of Dave Hadfield's review in *The Independent* which simply asks: How is it possible to resist a book with a chapter entitled *Kruschev and Rugby League?* Hadfield goes on to reveal that Tom was on first name terms with Pablo Picasso and King Farouk, a man with unlimited wealth, who was the tenth ruler of Egypt and fled the country after a military coup in 1952. The King was the proud owner of more than 30 aristocratic titles that left no-one in any doubt of his royal credentials including His Sultanic Highness, The Crown Prince of Egypt, The Sovereign Knight, His Royal Highness and The Grand Cross of the Royal Order of Ismail.

Tom contacts me again to thank me for my involvement and to ask if he can do anything for me, by way of a favour for my input, which didn't amount to much and was a thoroughly enjoyable experience.

Quite an invitation from a great man, whose nickname, by the way, was *The Godfather,* earned for his reputation as a benevolent and influential figure, most notably as the Great Britain manager on the successful 1958 tour to Australia.

For some reason an image of Boxer Walker flashes inside my head and I am transported back to Craven Park and all those painful defeats and I find myself wondering what kind of person he is, this crazy, unpredictable maverick of a player, with a gift to inspire those around him.

"Any chance of having a chat with Boxer?" I ask, without much conviction.

Tom is pessimistic about setting up a meeting and warns me that Boxer is well known for shunning publicity and that he has consistently refused previous requests for interviews.

"I can't promise anything, Mike," Tom tells me. "I will ask Boxer to meet you as a favour to me."

Two weeks later I am walking through the front door of Kells Rugby League clubhouse in Hilltop Road, a community club which was formed in 1931, and is situated 400 yards from Boxer's childhood home. I am seeing him close to, for the first time, and there is no mistaking him, even after all these years. He still has the same blonde hair but it is finer now, much shorter and there is a lot less of it. Boxer is wearing glasses and he looks anxious as he shakes my hand firmly before buying me a beer and waving away my offer to go the bar. He looks much smaller than I had imagined and I find myself wondering how he could have been such a courageous tackler and how did he knock down all those huge front row forwards, giants of the game who looked like they had the power to grab hold of an axe and knock down a Lake District forest.

We start chatting away as the Red Hot Chili Peppers blast out *Give It Away* on the piped music playing gently in the background. Workers are arriving at the bar, and many are wearing blue boiler suits with BNFL emblazoned on their pockets in large white letters. Occasionally they look over in our direction as they sup their pints, and you sense that Boxer's presence in the club is something of a big deal. He is more relaxed now and talking quietly and with great authority, reacting to all my questions with an honesty and openness that I had not expected. He answers everything, nothing is out of bounds, and the stories are flowing from him unhindered as he takes me with him on a journey through his life, all the highs and plenty of lows, and my hand is aching as I scribble in my notebook, struggling to keep up.

Boxer is a great storyteller and his descriptions are so compelling that if you close your eyes, you would be right there alongside him, watching the action and almost a part of it. You could be sitting in the Haven dressing room, flanked by Great Britain international Vince Gribbin, who once scored six tries in one match, and Milton Huddart, a fine back row forward who played for England. Boxer is issuing instructions and his words of encouragement are inspiring you, and if you look down you will be wearing the blue, yellow and white shirt, and you are seeing in your mind's eye, a team of Cumbrian heroes while the crowd cheers in the background, the sound muffled by the concrete walls.

He is asking me about my life and my family now and listening attentively. He nods occasionally and you can see he is taking everything in. My story doesn't amount to much and yet he is giving the impression that he is mightily impressed and genuinely interested and it is having the unexpected effect of making me feel good about myself as the interview flashes by. I have a sense, deep inside me, that he is my best friend, that there is closeness between us, as his life unfolds in front of me. Many of his tales are x-certificate and clearly unavailable for publication but he tells them anyway never bothering to indicate that anything is off the record. He trusts me. Boxer is laughing a lot and he is enjoying his recollections, and his admiration and affection for his team-mates are ever-present. So much so, that when I begin transcribing the three-hour interview the following day, I find out, to my surprise, that he has managed to say not much about himself, apart from his frequent confrontations with Widnes scrum-half Reg Bowden.

His account of their rivalry was literally gruesome and only suitable for adult readers and contained the inside story on how they would punch, gouge and kick each other in the pursuit of victory. Yet they always ended up, according to Boxer, shaking hands at the final whistle, before sharing a beer and a joke in the bar, their faces covered in lacerations, their eyes black and blue before they would limp back to the team bus.

I tracked down Reg and gave him a call. He confirmed Boxer's chilling description and like him, the violence was something he considered barely worthy of mention, and was just something that came with the territory. I guess he was saying: 'this is professional rugby league, we ain't choir boys, you'd better get used to it because it's part of the game.' He ignored my probing questions, preferring to speak with sincere admiration about Boxer and their battles, and I put the telephone down with a sense of accomplishment because opinions from such a powerful source are the lifeblood of sporting interviews.

"Boxer was the best scrum-half I ever played against," Reg told me. "There is no doubt about that. We had some great tussles. When I woke up in the morning and we were playing Workington, I would think to myself, 'oh no, not Boxer.' He was the only player I thought that about. I could handle everyone else. He's a great lad too, a complete player."

The interview, which was more than 2,000 words, appeared in a magazine called *Cumbria Life* and, like most writers, I was far from certain that I had done a satisfactory job. A few days later I received a message from a third party telling me that Boxer was happy with the accuracy of the article and how I had portrayed him which was pleasing to me and all I really cared about.

§

A year has passed by, and the *News & Star* is sponsoring a match at the Recreation Ground, Whitehaven, against Keighley if memory serves, and I contact Boxer to invite him to attend the game, to mingle with sponsors and select the man-of-the-match award in his capacity as a local hero.

He reluctantly agrees and we are shaking hands the following Sunday on the corner of Flatt Walks and Castle Mews and although it is a walk of less than 400 yards it is taking perhaps 30 minutes as he walks uneasily along with the local fans. The banter is flying thick and fast.

"I wish you were playing today, Boxer," someone in a Haven replica shirt shouts, the name SEEDS standing out proudly in large blue letters on his back above the figure four. "Yeah, better than this lot," another fan says before thrusting a pen and a programme into Boxer's hands. "For my son, please marra."

He might have signed his name 20 times and though public adulation is uncomfortable to him, Boxer is always courteous and patient as the fans' warmth and admiration breaks through the autumn sun. He cuts a smart figure in his club jacket, Great Britain badge and tie and we arrive at the ground and head for the directors' box in the main stand. Everywhere we go, fans are staring and pointing at him and if I strain my ears I can just pick out what they are saying in a thick Cumberland dialect, and often it might be a father, who witnessed his genius first-hand, telling his son something along the lines of: "That's Boxer Walker. What a player." And Boxer walks on, pretending he hasn't heard.

The game kicks off and he is conducting his duties as a rugby advisor to representatives from a local double glazing firm diligently, explaining the intricacies of the game with great patience and understanding.

After the match, which Haven won convincingly, we are enjoying a meal in the clubhouse and Boxer is more relaxed after a couple of beers and he is looking right at home, recounting amazing stories of his own career and the wonderful players he shared it with. You have the sense that being the centre of attention, away from a rugby field, is not his thing but he slips into the role of entertainer and raconteur with an easy charm. At least a dozen people have joined us and they are listening to every word attentively with stars in their eyes. Spending time with him after a late afternoon drinking, and the unspoken incentive of a bar bill that will be the responsibility of CN Group Newspapers Limited, is an unforgettable experience.

He's in full flow now and recounting a story I have heard before, involving his close friend, Eddie Bowman, Town's international front row forward. According to the story, Eddie and Boxer are in deep conversation as they walk onto the Derwent Park field, to prepare for the kick-off and Eddie is playing a practical joke in a thinly disguised invitation that is guaranteed to make Boxer a hero, or so he says.

"Aye, he promised me that he had figured out the team we were playing and that all I had to do was back him up, you know follow him into a tackle and I would score lots of tries," says Boxer, his audience listening attentively.

"He promised me that if I did this, then once or twice out of every 10 times it would work and no one would lay a finger on me," and Boxer pauses for effect, as if he is figuring out the arithmetics of the situation, which, on the face of it, don't appear favourable to him. A frown appears on his face before he says: "That sounds great Eddie, but what about when I don't get the ball?" he asks, smelling a rat.

"Well, you'll probably get your bloody head knocked off," and everyone laughs loudly and there's a small ripple of applause and people out of earshot, perhaps at the far side of the room, look up from their plates of roast beef and Yorkshire pudding wondering what all the fuss is about. A few beers are enhancing the agreeable aspects of Boxer's character, which are substantial. He smiles more, laughs more and can't prevent himself from complimenting me and showing his gratitude. It is time to go home now and Boxer is suddenly looking very tired but he is still sparkling company and the laughs are plentiful as the empty wine bottles and half eaten sausage rolls lie on the table.

We are sitting in the back seat of a taxi and travelling away from the ground, taking him home and the drink is making him surprisingly affectionate but he is not making much sense.

"Thanks for a lovely day, Mike," he is telling me as the taxi climbs up the steep gradient along Rosemary Lane and High Road, the lights of the harbour shining brightly behind us, on the short journey to Kells. "You're welcome," I tell him but he continues to show his gratitude and he starts calling me a 'great author' as if his achievements on the rugby field, which culminated in an appearance for Great Britain, did not amount to much. By the time we arrive, I am starting to think I am Ernest Hemingway, as he shakes my hand and gives me a large hug and heads towards the house, a smile of complete satisfaction on his face as if his day has been so spectacular and unforgettable, he is thinking he is one of the luckiest men in the world.

We shared these wonderful Sunday afternoons together many times over the next few years and they always followed the same pattern though occasionally he might bring along an old team-mate who each shared Boxer's lack of arrogance and extreme discomfort with adulation. They would quickly get in the swing of things and chat comfortably about the golden days, while Cumbrian businessmen, directors and local dignitaries would sit back in their chairs, making themselves comfortable, in awe of them, eyes wide open, mouths slightly ajar as the laughter bounces off the boardroom walls.

Boxer likes to recount a story, about how Sol Roper used to call him George Best and it was a comparison that was not meant to be entirely complimentary but one for which Boxer had solid credentials. The nickname, which was used often, was as much for his fondness for skipping training, turning up late on match days and his occasional binge-drinking, as it was for his unpredictable and formidable capabilities on the field.

On the following pages you will discover the inside story of an incredible man and you should know that it is entirely truthful and full of extraordinary deeds which are often accompanied by irresponsible behaviour. He acknowledges this with great honesty, yet it is as if he is saying... this is me, this is my life, take it or leave it. But ordinary people who have not been touched by greatness should not be quick to criticise. We can't begin to contemplate how it feels to put on a theoretical Superman costume, which in his case came in the shape of a rugby league shirt with a large number seven on the back, and walk out in front of 10,000 people and perform deeds of unimaginable courage and skill.

Whatever you may think of Arnold 'Boxer' Walker, who was once rated as the greatest scrum half in the entire world by the respected rugby league magazine, *Open Rugby,* he is a genuine, authentic, unquestionable, actual, bona fide, indisputable, absolutely without doubt, 100 per cent believable and true Cumbrian rugby league legend.

Now you are going to find out why.

CHAPTER 1

A Star Is Born

William John Walker was born on November 7, 1907, in a tenement building on the south side of Whitehaven on a steep hill, where The Beacon Museum overlooks the harbour today. You could purchase three pints of beer for a penny, a dozen eggs for two pence and a miner earned five shillings (25p) for an eight-hour shift hacking away at the coal face, five miles away, deep below the Irish Sea. The estate, which was known as Mount Steps, provided cheap and basic accommodation for miners and their families.

Basic perhaps doesn't quite describe the poverty and hardship that was a part of daily life. Families lived without the benefit of mains electricity, which would not be introduced into West Cumbria for another 20 years. There was an outside toilet, or rather what passed as a toilet, and no bathroom. Tallow candles, made from animal fat, would try and fail to light up the evening gloom and the whole house would be perpetually infected by the stink and smoke that was an unwelcome by product of burning candles. The favourite pastime for front-line miners, who would arrive home exhausted from a shift below the sea, was falling asleep.

The estate took its name from the steep steps leading up to Mount Pleasant, a hillside development of small, whitewashed terraced houses which had been built by linen manufacturer and philanthropist James Hogarth, for workers employed in his factory.

Mr Hogarth was a remarkable man who carried out his responsibilities as a practising Christian with great enthusiasm. He was a benevolent presence in the community and he erected the Hogarth Mission on Rosemary Lane, to ensure his workers would have the opportunity to follow the word of God and become good Christians. Mr Hogarth, who was known affectionately as the King of the Mount, also donated a house in Queen Street where poor people had access to medical care.

When he was a small boy, William's friends began calling him Duncan, no one can remember why, and the name stuck. He left school at 12-years-old to start work in Haig Colliery, where he began caring for pit ponies on the surface and he would watch in wonder at the great spoked wheel of shaft number five, rising above the red-brick buildings. In the late 19th century more than 200,000 pit ponies were worked to death in British coal mines with an average life expectancy of only three years.

Outside the stables, large locomotives would be waiting, great clouds of steam rising into the Cumberland air, before a loud whistle signalled the beginning of a short journey to the Ladysmith washery, less than half a mile away, then along to Howgill Brake. Tubs of coal were taken down into the 'Hurries' in Whitehaven harbour, where they would be upended into the holds of waiting ships.

Duncan watched workers burst out of the metal cage, as many as 20 at a time, emerging together, their entire bodies and clothes blackened by coal dust, all wearing helmets, their lights still blinking in the darkness, before heading along Wagon Road, towards their homes.

He was soon pressed into service among the 'screen-lasses' who graded the coal alongside sheds where brakemen controlled the loading of tubs. Less than a year later he was working alongside powerful colliers deep below ground, in cramped and dangerous conditions, living under the daily threat of methane explosions and poisonous carbon monoxide, with nothing to protect them other than canaries which would hang in cages above the miners, chirping away. The birds, which were highly sensitive to dangerous and adverse conditions in the atmosphere, might doze off or die in the presence of lethal gases and miners would blow whistles and shout warnings which would echo along the narrow tunnels.

He grew into a man listening to chilling stories of workers being gassed and killed, or making miraculous escapes from the many explosions and fires. Women were a common presence too, some heavily pregnant, pulling or pushing trams laden with tons of coal and they were often seen controlling large ventilation doors.

§

Sir John Lowther, whose official title was the 2nd Baronet of Whitehaven, had made a vast fortune from owning large coal estates in the middle of the 17th century. He oversaw the growth of Whitehaven from a small fishing village to a planned town centre, exclusively for merchants, ship owners and industrialists. Sir John is described by one modern historian as 'a polymath interested in any industrial or commercial enterprise which seemed likely to bring a profit.' Compassion was low on his list of priorities but Sir John did find time to erect 260 small cottages close to Preston Street for his workers, who faced a life expectancy of 38 and often succumbed to plague, tuberculosis and other urban pestilences. The homes had poor sanitation and are best described as slums and they were soon demolished as the town centre expanded.

In the middle of the 18th century several new streets were built including Charles Street, Scotch Street, Catherine Street, George Street and Newtown. By the late 18th century Whitehaven was the sixth largest port in England with a fleet of 448 ships.

§

Duncan's parents were devout Roman Catholics and he shared their faith, which had sustained and blessed him with a pleasant personality. The family attended Quay Street Chapel, the first catholic church to be built in Whitehaven. They worshipped there every Sunday, and it was here where Duncan was baptised and confirmed and where his Christian beliefs provided him with an inherent sense of right and wrong. And he had other gifts that his parents had cultivated in him - he was smart and resourceful and Duncan never lost his temper. He would deal with problems with patience and understanding. It was said that Duncan was so low key he was in danger of falling off the end of the piano.

Everybody liked him. He had a decency inside him that set him apart, an unstated confidence that was never arrogant but still, nevertheless, Duncan was considered a knowledgeable person and his friends and work colleagues would listen to his opinions, with great concentration knowing they were coming from such a powerful source.

Esther Bitcon was born on February 9, 1910, in 1 Basket Road, in another miner's cottage less than 50 yards from the entrance to

Haig Colliery, which had provided employment for her family and generations of miners before them from way back before anyone could remember.

Like Duncan, Etty, as she would always be known, left school at 12, and she began employment at a bakery in town, developing a skill she had inherited from her mother as a producer of quality confectionery. She was a popular young girl, barely five feet tall and she would break into a smile without much encouragement. Etty had a soft laugh that made her immediately likeable and as she tiptoed into adulthood, she was known for her good looks and pretty doesn't begin to do her justice. Etty had a dark complexion and her hair, which was always pleasantly arranged, was as black as the darkest night and gave her an almost Latin appearance. She wore her hair short with a large curl above her right eye and she was known around the town for her resemblance to Vivien Leigh.

Duncan and Etty had known each other from a distance since they were children and they first met as teenagers on one of the dance floors in the town centre, where young people would display their ballroom dancing skills to the accompaniment of local musicians. Duncan Walker, who was by now a face worker, had always had a soft spot for Etty. So no one was surprised when the young couple began 'courting.' They made a handsome couple, Duncan with his athletic build, constructed on a welterweight scale and Etty with that captivating smile and gentle nature.

They might hold hands as they walked along the footpath alongside The Candlestick Chimney, which was a ventilation shaft for the mine and marked the northern end of Kells. The young couple would enjoy the panoramic and spectacular views, over to the Isle of Man to the west, where today you would see the wind-turbines of Robin Rigg, and the distant mountains of Galloway to the north, and there below them, perhaps less than a mile away, was the centre of the town, which contained the imposing mansions of Church Street and Lowther Street, built by wealthy mine owners and leaders in the tobacco industry in the 17th century. They were in clear view and made an impressive sight though in comparison to the poverty in the miners' cottages, they might be from another planet.

In the 1920s the pursuit of a wife was a lengthy process and followed certain rigorous social restrictions which included the prohibition of shows of affection that will seem medieval in comparison to today. But the couple's families quickly accepted that Duncan and Etty were in love and well suited and their courtship proceeded without incident.

Etty's parents were fond of Duncan and his kindly personality and placid nature but as a face worker he was not considered much of a catch. They had harboured hopes, unlikely though it may have seemed, that their pretty daughter might attract the attentions of an alternative suitor with a less dangerous occupation, a school teacher perhaps, or a farmer.

Extracting coal from deep below the sea was an enormous enterprise and an unimaginably complicated procedure that involved many hundreds of workers doing no end of things – trappers, hurriers, thrusters, getters, brushers, hauliers, onsetters, banksmen and engine men. And work never stopped, not for a moment – it was a continuous process, on and on, never ending, not for a moment, 24 hours a day.

Miners went to work knowing it was far from certain that they would return home safely. More than 1,700 men, women and children have lost their lives mining coal in Whitehaven collieries and an average of four workers were killed and 517 injured every day throughout the mines in the United Kingdom at the height of the industry before the First World War when Duncan and Etty were born. Death and serious accidents were so commonplace that owners were indifferent to them, so much so, they would not permit an incident to be referred to on official paperwork as 'a disaster', unless more than 10 people had died.

Sheep and cattle would graze on the green fields close to the Cumberland coast and all the time, deep below them, men and children, some as young as 10, were removing the black rocks, which had taken more than 350 million years to form. Recently discovered records have revealed that very young boys and girls were a constant presence at Haig Colliery and in the early 19th century, a young boy called Jonathan Johnston was employed as a trapper – he was just six-years-old. Coal mines were hazardous places of employment but even judged by the normal dangers that confronted colliers throughout the country, Haig Pit was a whole new ball game on account of the regular occurrence of methane explosions.

Mine shafts collapsed, the Irish Sea infiltrated pits, miners were buried and never seen again, there were frequent and unexpected explosions, fatal accidents were commonplace and most miners, should they survive the rigours of such a dangerous occupation, would most likely succumb to an early death from emphysema and chronic bronchitis pneumoconiosis, also known as black lung disease.

Less than two years after they first met, William John Walker and Etty were married at St Begh's on Boxing Day, 1934. The best man was Duncan's younger brother Edward who was more popularly known as Polo. They moved into 111 Windermere Road, Woodhouse, just a few hundred yards from Etty's childhood home.

Duncan was now an experienced face worker and a fully paid up of member of the National Union of Mineworkers which was still fighting to improve the working conditions of miners.

The hourly rate was not introduced into Cumberland coal mines until 1969 under a new industrial law called the National Power Loading Agreement. Until then, colliers were only paid for the weight of coal they produced. They worked in what was referred to as 'gangs' with the money shared evenly every week after being distributed by who might be referred to today as middle management but back then were known as 'deputies.' Miners would often spend large parts of their shift on vital safety and maintenance work on which their lives depended and was always conducted with great care. To make matters worse, miners were forced to hire their tools from pit owners and were also subject to weekly charges for their maintenance.

The favourite topic of conversation among miners was something referred to as 'travelling time' which was the average time it took for colliers to arrive at the coal face, from the moment they arrived at the pit head, prepared themselves for duty, entered the cages, which descended at speeds approaching 60 miles an hour, checked the safety equipment, reached the coal face and began hacking away. At Haig Colliery that journey was as lengthy as it was possible to get and second only to pits in Ashington, in Northumberland, which was referred to as 'the world's largest coal-mining village'. The official distance from the surface to the blackness under the Irish Sea, which was always measured in fathoms, in Haig's case came in at 160 fathoms, almost 1,000 feet, and is just a few storeys short of the height of New York's Empire State Building. Duncan and his colleagues were faced with an hour's walk there and an hour's walk back, without pay - that is, of course, using walk in the loosest possible sense of the word. They stooped, crawled and shuffled along the passages, unable to see a man in front of them, stepping under craggy ceilings held up with wooden props and over rats and railway tracks and slime and pools of black rancid water among the constant noise, oppressive heat, foul air and cramped spaces. Then, finally, they arrived, peering through the gloom using the weak light from their Davy lamps, and they would take off their shirts, pick up their axes and begin chopping away at the face, blackened to the eyes, throats and nostrils filling up with the black dust, penetrating deep inside them, the silent killer, before loading up the coal on conveyor belts that whistled above.

A report commissioned by mine owners, who always felt they had more to learn in the area of productivity, discovered that an average collier could load coal at the rate of two tons an hour, which seems an astronomic and wholly incredible figure. Friday was pay day and Duncan and his gang would join other miners heading for the public houses on the corners of the winding streets that spread out from the pit entrance to the cottages in Kells and along to Woodhouse and down into the town centre.

On their departure, and in various stages of intoxication, miners would be surrounded by poor children, some without shoes, and pennies would be distributed among them, like a scene straight from a Charles Dickens novel. Their marriage was happy and fulfilling - the one thing missing was children. They were thrilled when Alan was born on December 7, 1936, the year Nazi Germany held the Olympic Games in Berlin.

Four years later, Alan's sister Margaret was born with the Second World War well under way. Whitehaven was unaffected by raids from the Luftwaffe and only a solitary bomb was dropped on the outskirts of the town on an estate called Moresby. As a miner, Duncan was in a reserved occupation, and the pit was churning out coal for the British war effort.

Nevertheless, the town was subject to food rationing and blackout restrictions – lawns were dug up and potatoes, cabbages and other vegetables were planted. Everyone was issued with gas masks and identity cards and the main entertainment was provided by visits to Whitehaven's three cinemas - The Queen's, The Empire and The Gaiety.

The family still yearned for more children and to everyone's delight and surprise, Etty was pregnant again, 12 years after Margaret was born. She was now 42 and her pregnancy was difficult and uncertain. Arnold was born on April 15, 1952. He was eight weeks' premature, weighed less than four pounds, and fighting for his life.

CHAPTER 2

Leets and Sheep's Trotters

Arnold was delivered by a midwife in the tiny miner's cottage sometime in the early evening. The family were unprepared for his arrival and a doctor was called to examine the baby who weighed less than two bags of sugar. There wasn't much they could do but pray for his survival.

"Arnold was what they called a seven-month baby," remembers sister Margaret. "The doctor and nurse came every day. He was so tiny. He slept in a little basket at first and then we moved him to a drawer in the sideboard. I remember how much he struggled to breathe. We weren't allowed to nurse him or hold him because he was so small."

Their prayers were answered and Arnold made a full recovery and life returned to normal in the Walker household and he was soon developing a reputation for mischief and a disregard for authority. When Boxer was four-years-old, the family moved a few hundred yards to 18 Mid Street, Kells, where they paid five shillings and sixpence (28p) a week to rent another miner's house which was slightly bigger but not much.

Mid Street was around 120 yards long with 18 terraced houses on either side of a narrow track where a car was a rare sight and children played long into the night under the dim light of the street lamps. The dimensions of the properties could hardly be described as spacious – they were 18 feet wide and 22 feet deep and there was a small concrete yard at the rear where the toilet was situated. There was a gentle grass slope behind the properties, perhaps 50 yards wide, right up to the rear of West

Row, a street built to more well-appointed specifications and exclusively occupied by colliery managers. Occupants enjoyed unhindered views of the Irish Sea and the use of long allotments in the front of the houses, with the cliffs above Barrowmouth, less than 100 yards away.

One benefit to working miners was the opportunity to buy coal at a discounted price, which, in the late fifties, Arnold remembers cost 11 shillings (55p) for five hundredweight bags which would last around two weeks in the middle of a long winter.

Etty and Duncan were loving parents and their home was always full of children of various ages, friends of Margaret, Alan and later, Arnold, who prospered in the relaxing environment, enjoying the home cooking and cakes that Etty would make every day. Arnold remembers kindness glowing inside her and how much she cared for him and his brother and sister. Surprisingly, although Etty could hardly be called a strict disciplinarian, she was the parent who would administer punishment. This didn't usually amount to much although she was not the kind of mother to be appeased merely by Boxer's attendance at church and his respect and courteous behaviour among adults. Etty demanded more. He was the perfect son in many ways but he fell short, way short, in the department of education. The same lack of respect for authority which was about to be in much evidence in school, would be replicated as an adult among various official organisations including chairmen and directors of rugby league clubs and selection committees.

"Our dad never laid a finger on us," says Arnold. "None of us - not me, or my brother or sister. It was our mum who used to do that. She used to give it to me when I was naughty. She could be a bad 'un. Our mum had a special soft spot for me. I was known in the family as mammy's blue-eyed boy. We couldn't have done without either of them.

"In those days it took a really good family to clothe you and keep you fed, to buy us all our school uniforms. Everyone was in debt. My old lad used to flog himself down t'pit to get the money we needed. She was never out of debt, my old lass."

Etty had three jobs, as well as feeding and caring for the family. She was a baker at two shops in Whitehaven town centre, now no longer there – Batties and Todds. At night she was employed as a cleaner at a pub in Harras Moore, on the outskirts of the town, called the Hope Inn. The house was always clean, the windows sparkled and the cutlery gleamed and each day she would prepare stupendous meals for the family. Arnold's favourite was Tatie Pot, a traditional Cumbrian stew, made from braising steak, lamb, black pudding, leeks and carrots. The small lounge was often full of the chatter of children and back then, when the effects of passive smoking were unknown, a blue fog would hang in the room, while Duncan puffed away at his pipe and Etty chain-smoked her untipped Woodbines, which cost three shillings (15p) for a pack of 20.

The centre-piece of the living room was a brown, tiled fireplace with a mantelpiece on top, decorated with a large clock and small ornaments. There was a white three-piece suite and in one corner was a mahogany radiogram manufactured by His Master's Voice and containing a radio and record player on which Etty would listen to Doris Day and Alma Cogan, a British singer of pop songs, known as The Girl With A Giggle In Her Voice.

"On Sundays we used to get pig's trotters and pig's heads," says Arnold. "I remember coming home from infant school once and there was a beautiful smell in the house. I said: 'Mam that's gorgeous, what is it?' She answered: 'It's int'oven son. Have a look.' I opened the oven and jumped right back. It was a big pig's head with these big eyes staring right back at me.

"I remember there was an abattoir just down the road from us, next to Whitehaven Rugby League ground. My mam knew this butcher there who sold sheep's heads. I remember, even now, how much they were - a shilling (5p) for a head. He used to skin them for me, take all the fur off and I used to boil them for my dog. But my poor dog never got them. My mam used to use them for the family.

"I was only a kid but I remember my mam would send me down there and the butcher would fetch in the sheep from the back when they were still alive. The butcher would hang them up on these big hooks on the wall behind him, and put these electric clamps on their ears and press a button. The sheep would kick a bit but he told me that was just their nerves and that I shouldn't worry because they were definitely dead. He would get this massive sharp knife and cut the head off for me. It was still steaming when I put the head in my bag.

"My mam was fetched up to cook offal and liver for the family. We had everything – as well as the sheep's heads, we ate sheep's trotters, liver and the old lass used to love the heart of the sheep and sometimes cows.

Hearts and leets we called them. You could get them both for four shillings (20p). She would cook lungs too. She loved them. There was no waste at all. She used to make a pudding called herb pudding from barley, nettles and dock leaves that we picked from the fields.

"We were all surrounded by love in the home. Many a time, when any relations came and stopped, they had to sleep on the floor. I used to have to sleep in a sideboard drawer. My dad was friends with everybody. He had loads of friends. He was the life and soul of the party."

Duncan worked long hours and as much overtime as he could get to provide his family with the best life possible. He was a man of simple pleasures who asked for nothing but the continuing health of his family who he always looked upon with fatherly pride. He was rarely seen without a pipe in his mouth and the only time he wasn't chewing tobacco was when he was sleeping. Sometimes it was referred to as 'loading a fat one' and it was the number one hobby of miners who didn't worry much about a detrimental long-term effect on their lives. This was hardly surprising considering their occupation and the near certainty that they would die prematurely, assuming they survived the dangers 'below ground', from a range of particularly debilitating illnesses that lay in waiting, deep inside the blackened lungs of face workers.

"My dad always had a lump of baccy in his mouth," remembers Arnold. "Everybody chewed tobacco dow't pit. I tried it once and I spewed up all over the spot. His favourite make was Aromatic Twist, and I remember going to the corner shop to get it for him. One of the pubs my dad and his mates drank in was called The Ship in Whitehaven. I remember the landlady was called Mary Waddington and one day, when my dad was retired, she changed her coal fire into an electric fire. And my old lad and his mates kept forgetting about it, and spitting in the fire. They just couldn't stop themselves. All the electric fire was full of brown marks."

Miners never considered the dangers of their working lives or how the coal dust, that hung in the air in great black clouds, was destroying their lungs and their capacity to breathe. It was better to develop a kind of amnesia for that kind of thing. Duncan and his colleagues were given a chilling reminder of their precarious occupation in 1947 when 104 people were killed in the William Pit disaster, on the other side of the harbour from Haig Colliery and less than a mile away.

Dogs were used for the first time to locate bodies buried under falls. Miners cleared blocked tunnels, moved equipment, restored ventilation and carried away the bodies of their dead comrades, all while wearing heavy breathing apparatus and in stifling heat. The work was physically shattering and mentally harrowing. In all 35 rescue teams made 105 underground rescue visits, 75 of which were made by 14 regular Cumberland teams.

To put human faces on those cold statistics, Edward Glaister, 48, left a widow and nine children and another victim worthy of mention is William Harker Lee, 27, who had been severely wounded at Dunkirk in 1940. He had made a daring escape from a German Prison Camp via Belgium, France and Spain for which he was awarded the Military Medal in 1941.

The Bishop of Penrith appeared at the mine and prayers were said in the hope of divine intervention but the death toll kept rising. A government scheme called Workmen's Compensation calculated in financial terms at least, the value of a dead collier and came up with the unimaginably small amount of £538 each. A court case was brought against the National Coal Board by the National Union of Mineworkers for negligence in January 1949 and the compensation was set at £1,809 per miner.

"Our dad was a good old fella," remembers Margaret. "Duncan liked a pint. They all did and he was a typical pit man. He took us all to Mass every Sunday and I know Arnold loved his mother and father very much. Arnold has always been a good little lad but cheeky. Our mum was just an ordinary housewife. She was a good cook and she baked lovely teacakes and plain cakes. She wasn't one for making sponges. They were devoted parents. Christmas was a special time for our family. Dad was a dominoes champion and most years he would win a turkey at one of the local pubs and bring it home for Christmas. Arnold was spoilt. He got everything. On Christmas Day, we all got fruit, usually an apple and an orange, and a few nuts in one of dad's socks. We would get a few annuals too."

Duncan was a man of his time. He couldn't drive and he never owned a car, preferring to travel around Whitehaven on one of the red buses operated by the Cumberland Bus Company. He would wait patiently at the bus stop in the centre of the village and purchase a ticket to the town centre for a penny and take the short journey to the town centre to enjoy a drink with his mining friends in his favourite pub, The Ship in Duke Street. When he wasn't in his pit gear, he would always be seen around the neighbourhood smartly dressed in his navy blue suit and a white shirt and tie. The family did not own a television until many years later, but they enjoyed family evenings around a coal fire playing card games, darts and dominoes. They had a large radio and the family listened to The Archers and Billy Cotton.

Arnold was almost five-years-old and about to begin his education at St Mary's Catholic School but before that he would acquire a nickname that would stay with him for the rest of his life. Wherever he went, down a mine, along the streets of Whitehaven or in the great rugby league stadiums across the country, he would be forever known as Boxer.

CHAPTER 3

Growing Up with Billy

Arnold wasn't going to be Arnold for much longer. He had been named after a close family friend, who was a consistent and positive presence in the young boy's life. Although he wasn't a blood relative, he was referred to affectionately as Uncle Arnold, and he accompanied the family on holidays and would drop in unannounced at meal times when Etty would just pull up another chair and serve him her delicious home-cooked food. Arnold looked up to his 'uncle' who had recognised his early gift for athletic promise even at just five-years-old.

Uncle Arnold would spend time with the youngster, encouraging him – at football, rugby, cricket, any sport – depending on the time of year. So it was no surprise to the family when he turned up with an unusual Christmas gift and within 24 hours, outside the family, at least, Arnold would be forever known simply as Boxer.

"A lot of people think I was called Boxer because I was a bit of a madhead on the rugby field," he recalls. "They think I used to like a scrap playing rugby but it had nothing to do with that. My Uncle Arnold, who was also a miner, lived around the corner and was always in our house. There used to be a shop in Kells with pictures of famous fighters like Randolph Turpin and Freddie Mills in the window. So I asked Father Christmas for boxing gloves and a punch bag.

"On Christmas Day, Arnold had bought me the gloves and the bag. I was so chuffed and I went outside in the street and put on the gloves and started hitting this punch ball. I was thinking I was the bee's knees and these two old fellas walked by and said: 'Oh, it's la'al Boxer. How's your fettle.' And that was it. From then on it was always my name."

Boxer's mischievous disregard for authority, that would manifest itself as a vital component in his rugby league development, first began in St Mary's Church, or more precisely, St Mary's Roman Catholic School. He was an altar boy, which was a natural progression for young catholic children, although he was not given to conducting his ecclesiastical duties without incident.

Corporal punishment was administered with great enthusiasm by the teachers, who happened to be nuns too, and it was a regular occurrence in the classrooms of St Mary's. The nuns had one eye on redemption and an unerring faith that mortal sin carried with it consequences. It was their devout responsibility to discipline children who were reluctant to adhere to the strict catholic code of behaviour. And when it came to 'naughty' boys in need of redemption, the cheeky kid with blonde hair was at the top of their list of lost souls. They were looking out for him, they thought, as the bamboo cane thudded into his backside or across his fingers depending on the scale of his misbehaviour. The nuns held an unshakeable belief that they were performing their righteous duty that, in the long run, would prevent Boxer, or rather his eternal soul, from burning in hell for all eternity.

But the long-term destination of souls was not a priority for young boys, especially Boxer, who wasn't troubled by such sacred matters. And his liaisons with his best friend Billy Starkey, who lived around the corner in Loweswater Avenue, did not help matters.

"My father was my mentor," says Boxer. "Every night, before he went to bed, my old lad would say a prayer. My mam always made us go to church. When I was young, a little kid, sometimes, if I had nightmares, I would go into my mam and dad's bedroom and sleep with them. Many a time, I used to watch him get on his knees and say his prayers before getting into bed.

"When we went to school on Monday mornings, if we hadn't been to church, we got six of the best. Once, I remember getting caught out because the nuns used to ask us the name of the priest at Mass. I stuck my hand up with everyone else to say I had been but I didn't know the name of the priest so I was taken out of the class and whacked. There were a lot of nuns who were school teachers but I learnt right and wrong from my mam and dad.

"I remember the laughs me and Billy had when we went to the swimming baths, after we had been in front of the headmaster and got six of the best. We would get changed on the balcony with a towel around us, and you could see six red lines on our arses. Six very clear lines. I used to say to Starkey: 'They are still on marra.' They stayed on your bottom for hours.

"If I did something wrong but it wasn't really serious, my mam and dad would have a word with me. I remember once I was supposed to go for my sister's wages to Marchon, which was a chemical factory around the corner that made things like firelighters and detergents. I think I was about nine. I went over to Barrowmouth looking for grass snakes and I forgot all about my sister's wages. My mum needed that money for my dad finishing the first shift. She had to have it to buy some meat from the butcher's for his meal. But he didn't get anything for his dinner because I had forgotten. I got butched for that. My mam battered me with a wooden coat hanger."

When Boxer is recalling his school days, and his life growing up in Kells, a smile shines on his face. His recollections are clearly a pleasant experience to him, as he describes his escapades with Billy, his dislike for the teachers and the nuns and his reputation for irresponsible behaviour. He admits he was not known among his friends for a sense of caution but a theme that is constant in his stories and reminiscences is the deep love he had for his parents, their pride in his achievements and the role they played in making him a decent person. He would become one of the world's greatest rugby league players but there were other gifts his parents had cultivated in him – generosity, a kind heart and an inherent sense of right or wrong.

Billy, who is the present steward at St Mary's Catholic Club, has been Boxer's best friend for more than 60 years, and he, too, remembers fondly their time as young boys in Kells and how Boxer was always destined for greatness.

"We've always had a special bond," says Billy, who was a champion cross country runner. "I remember, we copied off each other regular in class and there was one particular lad who was the cleverest lad in the school, Peter Atkinson. He moved away and he went on to do big things in his life. We used to say to each other: What's Peter got? And I would write it down and Boxer would copy it from me or vice versa.

"We were doing a test one day, and this is how we got caught out. Boxer wrote down: *I don't know* and I wrote down, *neither do I*. I guess that gave the game away and we got put out of class for that. That was always happening. We used to stay at each other's houses. My mam would let us camp out in our shed in the garden. We used to do that a lot. She would bring us chips and drinks. I always remember playing table tennis in his mam's house. We used to smash balls at each other. It was only a tiny room. His mam and dad used to just put up with it, they never complained. They were strict, like all parents were in them days, same as mine. We didn't get away with anything. They were quite firm with him but lovely people though."

Boxer was a familiar presence at the Welfare Ground, alongside his father, watching their team of heroes, most of whom were born less than a mile from the ground. Kells Rugby League Club, which can trace its origins back to 1931, have appeared twice in the first round of the Challenge Cup and have provided dozens of professionals and internationals. The most notable is Paul Charlton, who would become a towering presence in the history of rugby league, playing more than 700 games, included 19 appearances for Great Britain and scoring 234 career tries. Paul, who was born in Kells in 1941, is everywhere respected and could quite possibly be the greatest full back in the history of the game.

Boxer and Paul would go on to play together in Town's glory years of the 1970s, which must have been a difficult achievement to contemplate when they first met when Boxer was six-years-old and Paul was breaking into Kells' first team. Paul would spend hours improving his goal-kicking on the Welfare ground, while this tiny boy with long blonde hair would run around collecting balls that flashed by the posts as dusk gave way to another moist Cumbrian night, the field lit up by the orange glow from the street lights on Hilltop Road.

"My father was the chairman of Kells," says Boxer. "I was mascot and it was great to lead my favourite team out before matches. It was a fantastic experience for a young pup like me. I looked up to them all. They were my heroes, every one of them. Kells used to hammer everyone. They had amazing players like Paul Charlton, Spanky McFarlane, Jackie Nicholson, Alan Garratt and, of course, my brother-in-law Les Herbert. Most of them turned professional.

"I had to go to every match, and every time the ball went over the walls, I had to jump over and get it. I used to go into the dressing room and the players would all pat me on my head. Kells won everything - nobody could get close to them. They won this one big trophy and it was bigger than me and they would fill it full of beer and spirits and I was too small to lift it up. To be among them made me feel brilliant."

Duncan and Etty recognised that their young son was different, that he had a gift for sporting excellence. There wasn't much Boxer couldn't achieve when he put his mind to it and his modest dimensions were no handicap. Duncan was of the opinion that the gifts that had travelled through his genes came directly from a higher source and that they must not be wasted.

"I used to play on The Welfare and a lot of the time I would be on my own," recalls Boxer. "My mam would make me do my homework before I went out but I would always say to her: 'Don't worry, mam. I'll do it when I come back.' They bought me a rugby ball and I took it everywhere. I was never without that ball. When I was on my own, I would talk to myself and pretend I was Billy Boston, diving over for a try. Sometimes, my mam and dad would have to come and get me. I used to come in late and my mam would say: 'Get in to that bath, you've got school tomorrow.' I would have stopped there all night, just talking to myself about rugby. There would be nobody else there. Sport, sport, sport, I couldn't get enough of it. It's rugby that has carried me through my life. Me and my pals would play marbles sometimes but rugby was what I enjoyed most."

Boxer refers to himself as 'a dunce' when he talks of his time at St Mary's. That is way off the mark but sport was always his motivation and his strongest trait, the amazing talent that gave support to all the others derived from and fostered by his father. By the time he was 10 or 11 he was already schooled in the rudiments of rugby league but it was still unclear that he would make this sport his speciality.

His best friend Billy recalls with pride the athletic excellence of Boxer who arrived at secondary school with a formidable reputation. Boxer proudly represented the school at every sport. He was the captain of the swimming team, football team, rugby league team and cricket team. He was a natural swimmer who specialised in the breaststroke and he won many representative events at Whitehaven Baths. He was an all-round cricketer too who specialised as a wicketkeeper.

"When we first went to secondary school, at 11 or 12, that was when Boxer started to show everyone how good he was at sport," says Billy. "He started to show a bit of fire and he was good at everything. He was especially good at football. Even at that age he was one of those lads who hated to lose at owt. He had a winning mentality, we could all sense that. He had a la'al streak in him to win. Boxer was a very popular lad at school. Everybody liked him.

"The top and the bottom of it, is that he was just one of the lads, as great as he has been as a rugby player and as well-known as he would become, nothing ever went to his head. He was a great player but nothing ever fazed him. He was always just Arnold. He was actually pretty quiet when he was younger.

"Sport was in Boxer's blood. There were so many outstanding rugby league players from where we were born. Our games' master, Kevin McIlroy, was a big influence on Boxer. He couldn't be bothered with timewasters but any kids who were talented and wanted to do well, he would give them every opportunity and look after them. Mr McIlroy had a real soft spot for Boxer."

The school football team were especially successful and Boxer was invited for trials with Carlisle United where he spent the day at Brunton Park and soon after with Workington Reds where manager Dixie Hale, who was a Republic of Ireland international, was an admirer of the youngster.

Boxer's many skills guaranteed him a large measure of success in whatever took his fancy but given the influence of his family and those he looked up to as heroic and influential figures, namely Kells rugby league players, he was about to abandon all other sports. His abnormal disdain for defeat and his acceptance of the game's violent excesses had already given Boxer a measure of unwanted fame.

He was held in the highest esteem throughout the village of Kells, which at that time had a population of around 2,000. At the age of 15, Arnold was barely nine stones and he clearly qualified for service as a scrum half. He still had the face of a choir boy, but choir boys, in the natural order of things, did not normally play the hardest sport in the world with distinction.

The Mount Steps, where Duncan Walker was born in 1907.
The estate, which was demolished many years ago, provided cheap
tenement housing for miners, who would walk up the steps every day
to Haig Colliery, on the cliffs, overlooking Whitehaven harbour. It
was situated close to where The Beacon Museum is today.

Photo by Ivor Nicholas

Screen lasses at work at Haig Colliery. As women were forbidden by an Act of Parliament from working underground in British coal mines, this often meant a miner's widow was offered a job as a screen lass, sorting stone from coal. Some screen lasses had to work into their 80s.

White School Road, in Kells, in 1927. A typical row of miners' cottages, 200 yards from Haig Colliery, where face workers could earn £5 a week.

William John Walker and Esther Bitcon were married at St Begh's on Boxing Day, 1934. Boxer's father, who was known throughout his life as Duncan, earned nine shillings (45p) a day as a front line miner at Haig Colliery.

The West Strand, alongside Whitehaven Docks, around the turn of the century. The building on the left is the Blue Anchor Inn, one of 20 public houses which used to line the docks.

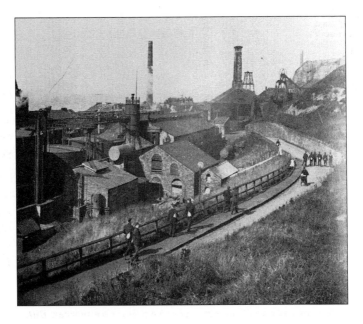

William pit miners on their way to work around 1900, seven years before Boxer's father Duncan was born.

*Whitehaven's legendary forward Bill McAlone, outside
the entrance to Haig Pit, where he was a face worker. Bill,
who was known as The Rock of Gibraltar, played 327
games for Haven and 11 times for Cumberland.*

One-year-old Arnold Walker with his sister Margaret in 1953.
He weighed only four pounds when he was born. 'Arnold was
what they called a seven-month baby,' says Margaret. 'The
doctor and nurse came every day. He was so tiny. He slept in a
little basket at first and then we moved him to a drawer in the
sideboard. I remember how much he struggled to breathe.'

Arnold with his sister Margaret and brother Alan. 'My mother was fetched up to cook offal and liver for the family,' he says. 'We had everything – as well as sheep's heads, we ate sheep's trotters, liver and the old lass used to love the heart of the sheep. You could get them both for four shillings (20p).

  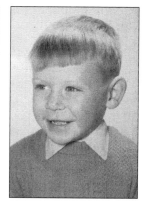

Arnold growing up outside his Mid Street home in Kells, where the family moved in 1956. 'My old lad used to flog himself down t'pit to get the money we needed,' he remembers. 'She was never out of debt, my old lass.'

Kells playing in the National Conference with the wheels of the pit head winding gear of Haig Colliery rising up behind the field. The club, which was formed in 1931, has produced more than 100 internationals, including two full Great Britain professional players – Phil Kitchin and Arnold Walker.

Kells all-conquering Under-19 team from 1960, with their winning trophies. The young boy sitting cross-legged on the front left, is eight-year-old Arnold Walker. Back: Jackie Brennan, Duncan Walker, Derek Rae, Ken Sloan, Pop Philips, Roland Johnstone, John Hornsby, Billy Davidson, Gilbert Martin, David Coward, Paul Charlton, Vic McFarlane, John Thompson, Jim Kitchin, Watson Lightfoot, Paul Pedersen, Bill Gainford, Eric Rae, Bill Proud. Front: Billy Pickering, Joe Scott, Geoff Sewell, John 'Spanky' McFarlane, Raymond Douglas (captain), Albert Adams, Matt Black and Tom Wren

St Begh's rugby league team: Back – Harold Haldane, David Rudd, Michael Taylorson, Stephen Bound, Wolfram Cook, James Blayney, Peter Atkinson, Robert KirkBride and Keith Goldsworthy. Front – Arnold Walker, Tommy Brannon, Dennis Wand, Joe Murdock, John Tubman.

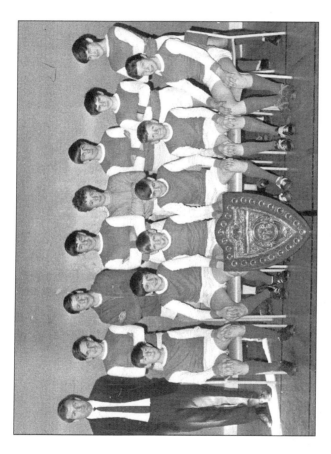

St Begb's Roman Catholic Secondary School football team, winners of the Moss Shield in 1967. Back: PE Teacher Kevin McIlroy, Robert Kirkbride, Wolfram Cook, John Regan, Alan Bonner, John Tubman, Billy Starkey and David Rudd. Front: Tommy Brannon, Paul Thompson, Arnold Walker (captain), Terry Bertram, David Murdoch and Michael Bird.

Kells Under-19 Cumberland Shield Winners in 1960 – Back: Jackie Brennan, coach, Joe Scott, Alan Garrett, John Thompson, Raymond Douglas, Matt Black and Tom Wren. Front: Paul Charlton, Tony Murdoch, Pat McGarry, John 'Spanky' McFarlane, John Davidson, Roland Johnson and Les Herbert.

Kells Under-19s in 1959, included three wonderful players who would pass on their knowledge to Boxer Walker a few years later – Les Herbert, Paul Charlton and Phil Kitchin. Back: Ralph Watson, Alan Garrett, Alan O'Fee, Geoff Sewell, Eddie Brennan, Michael McFarlane, John Thompson, Vince Corkhill. Front: Les Herbert, John Kirkbride, Alan King, Watson Lightfoot, Phil Kitchin, Raymond Douglas, Roland Johnstone, Paul Charlton, Billy Vaughan. The team won the County Championship and the Lockhart Trophy.

This photograph is on the wall behind the bar in the Kells clubhouse. Les Herbert, the captain, is holding up The Cumberland Cup: Bill Garratt (coach), Bunny Doran, Matty Glaister, Joe Wignall, Dennis Hugo, Teddy McAllister, Les Herbert, Jeff Doran, Tony Murdoch, Colin Murdoch, Raymond Martin and Ralph Holliday. Kneeling: Barry Smith, Michael Gracey, Michael Watson and Jim Kitchin (committee).

Kells captain Les Herbert receives The Cumberland Cup from a county official at The Recreation Ground. Standing above the top of the cup is Arnold Walker.

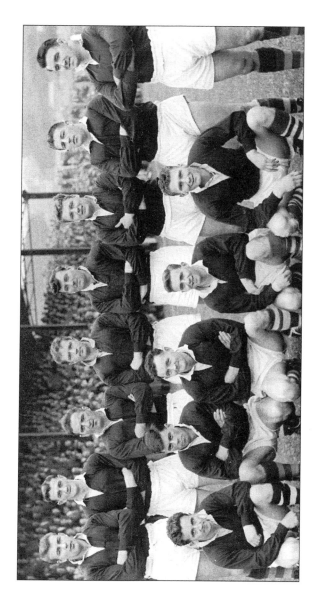

Cumberland's county side in 1960 – a formidable team containing two Great Britain Ashes-winning stars, Dick Huddart and Ike Southward. Boxer used to watch most of these players when he was growing up in Kells. Back: Dick Huddart, John O'Neil, Alvin Ackerley, Derek Hurt, 'Tedser' Stephenson, Billy Garratt, Ray Donaldson, Bill McAlone. Front: Ivor Watts, Louis Shepherd, Syd Lowdon, Sol Roper, Ike Southward

*Les Herbert celebrates yet another cup victory for
Kells with his three-year-old son Gary.*

CHAPTER 4

French Connection

It seemed like everything was falling in place for Boxer to begin a long journey that would take him to the pinnacle of rugby league where he would be the best scrum half in the world and go on to play for Great Britain. All that must have seemed a long way away when he was 14-years-old and training for St Begh's Under-15s – and he couldn't get in the team.

"I couldn't get my spot in the side," remembers Boxer. "There was a lad called Tommy Brannon and he was the scrum-half and a really good player. I was the captain of the football team but I was struggling to get the shirt from Tommy. I remember that I didn't lose heart and I just kept training.

"Then poor Tommy got injured and that was my chance. I played OK and ended up being selected for Cumberland under-15s twice before I was too old. I remember playing against Yorkshire Schoolboys at the Recreation Ground and they had this huge stand-off who pulverised us. It was John Holmes who went on the play for Leeds and Great Britain. He was as tall then as he was as a pro."

The development and nurturing that would take Boxer into Kells first team at the age of 18 began at what might loosely be referred to as a youth club, in the middle of the estate called Arrowthwaite. It was not much more than a shack in a bad state of disrepair. The building had formerly been in use as a cobblers which specialised in the repair of miners' clogs and young boys and girls would pay a shilling (5p) to play darts and table tennis and listen to pop records from bands such as The Troggs and Manfred Mann. An Under-17 rugby league team operated from within the hut and though it was not officially affiliated to Kells Amateur Rugby

League Club every player knew that their natural progression would take them along the road to one of the greatest amateur clubs in the country which had a proud history of developing international players.

The rugby league side was started by John Bell and John Mean as a continuation of the Richmond School team. John Mean would go on to become a senior referee and John Bell a senior touch judge, and secretary of The Cumberland Amateur Rugby League and Workington Town. After the first season they left and the team was taken over by Allen Banks, a council office worker, and the late Richard Eaves. They formed a great partnership - Allen was the organiser and Richard would be among the teenagers, encouraging them and arranging coaching sessions which were always enjoyed by the youngsters and focused on teamwork and having a good time and were not especially complicated.

Allen saw only goodness in young people and he regarded the teenagers with great affection. He was always there for them, solving problems and dispensing advice with patience and wisdom. It was not unexpected when he qualified as a clergyman and he is presently the vicar of St Peter's Church in Cliff Road which is less than 100 yards from the location of the hut which had such a positive effect on the lives of so many youngsters almost 50 years ago. The building was demolished sometime around 1977 and in its place now stands the imposing club house of Kells Rugby League Club where rows of Great Britain shirts and caps adorn the main lounge.

"John Bell started off the youth club with a few friends from school because there was nothing to do around Kells," recalls Allen. "There was a youth club connected to the Methodist and Anglican Church and perhaps that was a bit too regimented. We didn't say prayers or anything like that and we would occasionally go across the road to a pub called the Brewers Arms and the youngsters might have a soft drink. It was known as Toolses because it was run by two elderly ladies both called Miss Tooles.

"We had groups there and one time The Merseybeats came from Liverpool. We started off as just Arrowthwaite and we changed the name to Arrowthwaite Youth Club. John Bell played for the team and it was all good fun and nothing too serious. As a young teenager Boxer was a bit of a jack the lad character who was always having a laugh and I remember everyone liking him. He was always respectful and courteous to everyone and we never had any bother with him. When I first saw him play I could see how good he was – he had something about him. He just had it and I wasn't surprised when he went on to be a great player. At Town he had all those big forwards around to protect him.

"We were all proud of Boxer. It is always good when someone from Kells gets that far. I was born and bred in Kells. Over the years he should have been going into the local schools to inspire the kids. He should have been saying to them: 'Look, I am one of you, I came from here and I played for Great Britain – if you put your minds to it you can achieve whatever you want. If I can do it, you can all do it.' This is what I always wanted him to do but it never happened. He is a generous person who had a lot to give and he would have been good at it. I don't know why it never happened but I just wish it had – Boxer would be a great role model."

Boxer played for Arrowthwaite for a season and he also represented Cumberland Under-17s, alongside his close friend Raymond Morton, a powerful prop forward who would join Workington Town at the same time, two years later. His stand-off was Ronnie Connor, who lived in the same street and the team's full back was Allan Rae who would go on to play for Town too. Most of the side moved on to Kells the following season where they would play for the Under-19s.

Boxer left St Begh's when he was 16-years-old to begin working at Sekers, a fabrics manufacturer that had been created in 1938 at Hensingham by Sir Nichols Sekers. He was a fitter's mate earning £5 a week and though the company's directors were happy to allow him occasional time off to play rugby, this support was not shared by the personnel manager who told him bluntly: 'We want workers here, not rugby players.' He left Sekers after two years.

"It was great at Kells," says Boxer. "The Under-19s and Open Age side were coached by Billy Garratt who had been the Whitehaven stand-off. We all trained together on Tuesday and Thursday nights and there were lots of experienced players who would help us. I managed to get in the Under-19 side and we had an amazing season. I think we won five cups. We had matchwinners everywhere. My stand-off was Harold Rudd, who was a brilliant player who was great at tactics and reading a game. We didn't have floodlights back then and in the winter we would train in the gym of Kells Secondary Modern which we called The White School.

"Back then we were given permission to use the miners' showers at Haig Pit. We used that as our dressing rooms and we had to walk along High Road and Hilltop Road to get to the Welfare ground. When we played away, all the other clubs had big tin baths in the dressing rooms which were OK if you were first in but if you were fourth or fifth in, the water would be all black. There was nowt you could do and you just had to put up with it. Around that time, I remember once being asked to play rugby union at Egremont so I thought I would give it a try but I only played once. I hated it. I would go and watch Haven play with my mate Billy Starkey and I remember seeing two of the club's greatest players Bill McAlone and Dick Huddart. If Billy couldn't go I would still watch the match myself."

Boxer was already establishing a formidable reputation. There was something inevitable about his progress, his confidence and his willingness to accept responsibility and order older, more experienced players around. Looking back, years later and these experiences as a young teenager who was shining among his heroes are pleasant for him to remember and savour.

"I owe a lot to Billy Garratt," remembers Boxer. "Everyone looked up to him and respected him. Billy passed on his experience to the whole team. When he told you something you just did it. He made me the goal-kicker in the first-team but I wasn't consistent. He would take training wearing a long coat and wellingtons. He never wore a tracksuit and he wouldn't run on the field. Billy would influence us by shouting from the touchline and especially at half-time. He was really good then at telling us where we were going wrong. I learned a lot from him and he always looked after me."

§

He was now the captain of the Under-19s and the Open Age side and he was about to take his first trip abroad to Roanne, a beautiful medieval city in central France on the Loire river. The French side had travelled to West Cumbria the year before when the players and coaches had stayed in the homes of their counterparts in Kells. And now they were returning the favour.

"We had a great time," says Boxer. "One of their officials owned a big clothing business and he was really wealthy. They took us on a tour of the factory on the day of the first game and tried to stuff us with food and drink. But we weren't going to fall for that and we didn't eat much and no one had a drop to drink. We went out and slaughtered them.

"The same official took me out to a posh restaurant for a meal and made a big fuss of me. He spoke perfect English and began telling me that they wanted to sign me. They offered me all sorts, a good job and lodgings with a French family. They told my father too but I had to say no. I had already started talking to Workington Town around then. I remember a few years later, when I played for England against France as a professional at Headingley, I recognised one of the men from Roanne who had tried to sign me. He never said anything but I was sure he recognised me.

"When I came back I was made the captain of Cumberland Under-19s, and later that season we beat Lancashire at Craven Park, Barrow, before going to Yorkshire where we won to lift the county championship. After the match there was a reception and the three England selectors came out to name the team to play France in Avignon. They had watched all the matches. The main man told us all to stop talking and he starting reading out the team - you could hear a pin drop. When he got to number seven, he read my name out. I couldn't believe it - I was over the moon. Everyone was congratulating me and all the people in Kells were jumping around and making a big fuss.

"Geoff Rayshon, who played for Egremont, was in the team as well as Myron Bainbridge, who was my hooker at Kells and John Cunningham, who was a brilliant second row forward who went on to play for Barrow, Hull KR and England. We played together as pros for Cumbria and we have always been great mates.

"I remember going on the coach to catch the ferry at Folkestone and we passed this massive building in the middle of London. One of the directors, Joe Tyson, told me it was Buckingham Palace. My stand-off was called Johnny Blair, who went on be a pro with Oldham. I remember the French were a really dirty side and I think we got beat 19-3. What annoyed us was that when you stood up to them they didn't want to know but they did all the sneaky stuff like standing on your face if you were on the ground. Back then I was so fit – I was really bouncing.

"The biggest disappointment was the second game against France the following year which was played at the Recre. I was still Cumberland's captain and we had just beaten Lancashire, again at Craven Park. The same thing happened after the game and this official called everyone to order and read out the England team which would take on the French at Whitehaven the following week. They had picked the Lancashire scrum half and I was named on the bench. Everyone started booing. We had won the county championship twice on the row. The spot was in uproar. Harry Smith, who was the Whitehaven mayor, told the official from Lancashire that he should be ashamed of himself for leaving me out. We got hammered and they put me on with 10 minutes to go which was a waste of time. The scrum half who played was a decent player who went on to be a good pro with Swinton. I was big mates with him and he went to Leigh and partnered John Woods. Arthur Culnean, who was a great Kells centre, played along with the England vice-captain, Peter Whelan, who was a fine prop forward for Cleator Moor."

At the beginning of Boxer's second open-age season at Kells, Billy Garratt stood down as coach. He was a hard act to follow but his replacement was another example of Boxer's good fortune. He had much to learn and a man who was about to take him under his wing, and teach so much was very close to home – his brother-in-law Les Herbert.

"He was always my hero," says Boxer. "After my father, Les was the biggest influence in my life. Without him I wouldn't have amounted to anything."

CHAPTER 5

Local Hero

Kells Amateur Rugby League Club has been at the heart of the local community for more than 85 years. Wedding receptions are held in the lounge where birthdays are often celebrated, along with the occasional christening and it is here where the village's young men go to learn how to play rugby league and become better people.

The clubhouse is situated a short walk from Hilltop Road and as you walk through the entrance it is impossible for visitors to be unaware of the remarkable history of sporting excellence. There are examples of greatness everywhere. To the right, is a one-armed bandit with its red and blue lights flashing. It is called Cops 'n' Robbers and offers a £250 jackpot at 20p a spin, and there are small cartoons of thieves wearing flat caps being chased by dopey policemen. Along the corridor is a large wooden plaque celebrating the club's opening on September 19, 1980, by Widnes legend Dougie Laughton, a formidable international forward with hypnotic powers of persuasion and best known for luring rugby union legends Martin Offiah, Jonathan Davies, Alan Tait and John Devereux to the professional game. Further along, other plaques are attached to the walls, honouring senior officials who have given so much to create this special club where strangers are always welcome.

Inside the lounge you know you are somewhere special. Your imagination is not challenged because it is all laid out in front of you, rows and rows of international rugby league shirts and county caps behind glass cases with mahogany frames, each one bearing the name of the player and details of the honour on white cards. They adorn all three walls and there are exactly 68, going back more than 80 years and they all look the same, white with a navy blue and red V and the occasional sponsor's logo. The oldest was donated by

Joe Lancaster in 1935 and the most recent is the international shirt worn in 2016 by the present Kells captain and loose forward Tony Burns.

The uniformity is broken by three large television screens that are usually left with the sound turned off, flickering in the background unless there is a Super League match being shown or occasionally, at least, a Premiership football match. At the end of the lounge, there is a bar, and as far as bars go is nothing to make a fuss about and like any other such establishment in working class communities across the north of England. There is one difference however. And it is right in front of you, next to bottles of spirits, which are plentiful and all anyone could ever ask for, various bottles of vodka, whisky and brandy, turned upside down, optics hanging below them.

There is a large black and white photograph hanging on the wall. It is perhaps three feet wide and depicts a rugby league team celebrating - the players are shown accompanied by young children, grinning at the camera and there is a mood of jubilation.

The whole team is here, and if you look closely you can see many of the players are holding small trophies in their hands. Their shirts are in various stages of deterioration and most are covered in mud stains and in the centre, your eyes are drawn to three big men. There is no information to inform you who they are or when this happened but any of the older regulars would be happy to leap off their bar stools and start allocating names to faces and begin proudly describing what you are seeing.

They will tell you that the photograph was taken at Whitehaven's Recreation Ground in 1963 and Kells are celebrating winning the Cumberland Cup. And they will tell you that the two large men who are centre stage are front row forwards Teddy McAllister and Geoff Doran. Geoff's shirt is ripped almost to his waist and his broad chest is right there in front of you. He has a kindly expression on his face and there's something about him you can't quite figure out, the way he is holding aloft his captain, along with Teddy, an unstated confidence with just a hint of menace. They are balancing Les Herbert on their shoulders, and he is sitting uncomfortably, holding a large silver cup in his right hand.

The players are mostly smiling but you get the impression that public adoration is uncomfortable to them. There is awkwardness in their demeanour, and if you look closely, Les looks particularly ill at ease and you are left with the feeling that he would, right now, prefer to be somewhere else, as the cup shines in the afternoon sun and the houses of The Valley Estate are huddled together in the background.

The players look incredibly fit and athletic, almost Olympian, and you can sense, if you have a mind to, that there is something extraordinary in front of you. You know all about the comradeship and togetherness that kept miners safe hacking away at the coalface deep below the Irish Sea. The entrance to Haig Colliery is perhaps 500 yards away and you can feel that these brave men have brought that same togetherness with them, in great bucketfuls. They are saying in one voice, don't mess with us.

There can be no finer thing than to be one of these players, sharing this glorious moment, frozen in time forever, and it is all right here on the wall in front of you, a timeless image of heroism. The photograph has been chosen from dozens of memories of brave internationals who have worn Kells' red, white and black shirt with distinction for almost four generations. And Les is there, right at the heart of things, majestic yet humble, a true local hero.

§

Les is Boxer's brother-in-law but their relationship is much more complex than that. It is part older brother and all that might contain in the area of deep and unreserved affection and part surrogate father in the manner of Professor Dumbledore and Harry Potter. Whatever way you look at it, the two men love each other deeply and their common affection for the world's hardest sport provided Les with a unique opportunity to pass on his expertise to a young man who would be touched by greatness. No one knew this, of course, when they first met back in 1961 when Boxer was nine-years-old and his sister Margaret was falling in love with Les after they met at The Jazz Club in Whitehaven's town centre. Les would play patiently with Boxer in the Walker home in Mid Street, Kells, while the flames of the coal fire roared up the chimney.

"Les was always so kind to me and he was someone I really looked up to," recalls Boxer. "When I was playing football for the school but I couldn't get into the rugby team he would call me a sissy. He was always teasing me.

I loved football back then and I was a big Manchester United supporter when Les was engaged to my sister. When he came to our house he would play with me and we would be wrestling on the carpet while Margaret was getting dolled up to go out. I was only a kid. Then, later on, he always watched me playing for Arrowthwaite and then Kells Under-19s. When they got married they lived with us, with my mam and dad for a couple of years. That's what everyone did back then, to save up a bit of money.

"Les had a good job as a fitter at Marchon. I was told he was a great shop steward who always looked after the lads and gave a lot of stick to the bosses. I got a lot of rugby league advice from Les in the house. He would watch me play, taking it all in, and tell me what I should do and warn me about big forwards who might belt me. He knew all the hard players around here. Les was very strong, he had a good sidestep, he was fast and he was a great tackler. I remember Town signed a centre back then and everyone knew Les was a much better player."

Les had a great talent for listening and observing. His passion for the game and how he felt it should be played was infectious and he was appointed the first-team captain when he was just 24. He was a menacing centre threequarter who was strong and fearless, a 175-pound slab of Cumbrian muscle. He became a regular county player and in April, 1968, he played for England against France at Craven Park, Hull, where the programme notes, which listed Les as 5ft 10in, stated that he also represented Whitehaven at cricket and athletics. Later that year he played for England again alongside stand-off Ken Gill, who would go on to turn professional and play more than 300 matches for Salford and Widnes and 19 times for England and Great Britain.

Les's exploits as a formidable player are still talked about in the club today and reference is often made to an example of courage or stupidity, depending on your interpretation of what took place sometime around 50 years ago. Kells were playing a league fixture at Broughton Moor and Les broke his nose so badly, it would not stop bleeding and he was taken to West Cumberland Hospital, still wearing his blood-stained shirt and rugby boots. It was such a bad injury, Les was admitted overnight and he underwent some kind of complex operation to realign his fractured nasal bones before being sent home with a lengthy sick note. Kells were hit by an injury crisis, so the story goes, and Les turned up in the Welfare dressing room a week later, where he ripped off the plaster cast that had been applied to his face and turned out in the threequarters and proceeded to knock big men down and run with the ball as if he was the fittest man in the world. Those in the know, who were aware of what he had done, thought he was superhuman.

Everyone agreed that Les had the pedigree and star quality that gave him all the requirements to become an outstanding professional player - but it never happened. Directors came knocking, of course, but they didn't often return, not because they weren't convinced he could make it, which they were, but more because of the vehemence of his resistance to their open cheque books.

"Thanks for the interest," he told representatives from Whitehaven, Workington Town, Blackpool, Barrow and Warrington. "But please don't come again. I am not interested in playing professional rugby."

Howard 'Smiler' Allen, who played with Les for Kells before he went on to become an outstanding hooker for Workington Town, Barrow and Cumbria, is certain he would have been a successful professional.

"Les Herbert was so good at centre he should definitely have turned professional," Smiler recalls. "I know Haven and Workington were keen to get him and even though 10 or 11 of that great Kells side did turn pro, Les stayed as an amateur. I left Kells to sign for Town in 1964 and back then, Jim Graves was the chairman of Workington and they always seemed to have first pull of Kells' best players.

"Les had a great body swerve and he was a good sidestepper with it. His frame was perfect for a centre, he was strong and he never carried any weight. He wasn't a smoker and in his private life he was a good family man. He was an ever-present at Kells for years. He was a very tough tackler but never dirty. At that time Kells had a great open-age team. Les hardly missed a match and the team all played around him. When I was at Kells they had another good centre called Jim Powe, who went to Whitehaven. They dominated amateur rugby and won loads of trophies. Les would have been a very good pro."

Les's reasons behind his decision to stay with Kells were the subject of substantial debate and much speculation. Some said it was his job, others that he enjoyed coaching and there were those who believed he couldn't bear the thought of leaving his team-mates. There might have been some truth in all these opinions but Boxer, above anyone else, knew the real reason – it was him.

By now Boxer was the captain of Kells Under-19s and the Open Age side but he was barely 10 stones and he might have been subject to physical traumas from large forwards with mayhem in their eyes. He needed someone to look after him and that person was Les. No one was going to fool around with the kid while he was around.

"Les had gone into the pack at Kells as my loose forward and he always kept his eyes on me," says Boxer. "A loose forward is a protector for his scrum half and if anybody tried anything, Les was right at them. As an example, say a forward hit me, Les wouldn't just dive in fighting, no, he would bide his time and the next time that player got the ball Les would be right on him. He was never a dirty player, he didn't need to be, he would just tackle them really hard and sometimes he would keep hold of them and be right in their faces. Les would tell them: 'Keep off our scrum half or you'll get a bit more of that.' It wasn't just me, he did that for a lot of players in the team, especially the younger ones. Les was a hard player who really cared about his team-mates.

"He taught me so many things and I was more than happy to do everything he told me. I was playing good and I thought I was the bee's knees and I remember one time, Workington Town A team were short of a few men for an away match. I think I was about 18. One of the directors came to watch Kells and asked me to play and I agreed. I said I would love to.

"They said they would pay me, under the counter, of course, cos I was still an amateur. I thought I knew everything but I knew absolutely nothing. Les stopped me going, he just wouldn't have it and he was right on the phone telling them that I wasn't playing. He told me: 'You are stopping here. You're not playing. You are a stupid lad and you'll get your head ripped off. There will be players who are 15 years older than you and who have been a professional for all that time. You're only a kid.' In my last year at Kells, Les was the player-coach and everyone looked up to him.

"Les made me the captain in my last season and we won the league without losing a match. The amazing thing about that was what happened when we went to Seaton, who were second in the league - we only had 11 men and we drew. We were in four cup finals and somehow lost them all.

Our best player was Brian Chambers, who played in the second row. Brian had come out of the Army as a fitness instructor and he went straight into the Kells team. He was a fantastic runner and a great all-round player but he broke his leg and we weren't the same team without him. He was supposed to sign for Town at the end of that season but he didn't. I don't know why. We had a lot of good players - Bunny Doran, Harold Rudd, Harry O'Neill, Des Lightfoot and Raymond Agnew. I also played with Matt Garritty, who could play at stand-off or loose forward and rarely had a bad game. He loved all the hard work and knocking down big men. He never made a fuss about anything and just got on with it.

"I was literally surrounded by rugby league in my house. Sometimes we struggled to get a bath because my mam washed all the shirts. I have seen Margaret washing her feet in the sink because there might be 30 shirts in the bath, full of mud and soaking. Our house stunk of liniment. We used to laugh thinking of Margaret dancing down town and stinking of the stuff. You could smell it as soon as you opened our door. The corner flags were under the stairs. Every Saturday, which was matchday, loads of people would be knocking on our door, collecting things for the game – baskets full of balls, strips and medicines, our door never stopped knocking. Rugby league was everywhere in our house from when I was a baby."

In 1973, Boxer signed for Workington Town and within a few days Les quit Kells more or less immediately. "He never talked about that to me," recalls Boxer. "I think he just wanted to dedicate himself to helping me. That was the sort of man he was. From what I heard, Les told everyone at Kells: 'I've got the la'al fella where I want him and now I am packing in.'"

Les would never play rugby league again. He was just 29-years-old.

CHAPTER 6

The Godfather

Tom Mitchell was a Workington farmer and entrepreneur with an eclectic assortment of business interests throughout West Cumbria. He had an ego that can only be described as titanic, and he was a well-known celebrity around the town, not least for his flamboyant appearance, which included the wearing of broad-rimmed hats, the cultivation of a white beard of Robinson Crusoe proportions and his fondness for driving large American cars.

He had also been employed as a senior figure in the Ministry of Agriculture, which was an occupation that necessitated world travel and the opportunity to live an incredible life and cultivate friendships with public figures ranging from Nikita Khrushchev, King Farouk and Pablo Picasso, who once gave him a priceless ceramic. Tom was the founder president of the Traverse Theatre in Edinburgh and twice stood, unsuccessfully, for Parliament. He was a proficient arm-wrestler and included scaling the Matterhorn among his sporting achievements.

Tom was a major benefactor and driving force behind the formation of Workington Town in 1945 when he had lured Welsh great Gus Risman to Cumberland to coach and play for the team before he went on to skipper the victorious British Lions on the 1946 Australian Tour. Tom had a powerful and controlling personality and when it came to attracting talented young players to Derwent Park, he almost always got his own way. No one ever said no to Tom Mitchell.

The year is 1971, and you did not have to be a seasoned and knowledgeable rugby league expert to recognise Boxer Walker's genius. It was right there in front of you, the courage, the unpredictability, the playmaking, the will to win. Tom had been closely monitoring the youngster's progress and he liked what he saw. In his autobiography *The Memoirs and Sporting Life of Tom Mitchell,* he said: "I knew right away that I was watching someone with the ability and determination to go right to the top. Even at that age I was determined to get him to Derwent Park as soon as he was old enough."

His problem was that the kid's progress was no longer a secret. Contact had been made by Whitehaven and delegations from Barrow and further afield, from Warrington, Hull Kingston Rovers and Leeds. Tom wanted Boxer and he wanted him now. And he had a trump card in the negotiations that would take place imminently – Kells first team coach Billy Garratt.

Billy, who had been an outstanding stand-off half at Whitehaven, represented an England Under-21 side in an amateur fixture in France in 1950. He skippered Haven to a stunning win over the touring Kangaroos in 1956 and made 234 appearances for his home town team.

"As a stand-off, Billy had most of the necessary qualities," wrote rugby league historian Robert Gate in his excellent book, *100 Cumberland Rugby League Greats.* "He was elusive and creative, a good tactician who was adept at the cross-kick and an astute touchfinder. His side-on tackling was a feature of his play and many of the best stand-offs of his time came off second best in their clashes with him."

Billy was an outstanding coach who specialised in recognising and guiding young talent. Billy was known as a fatherly presence at Welfare Road, and as a purveyor of wisdom who would look out for juniors. When one of his players turned professional, he considered such a move a cause for celebration, and that it was the natural progression of things and he took pride and considerable interest in their progress. Billy and Tom were friends, or rather as far as it was possible to be friends for two people from as different social backgrounds as it was possible to get – Billy a collier and Tom a millionaire with friends in the royal family.

"Bill came around to my house to tell me that Tom wanted to sign me," remembers Boxer. "I didn't know Tom back then. Bill took me to see Tom at this big house at Calva and he offered me £500 right there and then but I didn't want to sign professional. I wasn't ready yet.

"A few weeks later, I was training at the Welfare and my mother sent someone around to the pitch to tell me that Tom Mitchell was at our house and he wanted to see me. Everyone must have known what was going on because he parked this big blue Saab car right outside our house. I was just a young kid of 19 and I was gobsmacked. I still wasn't ready but he told me to think about it. He offered me £500 again. The following week Bill took me through to Tom's farm again, but I refused even though he upped it a bit, I think to around £600."

The race for his signature was hotting up and parallel and equally lucrative talks had been opened with representatives from Whitehaven.

"Whitehaven wouldn't leave me alone," says Boxer. "Billy Lilly and Kenny Burns were directors of Haven and they were always asking me to sign. Kenny was a window cleaner for lots of town centre shops in Whitehaven and I used to pass him all the time. He would always shout over to me: 'Boxer, when are you going to sign?' He knew about Tom but he would tell me not to worry and that whatever I had been offered they would sort it out. Tom was very shrewd. Whatever Whitehaven offered, Tom would always up it."

The protracted negotiations that would take Boxer to Town were approaching the end game. Tom and Billy had a plan that would suit all parties and, most importantly the kid, who wasn't quite ready to leave his friends at Kells. He would make a definitive commitment to Town but delay the announcement for a season thereby enabling him to continue his development under the guidance and protection of Billy. It was a master stroke that was based on nothing more than a handshake and an independent signature that would in no way have been legally binding.

The story, as Boxer remembers it, begins when Tom gets wind of the scrum half's presence at an amateur game at Maryport, 14 miles along the coast. He immediately dispatches former Great Britain international Ike Southward to the ground to open up negotiations. Ike was a perfect go-between, in part for his standing as an indisputable rugby league legend but more importantly for his gentle, trusting and non-confrontational nature.

Everybody loved Ike who never considered his Town club records, of which there were many, or his 11 Great Britain appearances, as anything worth talking about and Boxer was quickly persuaded that the right place to foster his development was Derwent Park. Ike, who was a senior member of the coaching staff, took great care to explain the family atmosphere that would nurture and protect him. And the hint that Tom might be prepared to increase the cash payment, which at that time was standing at around £700, was all he needed to hear. A few phone calls later and Boxer is sitting in the front seat of Tom's car in a deserted car park in Grasslot, a working class district south of Maryport.

As we have heard, Tom Mitchell was a great character with many qualities but an ability to blend into the background was not among them. If he hoped that this meeting might have been clandestine, the car they were sitting in could hardly be described as inconspicuous. It was a white American Ford Mustang - left-hand drive, with a five-litre engine and it was 16 feet long. An identical car had appeared on West Cumbrian cinemas the year before, driven at speeds exceeding 100 miles an hour around the streets of San Francisco by Steve McQueen in the cult movie *Bullitt*.

They are behind a large factory, long gone now, that manufactured cigarette tips, their conversation occasionally interrupted as trains whistled by along the Cumbria Coast Rail line, the scenic coastline route that links Carlisle with Barrow-in-Furness. Billy Garratt was there too, overseeing the best interests of his teenage friend.

"I signed right there and then," says Boxer, who has a clear recollection of Tom taking the silver foil from the inside of a cigarette packet, tearing off any unnecessary paper and getting Boxer to place his signature on what was left, which can't have been much. Speaking in his book *The Memoirs and Sporting Life of Tom Mitchell,* he said: "When I first saw him play at 16, Boxer was already directing the efforts of a mature amateur pack, even then. I was at the corner flag when an opposition forward crossed and the dressing down he gave his team-mates behind the posts was unbelievable – a true competitor. I pursued his professional signature for two years – well worth the frustrating process."

Boxer remembers: "I got a cheque for £750 and we agreed the deal. It was kept quiet for a full 12 months. Bill had told Tom that Kells had lots of finals to play at the end of that season. He told him how young I was and that it was in everyone's interests if I waited another year before turning pro.

"It was like a handshake agreement. He kept the cigarette packet in his safe at his farm in Calva for 12 months and I signed the rugby league papers the following year. He trusted me. I gave my mam most of the money and rigged myself out in the top gear. And I bought myself a sheepdog that I had always wanted. She was a lovely dog who was brown all over with a white collar. I called her Kim.

"My best mates then were Ronnie Connor, Bill Starkey, Arthur Culnean, who later signed for Town, and Myron Bainbridge. We used to drink in a spot called the Towbar, in the town centre, which was a dancing club. None of us ever had any money and before I got this cheque all I ever had were a few shillings. This one night we were out and my mates kept asking me if I had signed for Workington. A few rumours were flying around but I still denied it.

"None of us had enough money to buy a round. So I said to them: 'I'll get these.' They couldn't believe it when I pulled a £20 note out of my pocket. I don't think they'd seen one before. They stood with their mouths open knowing then I had signed for Town. The A team coach at Town then was called Ecky Bell. He was a very good centre who played for Town in the great side of the 60s with Ike Southward, Brian Edgar, Sol Roper and Harry Archer. I was told he kicked up a stink because they were in a final against Whitehaven's A team and he was struggling to get a side together. He'd heard about my deal and he wasn't very happy. He wanted me to play for Town's A team in the Lancashire Shield final. Of course he couldn't do nowt about it and I remember Town got beat.

"The great Dick Huddart played in that match. He'd come back over from Australia and he went training with the Haven lads. I was very lucky because half the Kells team had gone to Workington Town. Most of them lived just up the road from me, great players like Spanky McFarlane, Howard 'Smiler' Allen and the Curwens. I knew they would look after me.

"Ike Southward was the A team coach when I first went to Town. Believe it or not I actually played with Ike. The A team played at Leigh one time and we only had 12 men. As there were no subs in them days, he ended up playing on the wing and actually scored the winning try. I think he was around 40. Ecky Bell was my stand-off when I first went to Town. He took over from Ike and was the player-coach. He was a great help to me and was always very encouraging. If I played OK he would always take me to one side and tell me how well I had done. He played alongside Ike when Town had a great team – he was a very classy player himself.

"As a coach he was always there, teaching us and showing us different moves. He went on to be part of the first team coaching staff and that was well deserved. One time we played Salford who had a full team of internationals including Kenny Gill. I remember Ecky teaching me about standing off players and letting them run across the field. He would say to me: 'Let him go, just let him go. He will just end up running into touch, he'll be lost.' We hammered them that day. Ecky taught me a lot. He wasn't a boozer, just the odd glass of lager. We all respected him and looked up to him.

"Last year I bumped into Ike's son David and he told me: 'Arnold, you used to drive my dad round the bend. He said he used to come in from training and say that he just couldn't handle you. He was laughing because he said that all the coaches knew they had to play you because you were so good.'

"Tom Mitchell was often around when we were training. One time I saw something called a Bullworker lying around. Some of the forwards used them to build up their muscles. Well, Tom caught me messing about with one and trying to figure out how it worked. He blew a gasket and started shouting at me saying that that he didn't want big muscles on me or any of the backs. I want you for speed he told me. All the forwards were on weights but he didn't want any of his backs to use them. Especially half backs, he said he wanted me to be fast off the mark. I remember he gave me a right tonking. I never went in the gym again."

A further incentive to lure Boxer to Derwent Park was the opportunity to serve his apprenticeship as an electrician at an electrical company owned by Town director George Graham. He soon discovered that the journeyman who would take him under his wing was Town's first-team hooker Howard 'Smiler' Allen, who would prove a suitable mentor in a wide range of other issues unconnected with conductors and copper wires. Smiler, who was one of the best number nines produced in the county, would teach the teenager many techniques to win possession from scrums, mostly illegal, and involving deceiving referees.

"I enjoyed helping Boxer," recalls Smiler. "He listened to everything I said and took it all in. We always got plenty of the ball when we played together."

At Kells and among all the amateur teams he played for, Boxer was the captain and the star player but now, among the professionals and internationals at Derwent Park, and for the only time in his career, he was crippled with self-doubt. At The Welfare Ground, even though he was just 19-years-old, he was obeyed without question and his instructions were followed dutifully. But at Town he was a nobody and it would take a pep-talk from his father to stop him walking away from Workington.

CHAPTER 7

I'm Not Good Enough

Boxer Walker had been The Big Dog at Kells even though he was barely 19-years-old. He was the star who would get out his magic wand and cook up unlikely comebacks and great victories. Yet he was still so young and he cut a fun-loving figure who often fooled around but no-one, ever, mistook his playful demeanour as a weakness. His team-mates knew how formidable he was. Boxer inspired those around him and the other players had started to rely on him, perhaps unfairly so, but they did anyway.

Now he was leaving his friends and his team to embark on a professional career in the hardest of all sports. His rugby league genius would be a cruel mistress that would take him on a bumpy ride to the pinnacle of the sport, where he would become a hero, someone special, an idol, followed in an instant by tragedy that would culminate with him lying in a hospital bed wondering if he would ever walk again. Of course, he knew none of this in the summer of 1971 as he arrived at Derwent Park for his first training session to experience, first hand, the gulf that separated a promising amateur and a seasoned professional rugby league player.

Workington Town were led by a group of proficient veterans who welcomed the cheeky teenager with blond hair with casual good wishes and not much else. They had seen it all before. He was a nobody here and something of a curiosity, on account of his size, which at that time was 5 feet six inches and around 142 pounds. Many of the players were county regulars and four more were full internationals, so promising performances against the likes of Wath Brow and Hensingham were never going to amount to much, not here. And the gap between evaluating Boxer's skills in comparison to Test rugby was a chasm of Grand Canyon proportions.

To begin with, there was the coach, Eppie Gibson, who was as high up on the totem pole of Cumbrian rugby league legends as it was possible to get. Eppie, who was inaugurated into Town's Hall of Fame in 2008, was an England international, who scored 145 tries in 335 games for Workington. He starred in Town's Challenge Cup final win at Wembley over Featherstone Rovers in 1952. And if his legendary status needed further confirmation, you need look no further than the Tom Mitchell lounge where Eppie's framed shirt from the Cup Final is still hanging on the wall today.

The pack included Bill Kirkbride, a Cumbrian second row forward who would go on to play for nine clubs and who had won the Lance Todd Trophy in Castleford's Challenge Cup victory over Wigan in 1970. Other notable forwards included Eddie Bowman, who also signed from Kells and would play four times for Great Britain, county hooker Howard 'Smiler' Allen, and full Irish rugby union international Ken Goodall, who represented the British and Irish Lions on their tour of South Africa in 1968. The centres comprised John Risman, a Welsh international and son of 1946 Lions captain Gus and his centre partner Alan Tait, father of the dual code international full back of the same name who played on the British and Irish Lions winning tour of South Africa in 1997.

"I remember once playing with Alan in the A team in my first season," recalls Boxer. "It was a club rule that if you had an injury that made you miss three first team matches you had to prove your fitness in the A team - it applied to everybody even some of our superstars. Often you might only have to play for 20 minutes. Alan was my stand-off after an injury and I put the ball in the scrum and we won it - I gave the ball to Alan he shouted in such a strong Scottish accent: cumarund. I honestly hadn't got a bloody clue what he was talking about. I just stood there and four great big forwards flattened him. The next minute Alan has me by the throat. Then I realised he was saying 'come around.' "

The regular first-team half backs were Harry Whitaker and Glen Turnbull, who had turned professional after outstanding careers at Hawick Rugby Union club. Hawick was 75 miles from Workington, and located in the Scottish Borders. Despite the town's tiny population of less than

15,000, its most famous claim to fame, apart from the manufacture of quality knitwear, was the consistent production of international rugby union players, which at the time of writing stands at 59, and includes three Scotland captains and nine players who represented the British and Irish Lions. Whitaker and Turnbull were both selected in Hawick's greatest ever team in a poll conducted by *Scottish Rugby* in 2013.

Try to imagine how daunting it must have been for Boxer to look around in the changing rooms and see how much star quality there was around him. They were so big, so strong, so fast and so skilful. That first night, Boxer watched in awe, his mouth slightly ajar, as the first team went through their defensive drills under the instruction of Eppie, a whistle dangling around his neck. And worse was to come when he took part in a game of tig-and-pass, right there in the thick of things, the ball flashing from one side of the field to the other, these giants of men towering all around him, making everything look so easy.

"I was only a little kid from Kells and now I was with all these superstars," says Boxer. "My nerves were killing me and that was just in training. I left for home and all I could say to myself was that I was never going to get in this team."

To make matters worse, Jackie Newall, who had starred for Maryport, was the serving scrum half for the A Team and understudy to Harry Whitaker, who was club skipper and leading playmaker. Jackie, who is described by Boxer as "a very tough player" was facing competition from another Maryport half back called Alan Ackerley, who had only signed professional forms the week before. So Boxer's chances of getting in the first team, even if viewed purely from a statistical standpoint, were close to non-existent, well that was the way he had figured it out – a one in four chance, with a one in three chance of just getting in the A team.

This was all so unlike Boxer. He was an unlikely sufferer of low self-esteem. Confidence had always been his greatest virtue. He had arrived full of self-belief but now it was all gone – *pop* – blown out of him as fast as you can prick a balloon with a pin and he was sure as hell going to struggle to get it back. All these negative thoughts were swirling around Boxer's head as he walked along Rosemary Lane and up the incline towards Solway Road and his parent's home in Mid Street, where Duncan and Etty were waiting for news of his experiences.

"I went in the house and sat in front of my dad and it all came out," says Boxer. "It's nae good this. There's no way I am ever going to get in this team, dad. I'm going to have to find a way to give Tom Mitchell his money back. I can't go back there again."

"What the hell do you mean?" his father asked, and his manner, which was quite caustic, took the youngster by surprise as he sat back, listening attentively. "What have I reared?" he asked and Boxer can recall the exact words he used which he repeated again for emphasis. "What have I reared? Are you a man or a shirt button? You're playing a man's game, son. Now get back there again and show them what you can do."

Boxer pulled himself together and he soon started feeling better about himself. There was something about the way he played, his cheeky persona and his willingness to learn, that is hard to define, a quality that older players and coaches could sense in him. He was about to make a new friend who would teach him many things. Harry Whitaker, the captain, could sense the kid was special and that he had greatness inside him. And he was going to do everything in his power to help him on the way.

CHAPTER 8

George Best

Harry Whitaker was Workington Town's official captain, and he took his responsibilities seriously, considering the appointment a great honour and much more important than tossing a coin before the kick-off and fostering a collective spirit in the first team.

As a former rugby union player, who had only been a professional sportsman for two years, it was a surprising decision but one that coach Eppie Gibson had never regretted, not for a moment. Seeing Harry conducting his duties, whether it was advising younger players, which he did often and with fatherly encouragement, or speaking to a seasoned front forward about how he must improve his tackle count, it was always a lesson in public relations. It wasn't so much what he said as how he said it. Such conversations were shared with a kindly and authoritative manner to prevent any possibility of misinterpretation that might have been taken badly, particularly among the older pros. Resentment might fester among them and could hinder the equilibrium of the team. But that was never going to happen, not when Harry was around.

Boxer's signing was low on the first-teamers' list of topics of conversation. Harry saw things differently – he could see something special in his raw technique and he made his mind up right away that he could help him. Perhaps he saw a younger version of himself in the unpredictable way Boxer played and the way he could bring big men down. There were certainly similarities in height but Harry had the advantage in weight - he was a full stone heavier.

"It is quite simple, as soon as I saw him, within two minutes I knew he had IT, and I want to emphasise the capital letters," says Harry, who is now 73 and happily living out retirement in his Hawick home. "I know that is very brief but it sums Arnold up perfectly. He was a genius and a tough kid and all he needed was a bit of experience. He was only a boy but he had it all, and I knew he had a great future in front of him. I'll admit I gave him a wee bit of a helping hand here and there – but all I had to do was try to keep him on the straight and narrow and that would be it. I thought to myself, this guy will take my place in the first team, no problem. One piece of advice I remember giving him was that it was fine, doing all his jinking and the moves that he became famous for, but he must not forget to do his share of tackling and that it was a big part of the game. I didn't really have to tell him that, because Boxer was a great defender. I told him he was a good player and he should be his own man.

"Even at 19, he had everything – he had good hands, was a great off-loader, a great line breaker and he was very fast too. He had a keen awareness of what was happening around him, which is the key thing for any good player. It did not matter when he was playing in lots of traffic with players all around him, he always knew what to do. And he was a terrific defender, and a tough wee guy. As we all know, rugby league is a hard game. You are not going to survive unless you can adapt.

"I knew he was something special, players like Arnold don't come along every day. I was very pleased when he played for Great Britain. I always knew he was good enough. He should have won a lot more caps. I just told him what to look out for and to go his own way. Boxer was such a natural. I think of him as a George Best, that was a perfect description of Arnold. He didn't need me, coaches or anybody. He would have made it without any help from anyone.

"I admit I really liked him but as I say, how can you improve George Best, you couldn't tell him how to play and that's how I will always think of Boxer. You have to remember it's easier to look good with better players around you. What I am trying to say is that if you put him in a team like Leeds or Wigan he would have been even better and won a lot more Great Britain caps.

"When I captained Arnold I was always aware of what a natural player he was and it was no good planning everything. We had certain moves but I preferred to let him play his own game. It didn't surprise me when he went on to be the captain because he inspired people by his own example.

He was his own man and he could lift the spirit in any side by scoring a try or doing whatever it took to win."

For his part, Boxer had always considered Harry a suitable candidate for admiration. He looked up to him, respected him and in some ways perhaps, tried to become him. Harry's pedigree as a rugby union star was as good as it gets. The only thing missing was a full Scotland cap, and many knowledgeable observers believed this omission was due to the higher social standing of his rivals, who might not have been as talented but could rely on the deep-rooted loyalty available for privately-educated sons of doctors, lawyers or high-ranking police officers.

Of course, Harry is having none of that. There is not a trace of resentment in him and he is happy enough with his career north of the border, which included a tour of South Africa with the Scottish Borderers, when they drew 23-23 with Transvaal and faced other powerhouses of the Springboks including Orange Free State. He had two trials for Scotland playing alongside legends such as Tremayne Rodd, who was also known as the 3rd Baron Rennell, and would go on to sit on the Conservative Party benches in the House of Lords. Barons were not too plentiful in the narrow streets of Hawick and the call never came. So he was ready for a new challenge when Tom Mitchell knocked on his door in 1968, waving a large cheque, promising a better life and making full use of his irrefutable powers of persuasion.

Harry was following a host of internationals who had left Hawick and the most notable among them was Dave Valentine, the Scottish International flanker who played 15 times for Great Britain, made 379 appearances for Huddersfield and skippered GB to victory in the 1954 Rugby League World Cup.

Harry played 86 times for Town, scoring 24 tries and kicking 54 goals, and although these statistics, which do not begin to do him justice, may not provide compelling proof of his true worth to Town, his critical role in the early years of Boxer Walker's development are a fitting legacy.

"All the players, everyone at the club and the fans treated me very well," recalls Harry. "We really enjoyed living there - my son was born in Workington. The people were great. I loved it. When I came back to Hawick, I followed Boxer closely and I had a few friends who went to watch Town and they would always come back saying what a great player

Arnold was. As soon as I met him I liked him. We hit it off right away. I could see what a character he was. Looking back now I would say Boxer Walker is up there in the top three of any player I played with or against in my career."

Boxer has an altogether different account of his relationship with Harry Whitaker and the great debt he owes him which is of such magnitude, he says with great certainty, that he might not have made it without him.

"If Harry had taken a dislike to me I would have been in serious trouble," says Boxer. "But he was really kind. On the first training session, he put his arms around me and made me so welcome. My own personal opinion of why he did that was that he had seen summat in me. I was someone he could help out. I was inexperienced and he was a special player and I think Harry felt he could help fetch it out of me.

"After a couple of weeks, he told me: 'I'm going to look after you.' There was strong talks about me playing well in the A team. So I think it must have clicked in his mind. I was told he was saying to the other players that I was doing OK. You don't get captain of a team without being a special player. Harry wasn't big, only slightly bigger than me. He was good with his hands and he was playing behind this big Town pack but Harry was a hard player in his own right, really fearless. He was quick too and I knew that when I first started training with him, if we had had a race, I would have had no chance.

"This one night in training, Harry came up to me, and I've never forgotten what he said: 'I'll go stand-off Boxer and you go scrum-off. I think we can make a good partnership.' This was in the first team and he was captain. I couldn't believe it, without him I might never have had a chance.

"There was another player from Hawick who was good to me as well, Glen Turnbull, our first-team stand-off. Glen was a very, very gentle man, who was a clever player. Some said he was too gentle to play rugby league. He didn't have a bit of dirt in him, whereas I would have done anybody to win. But Glen, if he saw an opponent was hurt, he would help him up. That's how much of a gentleman he was. He was the kindest and cleanest rugby player I have ever seen in my life.

"Glen was a bit older than Harry and his legs were going because of his age. Your legs are the first to go. But later on in your career it's your head that carries you through, your knowledge of rugby, being in the right place at the right time - it can give you another two years at the top. When Glen finished with Town, he spent a couple of years with the amateurs at Seaton, where he lived and he loved bringing all their players on. He did really well there."

After a handful of games for the A team, Boxer made his debut for Town against Huyton in October, 1971. He came on as substitute and scored the winning try in the final minutes, prompting a reporter from the *Workington Times & Star,* who went by the wonderful name of Eric B. Easterbrook, to write this prophetic account: "Walker has thrilled the band of die-hand spectators at A team matches. He is only small but he is a quick thinker who gets through more work than anyone else on the field. His tackling is superb, often pulling men down twice his size."

The following week he would be back in the A team, out of the firing line and about to play alongside a new stand-off half who didn't know much about rugby league. "You'll have to help him out, Boxer," he was told. "He doesn't know much."

§

When Harry Whitaker retired from professional rugby league in 1973, he returned to Hawick where he spent several years diligently training as an osteopath and he was soon credited with great powers of healing. He retired seven years ago but still cares for a small number of patients who he treats in his surgery in the back room of his home where the walls are festooned with signed photographs of well-known sportspeople including a framed Great Britain shirt from a rugby league great.

Last year Boxer travelled to the Scottish Borders to catch up with his old mentor, the first time the two scrum-halves had seen each other for 43 years. They chatted together for several hours, mutual respect and affection flowing between them.

"I was always in awe of Harry," recalls Boxer. "I was so nervous about seeing him again I had butterflies in my tummy all the way up. We had a great time. He was brilliant with me when I first joined Town, without him I would never have made it."

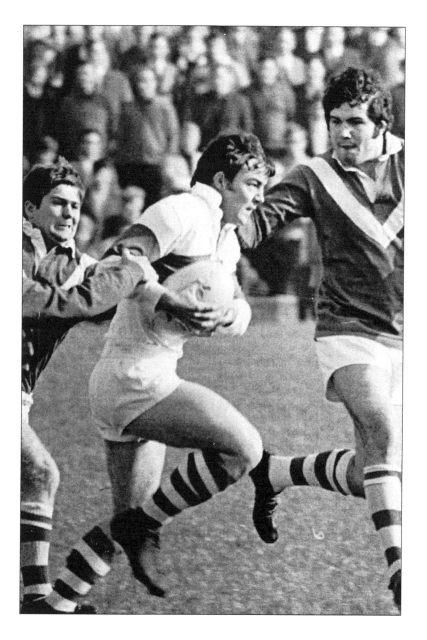

Harry Whitaker, Workington's scrum half and skipper when
Boxer Walker signed as a teenager. 'If Harry had taken a dislike
to me I would have been in serious trouble,' says Boxer. 'But he was
really kind. On the first training session, he put his arms around
me and made me so welcome. I think he saw summat in me.'

*Ike Southward, Town's Great Britain winger, who scored
376 career tries. Ike played an important part in Boxer's
development throughout his time at Derwent Park.*

When Boxer made his first away trip in Town's first team, he was taken to one side by the captain, David 'Jazzer' Curwen, and told he had to honour the club hierarchy and keep away from the back of the bus, which was exclusively for the senior pros, like the players pictured here. Above: Ken Goodall, the British and Irish Lions tourist and to the right, Jazzer Curwen, who had been Kells skipper, Rodney Smith, Town's powerful back row forward and Smiler Allen, who would go on to make 384 career appearances.

Jackie Newall, who was the
A team scrum half when
Boxer joined Town in 1971.

Derek McMilllan,
Boxer's close friend and
Workington stand-off.

Alan Banks, the Workington hooker, who
made 285 appearances for the club. 'Alan
really put himself about, he was a great
tackler,' says Boxer. 'I don't think he would
get away with it now because every tackle
was high on the chest. And he was always
there backing up, looking for a break.'

David Collister, Town's
Lancashire Cup winning
winger who was a
ferocious tackler.

Boxer Walker sets up an attack with Paul Charlton looking on. Boxer played for Workington for nine seasons before being transferred to Whitehaven for £30,000 in 1980.

Boxer Walker followed his father into the colliery at Haig Pit
when he was 21. 'Town always looked after the pit bosses,' says
Boxer. 'I would see a director at the start of the season and ask for
four or five season tickets and they would give the OK. They loved
the game and would do anything to help the rugby players.'

Blind side prop Eddie Bowman looks around with Billy Pattinson and Derek McMillan backing up. 'Eddie was the best ball player I have ever seen from all the players I played with and against,' says Boxer. 'He was so clever with his hands. I wouldn't have been half the player I was without him. If he was playing today he would be priceless and the best player in the Super League.'

Centre Ian Wright scored 170 career tries and was Town's top try scorer in a season eight times. 'He was our Golden Man,' says Boxer. 'Ian was always the fastest man on the field, whoever we were playing. Once he got a yard in front, he was gone and no one would catch him. What a marvellous player.'

Les Gorley was shipped out to Widnes in 1979 for £18,000, amid rumours of a back injury. He went on to play for Great Britain, and 162 times for the Chemics. 'Les was one of the best second row forwards of my era,' says Boxer Walker.

Tommy Raudonikis, the Australian half back who was once quoted as saying: 'I hate Poms as if they had done something wrong to my family.' Boxer made his county debut for Cumbria against the touring Australians in Whitehaven in 1973. Raudonikis was marking Boxer and the two scrum halves spent a late night together in the pubs and clubs of the town.

Workington Town, 1974: Back - Eddie Bowman, Les Gorley, Ralph Calvin, Harold McCourt, Harold Henney, Alan Banks, John Risman, Tommy Thompson, David Atkinson. Front - Dave Curwen, Iain MacCorquodale, Ian Wright, John Dobie, Bobby Nicholson, Arnold Walker.

Louis Shepherd was a fearless protector of half backs and he always looked out for Boxer Walker. When Louis was 19, he was picked for Cumberland and was asked to mark a large Australian winger called Peter Dimond, who considered rugby league the perfect opportunity to show the world how tough he was. Dimond was carried off on a stretcher, unconscious after five minutes.

Alan Tait, the former Hawick skipper, who was Workington's stand-off when Boxer first signed

Eppie Gibson, Boxer's first-team coach at Town. 'I don't want you to get yourself killed,' he told him.

Tom Mitchell brought Boxer to Town for £750 when the scrum-half signed the back of a cigarette packet. Tom was on first name terms with King Farouk and Pablo Picasso.

Ecky Bell, who was an outstanding centre for Town, was Boxer's A team coach when he was 19.

Workington Town squad in 1976: Back – T. Graves (groundsman), Eddie Bowman, Bob Maxwell, Ken Groves, Eric Bell (coach). Second row - Bill Martin (club steward), Mrs Doreen Martin, Judy Hampson (physio), J. Martin (office), Rene Anderson (secretary), Tony Roper, Ralph Calvin, Les Gorley, Arthur Culnean, Ian Hartley, Peter Gorley, David Collister, David Atkinson, Dave Smith, John Kelly, J. Williams (Pools), W. Kennedy, John Fillingham (director). Third row - Ike Southward (youth policy), Alan Banks, Ian Wright, Stan Pattinson, Paul Charlton, Jack Atkinson (director), Tom Mitchell (director), Harold Henney, Raymond Hurst, David Wright, Andy Key (trainer). Front - John Risman, Harry Marland, Arnold Walker, John Dobie.

Billy Garratt played 234 games for Whitehaven and he was an inspirational coach for Kells when Boxer was a teenager. 'I owe a lot to Billy,' says Boxer. 'Everyone looked up to him and respected him. I learned a lot from Billy and he always looked after me.'

Town won the Wigan Sevens tournament in 1978. Back: Billy Pattinson, Alan Banks, Ian Hartley, Iain MacCorquodale , George Graham (chairman). Front: Arnold Walker, Paul Charlton, Ian Wright, missing Bob Blackwood.

CHAPTER 9

There Are No Helmets, Marra

There was a rumour circulating Derwent Park about the imminent arrival of a stand-off half. More information was hard to come by and the only thing anyone knew for certain was that he went by the name of Ricky and was short on experience. Boxer was anticipating that Ricky would likely be a young half-back from one of Cumbria's top amateur sides or, heaven forbid, a rugby union trialist from across the border. Either way he wasn't too fussed.

Ricky, as it would soon become clear, was as low on the rung of rugby league knowledge as it was possible to get. He was an American Footballer. It later came to light that Ricky was an outstanding running back in College Football or so he claimed. He was something of a star with Oklahoma, Notre Dame or Nebraska, the exact university was unclear, so they said. There was talk about some kind of report that provided incontrovertible evidence of his ability, facts about his speed and athletic prowess.

It was a project that had Tom Mitchell's finger prints all over it. He had always been known as a wizard when it came to evaluating talent. But Ricky was something else. And to say he lacked experience was misleading to say the least and was comparable, say, to describing the maiden voyage of the Titanic as disappointing. The following Saturday, the Workington A team is preparing for the kick-off when Ricky walks into the Derwent Park dressing room holding a holdall and chewing gum. A director takes him around the team making formal introductions but no one is taking much notice.

Boxer welcomes him warmly but he is preoccupied with his own preparations. Ricky, so the story goes, begins to put on his boots and shorts, while his new team-mates are talking among themselves, the air resonating with Cumbrian accents as thick as maple syrup.

"Hey guys, can someone tell me where the locker room is?" says Rick. "Where do you keep the helmets and shoulder pads?"

"This is it marra," says Boxer, we have to play like this. There are no helmets in rugby league."

Rick sits down on the bench, a look of utter bewilderment on his face. He begins pulling on his Town shirt, and there's a knock on the door, indicating that it is time for the kick-off. Rick knows about first downs, linebackers and blitzes but he doesn't know much about rugby league.

He has never held a rugby ball before, knows nothing about scrums, play-the-balls or offside. And to make matters worse, the opposition have heard about the presence of a grid iron star over from the USA 'to show the Brits how it should be done.'

Rick's contribution didn't amount to much, apart from a few offside penalties. The one time he actually touched the ball, he was gang tackled by three big forwards that left him momentarily unconscious as if a small wall had fallen on top of him.

At half-time, Town's players are sucking oranges, and Ricky is looking worse for wear. His mouth is bleeding and he has a large bruise around his right eye. Boxer is about to ask him what he made of rugby league, the irony of the situation not lost on him, but the American has already taken off his kit and is limping towards the dressing room door carrying his holdall.

"No helmets? You guys are all crazy. I'm outta here," he says, before slamming the door behind him.

§

Boxer had become bored with his occupation as an apprentice electrician under the instruction of team-mate Howard 'Smiler' Allen. They were often working away, and staying overnight, refurbishing old buildings, and he was fed up with all the travelling and talk of power triangles, earthing systems and radial circuits. So he followed his father into Haig Pit where he became an unreliable member of the supplies team, with a fondness for sleeping on the job. His celebrity status as a Town player afforded him lenient management and, in fact, the hierarchy were so proud of his employment, his large framed photograph was placed in the entrance.

"I was always getting caught sleeping," remembers Boxer. "I liked my kip. I just found a nice warm corner in what we called a manhole. I had a big battery on my back, so I would turn off my lamp, take off my battery and make myself comfortable. If you were found sleeping down't pit, it was instant dismissal. I got sacked at least 10 times. The night shift manager was called John Skelley, who was my next door neighbour at Mid Street - he never sacked me, he just woke me up and gave me a roasting. This is what would happen. When I was sacked and told to get out of the pit, all my mates would say that they would walk out too. There might be six of us and when we all stuck together it just blew over and I went back to work.

"I was on supplies, loading up girders and stuff like that. When anyone started down the pit they had to spend 20 days training and the youngsters often did that with me. I was their boss, I suppose. I was one of the lads and they all wanted to stay with me. They would bring me chocolates and biscuits every day – I never had to bring any bait.

"The back shift was 12 noon until 7 and that was no good for the rugby players, we would miss training. But all the managers really looked after us and they would let the rugby players start at 9 so we would finish in time for training. So Town always looked after the pit bosses. I would see a director at the start of the season and ask for four or five season tickets and they would give the OK and I would get them from the secretary Rene Anderson. Brian Carrey was the general manager and Jim Brennan was the under manager and they were from Leigh and were big rugby league men. They loved the game and would do anything to help us."

§

Boxer was feeling right at home with the A team and the player coach Ecky Bell who had taken over from Ike Southward. And already, after only a few months, heads were turning, opinions were forming and there was a buzz around Derwent Park that there was a chance that a very special player was among them. Harry Whitaker saw him more as a project than a threat to his position at the club and he knew that young players coming through to replace older pros approaching the end of their careers was the natural order of things, and any way there wouldn't be much he could do about it as Boxer's artistry was there, in front of everyone, every week in training.

It was hard to believe that only a few weeks before, Boxer was stricken with self-doubt and only the wise and firm intervention of his father had put him back on track. He was now in the right frame of mind and all the old arrogance had returned and if anything, he had even more of it.

"Looking back all those years ago, I can remember the first pay packet I got playing for the A Team - £2.50 and that was winning pay too. A few years later, when I was an established first-teamer, it was great. I think we were on around £50 for a win and I was getting £9 for a full week down't pit.

"We had some great players in the A Team. I remember at the end of that first year we got into a cup final, I think it was called the Lancashire Shield. Well, one of the superstars of the first team was called Ken Goodall, who signed from rugby union, and he played for the British Lions. He had been injured for a while and hadn't played many first team games so he was eligible for the cup final. We played Salford over two legs and if I remember right, we only won the home leg by a few points.

"When we went to Salford, what happened? Me, the silly bugger only got sent off, for the first time in my pro career. It was a really long walk down the tunnel. I had let all my team-mates down and everyone was saying that we couldn't win, not a player down. Ken Goodall had an absolute blinder. They couldn't handle him and he scored the winning try and saved my bacon. I know if we had got beat it would have been my fault. We got £7 each for that."

The vets had tried to dislike him, this kid who already knew too much, but instead, Boxer had become an object of affection. Rather, they found his talent as something to foster and they had to admit that he had acquired a certain pugilistic competence that they found appealing and was further worthy of their respect. Apart from that, there was absolute indisputable evidence in everything he did that he would soon be among them, in the first team and driving them on to victory.

Earlier concerns that Boxer might be too small had long gone, though having said that, it must have made an interesting sight, especially seen from high up in the stands, watching him walk onto the field, perhaps sandwiched between his great friends Les Gorley and Eddie Bowman, who soared over him by more than seven inches. The three friends would be chatting casually and one of the big men, whose white shirts would be stretched tight over his broad shoulders, would be holding the ball, point down, in one hand, the Town coaches already taking up their positions in the dugout, exchanging small talk, knowing as they did, that the kick-off was only a few minutes away and nothing more could be done. Seen from the terraces he might appear like a boy scout or a choir boy but there was nothing remotely ecclesiastical about his fondness for punching, kneeing and a whole lot of other things that were a big part of the way he played. Patience was never among his list of virtues but he understood and accepted with good grace, that his gentle handling by the coaching staff was in his best interests - well almost.

"I was in and out of the first team before I really got my shirt," Boxer recalls. "I was mainly in the A team for a good 12 months. I can't remember my A team debut but my first start for the first team really sticks in my mind. When the first team substitutes were picked, one was a forward and one was a back. I got in as substitute for the first team at a place called Huyton, which has changed its name lots of times and used to be Liverpool City, I think, and then Runcorn Highfield. I came on as a sub and went straight to scrum half and I scored the winning try. We were pressing on their line, and there was a scrum and the ball was bouncing around a bit and all I had to do was fall on it right under the sticks. I was the hero.

"If I remember rightly, I think I kept my spot for the next three matches. Then Eppie Gibson, the first team coach, dropped us back into the A team again. I went straight in to see him and said: 'What's the score here? Why have you dropped me? I think I am shining in the first team.'

" 'Boxer,' he said. 'I know you're playing well but I don't want you to get killed. I want you back in the A team then back in the first team for a few matches then back in the A team again. Look, you haven't done anything wrong. I don't want to spoil you. You'll be in and out until I think that you can hold your spot.' "

§

On the subject of Boxer's modest dimensions it is interesting to look at the mountainous proportions of the biggest man who has ever played Test rugby, believed to be a currency manager who goes by the name of Bill Cavubati. The tight-head prop set a world record for an international player when he tipped the scales at slightly over 26 stones, playing for Fiji against the All Blacks in 2005. According to a report in the local paper, Bill, who is now 41, is considerably bigger and weighs in 'almost 30 stones.' Apparently, when he is not dealing with foreign exchange matters, he undertakes alternative employment as a bouncer at a hotel on the wrong side of the tracks in Wellington, New Zealand. The newspaper goes on to report that Bill is on call 'only on special occasions' which do not include brawls and knife fights and whatever else might be considered a normal night for such an establishment. Rather he is sent for only to deal with violence of an altogether different level of description, which the article refers to as 'a riot.'

§

Harry Whitaker was soon transferred to York to clear the way for Boxer's inevitable and permanent promotion to the first team. "I always look at experience in rugby league like this," says Boxer. "Imagine you are a tradesman - a plumber or a fitter or an electrician. Well, they have to serve a five-year apprenticeship and it's a bit like that in rugby. I came from Kells to Town's A team, and it is a big step up from the amateurs, in fact, it's a lot faster, so that's one year of your apprenticeship. The second year, if you are good enough, you get in the first team, that's your second year and that's a massive thing. It is 10 yards faster than the A team, you have to have eyes in the back of your head, you can't relax and you can't take your eyes off the opposition, not for a second.

"And then, after a few years more experience, you might break into your county and that's another year of your apprenticeship, another step up in class and then finally, England and Great Britain, that's the route to the top for the very best players."

In his first two years at Derwent Park he made 25 first-team appearances but despite what might appear as a lack of experience, Boxer made his debut for Cumberland in a 28-2 defeat by the touring Australians at the Recreation Ground, in October, 1973.

He was the best player in the A team and all their attacks revolved around him. Boxer would get the ball at first receiver, while the backs and forwards scattered around him, to the left and to the right, some to the blind side, some to the open, and he would fire out passes, long and short as Town pressed forward. The veterans in the first-team would monitor his progress and ask: 'how did the la'al fella do?' And the answer that would come back was almost always the same and along the lines of: 'Great, Boxer is going to be a special player.' But to the vets, he was still a cheeky kid, and though they took their protective duties seriously and when called for, violently, he still had to respect them, defer to them and do what he was told. That's the way it's always been, they told him. The hierarchy at a professional rugby club still had to be adhered to and Boxer was happy to embrace it, follow their instructions obediently and without question and show a respectful deference to the big men who looked after him.

"When I first played in an away game for the first team, I got a whisper in my ear from one of the first teamers," remembers Boxer. "It was David 'Jazzer' Curwen, a second row forward, who was the Kells captain and now the Town skipper. He took me to one side when we were waiting for the bus to pick us up and he said: 'Boxer, don't think you're going to walk to the back of the bus. It doesn't work like that. You need to get a newspaper, lad, get on that bus, sit on the front, read that paper and when you've finished it, read the bloody thing again and again. Don't think you are going straight to the back of the bus with the top boys.'

"That was like serving your time as well, only not on the field. There was a hierarchy, from the young 'uns at the front of bus, then it was the middle and then right at the back seat, where the likes of 'Smiler' Allen, Louis Shepherd, cousin of the great Syd Lowdon, Billy Kirkbride and Rodney Smith would sit. All the older pros would be there, the elite players, who had been here for a few years. Of course I did what he told me, I had to.

"One time we were in the changing rooms before a match. I can't remember where but I can remember what happened. One of the senior players called me over in the toilets and gave me a bucket full of water and pointed to a cubicle.

"He told me that Eddie Bowman was in there and ordered me to throw the water over the top, you know, for a bit of fun. Well, I wasn't too keen but I had to, you just had to do everything the seniors told you. I was only 19-years-old but I knew I always had to respect the old pros. I had to do whatever they told me.

"I'll never forget who it was on the toilet - poor Ike Southward with his club blazer on. He was the first team coach and a proper legend. Well, Ike came out and he was drowning in water. I had made a right mess of him. I just ran away into the changing rooms and the first person I saw was Eddie Bowman. I said to the old pro: 'I thought Eddie was in there.' And everyone just fell about laughing. I'll never forget that day. For the first few games, there were perhaps eight players in a drinking syndicate, and in them days, they would have a pile of notes on the middle of a table in a pub kitty.

" 'Boxer, go and get the beer in lad, and don't forget to get yourself one as well,' they would tell me. You had to do what the seniors said. I know I was a cheeky bugger but somehow I just knew I had to do what they told me and I am glad I did. Remember, I never paid for a drink - all my drinks came out of the kitty. Of course, it wasn't like that on the field. You played your own game for the good of the team. There was a great team spirit at Town and all the older pros looked after me.

"Louis Shepherd was unbelievable. I remember once playing with him in the first team in an away game. He was my stand-off. Well Louis tackled the other team's stand-off and knocked him out. He woke up straight away and they only stopped the game for a couple of minutes. Then we had a scrum and it was their put-in and I could see the stupid bugger mouthing to Louis telling him what he was going to do to him. 'I am coming to get you,' he kept shouting. They won the ball and the stand-off ran right at Louis again at full speed and he just decked him and he finished unconscious again. They carried him off on a stretcher and he didn't come back which was probably just as well for him. I think he must have been knocked out twice in about two minutes.

"I learnt so much from all these older pros but I have to admit that I was never intimidated by any big-name players and this even included the likes of Roger Millward, one of the best players ever. A few years later when I was an established first-teamer, Cumbria were playing Yorkshire at Hull KR. I remember our loose forward was another Kells lad, Tom Gainford - what a tackler he was. I was a lot more experienced then and if I remember rightly I was captain of the county team as well as Town.

"I went to the centre of the field to toss up for the kick-off and the referee said: 'Right lads, shake hands and have a good game.' And I wouldn't do it. I swore at Roger and refused to do it. I told the ref: 'I am not his friend, I have come here to win.' I don't think he could believe what I was saying talking like that to such a great player. I would do that with anyone, not just Roger. Once I was on that field, I had no friends on the opposition. It was psychological. I knew Roger was a legend and rightly so, he was a great player. When he died last year I sent a message to his family telling them how sorry I was.

"Later on that game, I will always remember it, Roger told me I would never play for Great Britain. 'Boxer you are far too dirty,' he told me. I will always remember him saying that. I think he was just trying to wind me up. Back then there were a lot of ways to wind the opposition up.

"Nothing like that really bothered me. Say we are in the dressing room before a big match and the coach shouted across to me something he wanted me to do in the game. 'Have you got that Boxer?' I would say: 'OK, I've got that,' and I would try to do my best and follow what he said. If he shouted at me or tried to tell me off, it didn't bother me at all, it was water off a duck's back. He was just doing his job and trying to help us win.

"But some players didn't like coaches shouting at them. The odd one might wonder why is he picking on them and they might take it to heart but none of that mattered to me. Some players need an arm around them but that kind of thing was a waste of time for me.

"Every year, before the season started we were given a talk by Doctor Walker. He would give us advice about how to look after ourselves, and to make sure we didn't drink too much, that kind of stuff. All the players were there, first teamers and A teamers and he said that he knew a few of us liked the odd pint. He wasn't including Ian Wright, of course, he only drank shandy. Doctor Walker's advice was always the same: I know many of you like a pint but whatever you do, keep off those shorts. The spirits are killers and they take a long time to get out of your system.

"At the end of his talk he asked us if we had any questions but no one said a word, so I put my hand up. I was such a silly lad. 'How can I help you, Arnold,' he said. I asked him: 'How safe is it before a match if I wanted to have sex? Would it drain all the energy out of me?' Everyone was falling about laughing. The club secretary was Bill Whalley, the mayor of Workington, and he said: 'I might have known it would have been you asking that daft question.' Doctor Walker was laughing his head off too."

Boxer's father Duncan had rarely missed him playing for Kells but for some reason rarely watched him play professionally. He was his harshest critic and this unsympathetic assessment was clear when he made a rare visit to watch his son face Leeds at Derwent Park. "I had a cracker of a game and scored two tries," says Boxer. "Everyone was patting me on the back and making a fuss and I was as proud as punch. I met my dad in the bar after the game, and I was expecting him to say to me: 'Great game lad, well played,' something like that. Well he knocked me right off my pedestal. He told me: 'There is room for improvement son.' My mam never watched me in the flesh – she was too frightened that I was going to get hurt. I think she watched me on the telly the odd time."

§

Boxer was quickly establishing a formidable reputation as much more than a promising rugby league player. He was a match-winner and the creative force behind most of Town's attacks. And while it was true to say he was a player of some renown, Boxer had also earned a name as a fearless defender who would punch, knee and kick opponents in his single-minded pursuit of victory. This fully-established reputation would follow him throughout his career. But it never troubled Boxer. He had a pack of mighty forwards behind him who saw his potential for greatness first-hand and they looked out for him as if they were saying to the world. "Mess with the kid, and you're messing with us."

Boxer's unique style of defending was an extraordinary thing that bewildered big men. They would see this small man in front of them and grossly underestimate his skill and courage. If they did not know him, their eyes would light up and they would hurtle towards him at full speed and most of the time they would end up flat on their backs, not sure what had happened.

"It doesn't take a genius to realise that if you went down below, you stand a big chance of getting size tens in your face," recalls Boxer. "You are probably going to get hammered by the knees and boots. Nine times out of ten, a rugby player carries the ball under one arm and hands off with the other. That suited me because I could grab hold of their shirt and drag them down – we used to call it the hand and foot tackle. If I got it right, I could knock the wind right out of them. You never see anyone do it now. They say that Dick Huddart used to run with his knees so high they were up to his chest, so how was I going to tackle a big forward running like that? Harry Beverley used to run like that, with his knees right up and he was one of the hardest men I ever tackled."

When he was around 20, Workington travelled to Craven Park, the home of Hull Kingston Rovers, for a league fixture. And what happened on that day was typical of the kind of violence he was bringing on himself through his fondness for the game's confrontational excesses.

"There was a great team spirit at Town and all the older pros looked after me," recalls Boxer. "I have a great story to explain this. Remember this would never have happened later in my career because I knew what I was doing. It was away at Hull Kingston Rovers and I am on the ground with the ball and this big forward came on top of me and pushed his elbow right in my face. Later on I would have known to keep my elbow up to protect myself - the elbow was a great guard against stiff arms. It saved a lot of trouble. But I was green as grass then and I left my arms down - I had so much to learn. He just flopped right down on me with his forearm in my face."

The unnamed forward had the misfortune to abuse Boxer in close proximity to the Town dugout where coaches, the sponge man and two substitutes were watching the game. One of the substitutes was a loose forward called Louis Shepherd, who was a ferocious tackler with a devout belief in retaliation. He had learned his trade under the wise tutelage of legendary Haven and Cumberland front row forward Big Bill McAlone, who celebrated his 90th birthday last year. Louis, still wearing his tracksuit, leapt from the sidelines, grabbed the offending forward by the neck, and hit him twice, right there in full view, without a moment's hesitation, as if it wasn't such a big deal, right square on the jaw - bang, bang. He fell limp in Louis's hands, and he finished the job by throwing him on to the pitch with great satisfaction, the offending player out like a light, as if a piano had fallen on top of him.

What followed can only be described as a mass brawl, with both teams exchanging punches and it was only stopped by the intervention of members of the Yorkshire constabulary. The referee was nonplussed for what seemed like a long time, as if he was giving careful contemplation to what had just unfolded in front of him, which was hardly surprising considering the rarity of the situation, and the fact that Louis was technically a substitute who was not, officially at least, permitted to take part in the match, not in any capacity, let alone assaulting an opponent. Then the referee came to his senses and began pointing to the dressing room and Louis nodded respectfully, without complaint, before walking along the touchline, accompanied by two police officers, one either side of him, as angry Rovers' fans hurled abuse.

His departure was not well received by the Town coaching staff as they contemplated how they were going to survive the rest of the match with 12 men and the loss of a powerful forward. Meanwhile, Louis is standing in the shower, though he probably didn't need one, and running through the incident in his head, and coming to the firm conclusion that the assault just had to be done. He had no choice - no one was going to mess around with the kid when Louis was around.

"Louis got right into him," says Boxer. "He was so angry that this big experienced forward had done that to me, a young pup, only 20-years-old who knew nowt about protecting myself. Luckily for me, he didn't quite catch me properly and I just managed to turn my head around so his elbow glanced around my ear and there was no big damage. Louis went to live in Australia and he is a big mate of Paul Charlton. They worked together at Border Engineers. I remember we went to a night club that night and I told him how grateful I was for him sticking up for me. 'You'll learn, son,' he told me. I played with Louis a few times and I'll never forget that day."

Louis Shepherd had an extraordinary will to win and he took the view that only victory was acceptable and that defeat represented a catastrophe. Intimidation radiated from him and his team-mates, especially the half backs, loved him for his extraordinary virtues of retribution and willingly overlooked his limitations as a reliable but unspectacular player. Anyone with his wits about him never, ever messed with him. Louis's career as a legendary hardman is quite something. He was appropriately named after Joe Louis, The Brown Bomber, who was the world heavyweight champion for 12 years, after winning the title in 1937 against James Braddock. When Louis was 19, he was banned from rugby league for life when he had been penalised for a late tackle and the referee asked him his name. 'It's in the programme,' he told the referee who didn't have much of a sense of humour and immediately sent him off. He was reinstated at the end of the season and went on trial at Warrington where New Zealand legend Ces Mountford was the coach.

Louis played for Whitehaven for 13 years before joining Town and if you believe the stories, he once introduced Vince Karalius to oblivion. Vince was the protector of Alex Murphy on the 1958 Australian Tour and the scrum half compared having his loose forward looking out for him to playing alongside the Kray twins – both of them. Louis played for Cumberland at the Recreation Ground against the Australian tourists in 1963. He was told to mark a large winger called Peter Dimond, who arrived in the UK with a fearsome reputation as a brute of a man who loved violence and considered rugby league the perfect opportunity to show the world how tough he was. Dimond was carried off unconscious after five minutes.

Another violent illustration of the protective nature of Workington packs occurred during a trip to Leeds that followed a dismal run of eight league defeats. Everything had clicked just so in the first half which resulted in a hefty and wholly unexpected lead for the Cumbrians. There was much recrimination and finger pointing in the Leeds dressing room which resulted in their forwards coming out all fired up, and the way things worked out, out of control. Town prop Harry Beverley came to the game with a large black eye after getting on the wrong side of Jim Mills, in an international match between England and Wales the previous weekend. Harry had an exceptional capacity to withstand pain and he had ignored pleas from medical staff to withdraw. Not surprisingly, his injury had deteriorated, and for his own good, he was taken off. This necessitated a shuffle in the pack which moved Peter Gorley to the front row. Leeds forwards Steve Pitchford, David Ward and Graham Joyce seemed to have been singled out for especially harsh criticism from coach Syd Hynes and in the first scrum they decided to forget about rugby and began an assault on the Town pack. This was not a particularly smart thing to do and within around 30 seconds, David Ward was out cold and surrounded by three other Leeds forwards nursing a variety of head injuries that required medical attention. The Town pack was standing together, all six of them, towering over their opponents, in perfect unison, blasting out in one voice that they weren't going to be messed with.

§

Paul Charlton was now the player-coach at Workington. All the team loved playing for him partly because he is probably the greatest full back in the history of rugby league and partly because he was never aloof and always humble and dismissive of his own accomplishments which include scoring 33 tries in one season and playing for Great Britain 19 times. Paul was one of the lads but he could always switch off and become an authority figure who demanded respect in an instant, if the occasion demanded it. Everybody listened when Paul was giving his instructions. "I was having a good run at Town when I was only about 23," recalls Boxer. "I had scored a try in a few matches on the run, not always down to me, of course - I might have just backed someone up and just been in the right place at the right time - nowt to do with me. Then I had a bad run - I was playing OK but I wasn't scoring tries and that turned the tables for the fans who were starting to have a go at me. They were asking me: 'What's the matter, why aren't you scoring?'

"It was getting me down so I went to Paul, and told him about the stick I was getting. He just laughed and told me not to worry about it. Paul said the same thing had happened to him when he went to Salford. Keith Fielding, Dave Watkins, Maurice Richards and Chris Hesketh were all scoring and not Paul. I asked him to drop me but he wouldn't, he said I was playing great and that he had great faith in me."

CHAPTER 10

Boardroom Backhanders

Boxer is enjoying a few beers in a town centre bar alongside some retired Town players after a hard night's training at Derwent Park. The mood is celebratory and there's a lot to feel good about if you are a Town supporter. The team has won three games in succession and everything is falling in place under the stewardship of Sol Roper, himself a successful scrum half who is taking great pleasure in passing on his wisdom to Boxer, who is settling in nicely to the role of playmaker among a team of stars. The atmosphere is suddenly conspiratorial and the old pros move closer before asking him discreetly, quietly, so no one would overhear.

"Have you been in for a backhander yet?" they ask, before beginning a lengthy explanation of what it is, how it works and how to acquire it, which goes something along the lines of this. A backhander, they explain, is an under-the-counter payment that it is possible for star players to receive from directors, providing a specific set of circumstances are met.

"You had to be a regular and well established in the first team," recalls Boxer. "You knew when you were playing well. You couldn't do it in the first few months - at the time I was playing great and scoring and making tries.

"I had never heard of a backhander. I didn't know what it was but these old pros were telling me. 'Get in there. It's a short career, marra. Next week you could break your leg and be finished.' "

They go on to explain that a player needs to be performing well, winning matches and playing for Cumbria and it would also help if you are being frequently linked with moves to other clubs. Boxer clearly qualified on all counts but the final requirement was to figure out a unique reason for a sudden and desperate need for money.

So the following week, Boxer is knocking on the boardroom door, following another five-star display at the weekend and he was getting right into the feel of things wearing a glum expression suitably appropriate for someone facing a financial catastrophe. Boxer recalls the identity of the director - Tom Mitchell, who had signed him less than three years before. Timing was everything he had been told.

"I plucked up the courage and went in to see Tom," says Boxer. "If I had been playing moderate I would not have got anything. I told him: I am in trouble. It's all my bills at home. I can't pay the electric, the rates or water bill. I have debts and I just can't pay them."

Tom goes to a large cabinet and returns with an expensive-looking ledger, the kind you might expect to find in use in a successful lawyer's office.

"How much do you need?" he asks. "You are playing well. I have to admit it."

"A thousand pounds should do it," says Boxer, who had been told that was the going rate.

The director writes out a cheque without a hint of negotiation, warning him that it will take three days to clear. Boxer signs the ledger and promises to keep the transaction confidential before he leaves with a huge grin on his face.

"I couldn't wait to tell Les Gorley," he says, as if it hadn't crossed his mind to keep his payment private, not for a moment. "He was one of my best mates and we both signed around the same time. I told him to get himself in. It ended up like a free for all between me and Les. We didn't start training until about 6.15 and I would be sitting on the forecourt at 5.30 so I would be the first one in to get paid out."

Les constructed a suitable sob story, which he had meticulously planned, and involved a lengthy list of expensive bills that he was unable to pay, related to his latest car, which on this occasion was a large green Triumph 2000. He needed four new tyres, an MoT and unspecified but highly expensive work on the engine, not to mention insurance and tax. The story goes that on his first trip to the boardroom seeking the 'backhander' he realised that he had already paid the car tax which was displayed on the windscreen. He quickly returned to the car park and covered up the disc with a Guinness beer mat in the event that a director might check the authenticity of his story, which was unlikely and would have made an interesting scene, you know, a director carrying out a thorough inspection of the car, wearing a smart suit, kicking the tyres and checking for oil leaks while the team looked across from the stadium windows.

Boxer continued to show his artistry to the unrestrained delight of assistant coach Ike Southward, and it was his professional opinion that the scrum half had all the requirements to become an international player. Support from such an authoritative source got Boxer thinking and before long he was knocking on the boardroom door again seeking his second 'backhander' to help avert another imaginary financial crisis. He had been told that a satisfactory payout was more likely if you could deal with the director who had signed you. The talk was that they might have a vested interest in your development and that match-winning performances were positive reflections on their contribution. Boxer had always been known as 'Tom's boy'. Tom had signed him personally and it was no secret that he admired him greatly and his veneration was in no small part due to Boxer's roots, coming from a local mining community.

"I'm in trouble Tom," Boxer pleaded. "Can you please help me out? I can't pay my electricity bill." And Boxer went on to repeat his story of financial difficulty, complete with a dejected demeanour, before waiting patiently for the answer.

"I'll have to a look at the book," said Tom, opening the ledger, before saying: "Arnold, you only got £1,000 a month ago. Is all of bloody Kells wired up to your electric meter?"

Boxer was beginning to lose hope of an agreeable outcome but to his surprise, Tom quickly began writing out another cheque, shaking his head but smiling broadly and Boxer was soon signing the ledger once again.

The problem was Boxer was not very good at keeping secrets. Word had leaked out but there was not much dissention in the team as his contribution was without question. But one county player, who held a high opinion of his own ability, took exception to the news. At that time, Town's training was held on a field to the east of Derwent Park, the present location of Tesco Superstore. It was a lengthy walk to return to the dressing rooms and the player in question, who took his absence from the 'backhanders' club' as a personal slight, took the opportunity to explain his grievances to several of the senior players, telling them of his plans to demand a similar payout, not thinking for a moment that he would not be successful. It was what he deserved, he told them.

"He was bullish," remembers Boxer. "He kept telling everyone: 'I'll get it, I'll get it. I'll show the buggers who the gaffer is. I'll show them when I get in. This isn't on this. I'm going in for my backhander.'"

His anger was plain to see and senior players tried to warn him that it was not a sensible plan and that he would be better off following their policy of claiming acute financial hardship. But he was having none of it and even though he was a fine player he was no Roger Millward or David Topliss.

After a quick shower, he was knocking on the boardroom door, water still dripping from his hair, demanding money and explaining, according to him at least, that it was no more than he deserves.

He was soon back in the dressing room, where the players were awaiting the outcome expectantly.

"How much did you get?" Boxer asked him.

"How much? Bugger all. I'm on the bloody transfer list."

Less than a week later, the player was running out at Craven Park, 50 miles down the coast, at the other end of the meandering A595, making his debut for Barrow, who were coached at that time by another Cumbrian legend, Frank Foster.

"I lost count of the number of backhanders I got," says Boxer. "I always hit them for a thousand. It was always Tom I saw. It was always said among the players, and I can quite believe it as well, that if Tom had originally signed you on, as he did with me and the Gorleys, that he would look after you.

"Tom Graves, who owned nightclubs in Workington was another director who you had a chance with, even if he hadn't signed you. I don't remember what I did with all the money, but I always looked after my mam and dad and quite often I would buy her some nice furniture or whatever she wanted. If she wanted a three-piece suite, I would buy her that. Or I might treat my sister and until all the money was gone I might drop her £40 every now and then, and the rest of it just went."

Town had become a powerful team and they won promotion to the First Division in 1976, the same season the Cumbrians played in the final of the Lancashire Cup, in their first of four consecutive appearances. Workington, who had been boosted by the arrival of 18-stone Welsh forward Jim Mills, were defeated 16-11 by Widnes at Wigan, which had created a big controversy in the press when photographic evidence later proved that Stuart Wright's winning try should not have been awarded.

The next season, Town faced Wigan in the final at Warrington but the Cumbrians were not given much hope of an upset against a team that had once won the trophy six times in succession and would go on to become champions 21 times before the tournament was terminated in 1992.

More than 6,000 Town fans travelled to Wilderspool to roar on their heroes in one of the most exciting finals in the history of the competition.

CHAPTER 11

Talk of the Town

Workington Town would not have won the Lancashire Cup without Boxer Walker. He was voted the man-of-the-match, he topped the tackle count, he kicked two drop goals at vital moments and he had a hand in both tries. Yet Boxer shouldn't have played. He wouldn't have been allowed anywhere near a rugby field using medical protocol which is in place today.

An England rugby union website, appropriately called Headcase, lists a chilling medical warning about the dangers of playing too soon following concussion. It warns: if a player returns too early, before they have fully recovered this may result in long term health consequences such as psychological and/or brain degenerative disorders and a further concussive event being fatal, due to severe brain swelling, known as second impact syndrome.

None of this was known back in 1977 and even if it was, Boxer would have ignored it. Two weeks before the final, Town were playing a First Division game at Headingley against Leeds. Town front row forward Harry Beverley and Boxer were involved in what was reported as 'an accidental collision.' A conservative estimate of their physical differences would give Harry an 80 pounds advantage and was the sporting equivalent of an articulated truck colliding with a supermarket trolley. The two Town players made a tackle together but Boxer got the worst of it.

He was left spark out and, not for the first time in his career, he was carried off on a stretcher. He woke up soon after and was given the all-clear to return home. His medical assessment was overly optimistic and he was admitted into West Cumberland Hospital later that night where he remained for three days undergoing brain scans and various tests. The scrum half was eventually released and his expected absence from the cup final was headline news in the *Workington Times & Star* which reported: 'Star scrum half Walker suffered severe facial bruising and concussion and was detained in hospital with pains in his neck and throat. He was detained for three days and was discharged with a surgical collar on his neck. He may need further specialist treatment, or a period of rest.'

Chairman George Graham was quoted as saying: "This couldn't have come at a worst time. Walker is now doubtful for the cup final and just at a time when he was getting back to his best form and when the side was starting to play around him."

Boxer's influence on the team was its vital component and much in evidence in the Lancashire Cup semi-final when Town had overcome St Helens 5-4 thanks to the scrum-half's late drop goal.

"We were pressing on their 25-yard line in the last five minutes," recalls Boxer, who won another man-of-the-match award. "I went acting half back which is normally the job of the hooker but I knew I had to drop the goal first or second tackle, when they weren't expecting it. There's always the temptation to have another tackle and try to get a bit nearer but things can happen quickly and a forward can be pushed out too wide.

"Saints weren't expecting it and they didn't even move up fast. I had plenty of time on my hands and it sailed over the sticks. I always remember Eddie Bowman lifting me right up in the air. It seems like it was yesterday. We had a great reputation back then and were everyone's bogey team. No one wanted to play us."

Four days after leaving hospital, Boxer declared himself fit and he attended a light training session at Derwent Park on Saturday, October 22, eight days before the cup final. It was here that the players learnt how much they would be paid if they were successful - £100. And Tom Mitchell, who was always looking for angles to give his team an edge, told his players that if they brought the cup back to Cumbria he would personally pay to take them all on a trip to Benidorm.

The team and coaching staff assembled in the lounge to watch Wigan's John Player Trophy match at Leeds which was being televised live by the BBC. There was a mood of anticipation as they huddled together but what they saw did not have a very positive effect on their chances of an upset, not according to the commentator Eddie Waring anyway.

Wigan had defeated a Leeds side, which was full of internationals including John Atkinson, Les Dyl, John Holmes, Roy Dickinson, David Ward and Steve Pitchford. South African winger Green Vigo was unstoppable for Wigan, and he crossed for three tries in the 25-22 win. Wigan were too big, too strong and too fast for Town, so everyone said, and the statistics didn't provide much comfort for Cumbrian fans – Wigan had appeared in 26 finals, and they had won the trophy 15 times – this was Workington's second appearance. The morning newspapers that were being read on the team coach as the party set off for Wilderspool did not carry optimistic predictions. There was one account, unattributed, that Wigan's talented second row forward Bill Ashurst had placed a large bet on Wigan. According to the report, the Great Britain international could not be deterred from his wager, despite the prohibitive odds-on prices. One reporter had installed Wigan as 16-point favourites but no one was taking much notice of that as a long line of cars containing Town fans, and bedecked in blue and white, flashed alongside the coach, waving scarves at their heroes.

The Town coach stopped at the County Hotel, in the centre of Carnforth, for a light lunch where a room had been reserved specifically for massage purposes. Andy Key, the former county forward who was part of the coaching staff, operated a useful sideline as a manipulator of muscles. He was considered one of the best on account of his own medical condition which involved acute arthritis in his fingers which were more like thick drum sticks, and apparently not much good for playing the piano but especially suitable for the pummelling of legs and arms. A queue of players, all looking smart in their new navy blue suits and Town badges, formed outside the room while Boxer and Eddie Bowman chose records to play on the hotel jukebox.

"No one gives us a chance, Eddie," said Boxer. "But I've got a good feeling about this. Something tells me we are going to pull this off."

Coach Ike Southward joined the players for a relaxing walk of perhaps a mile and soon they were back on the M6 and close to the Wilderspool stadium where they were assisted through the traffic by a police motorcyclist, yellow lights flashing and siren blaring, as the long lines of stationary vehicles parted in front of them. Behind the scenes, while the players prepared themselves, a legal row was going on between the competition's main sponsors Burtonwood Brewery and Matthew Brown, who had commissioned new tracksuits for the Town players. They would not be permitted to wear them.

"I remember waiting in the dressing room and I could hear the Wigan team walk out onto the field," recalls Boxer. "We could hear everyone cheering. Then someone on the tannoy said something like: 'Come on you Town supporters. Put your hands together for your mighty Workington team.' Paul Charlton was the captain and he led us out onto the field and all the cheers started. I was superstitious and I always insisted on being the last player even though it meant I would walk out behind the two subs.

"You could hear the crowd for a couple of seconds then it went so loud we all went deaf. It moved us, every one of us. We were all really nervous and we knew we were up against it. We just looked at each other and we knew we couldn't let all our fans down. We had to win."

The official attendance would eventually number 9,548 and a conservative estimate of the Cumbrian contribution was close to 6,000 and those who couldn't make the trip were huddled around their television sets while Eddie Waring droned on. The half-time score was 9-8 to Town who had scored two outstanding tries by Ian Wright and Ray Wilkins, following mighty play from Peter and Les Gorley, which was characteristic of the kind of running and support play, rarely seen in today's Super League, and which had always been right at the heart of Town's playbook since 1946. Wigan scored two tries from centre David Willicombe and forward Bill Ashurst.

The second half was especially notable for three long-range penalties from Iain MacCorquodale and a cheeky drop-goal from Boxer at a vital point when Wigan were threatening to take control. Scrum-half Jim Nulty scored a late try but Town had not come this far to permit a late comeback.

"I think the turning point was when we were defending our own line and Wigan really looked like scoring," remembers Boxer. "Billy Pattinson was tackled by Bill Ashurst, who lost his rag and nutted him. Now Patty was a good pro and I don't think he was hurt but he made a meal of it and the referee gave us a free kick.

"I remember grabbing Billy and saying: 'You bloody beauty.' That gave us the chance to clear our line and, of course, having Corky in our team meant he kicked the ball way into their half, where we had another six tackles. If Wigan had scored then we might not have gone on to win. My second drop goal was a pearler. It went so high between the sticks, not just half-way, it went right over the top. I connected perfectly. My mate Bob Blackwood, playing for Wigan, tried to stop me - he knew what I was going to do. As I turned around, a young Town fan ran on and grabbed hold of me. I just put my hand up in the air. It was a great feeling. At the final hooter I just fell on my knees. Our whole team had played fantastic. We had to.

"There was a pitch invasion of hundreds of Town fans. They came from everywhere and somehow I ended up being carried on their shoulders and bouncing up and down and when I looked around I could see Tom Mitchell being carried on someone else's shoulders. We looked at each other and I tried to stretch my hand across to him but then he was gone.

"We were celebrating that much that before I knew it, all the Workington players had got their medals and the cup had been presented. I missed all that - I was still on the field. I was surrounded by fans and loads of kids and I just couldn't get through. I remember Bob Blackwood got hold of my shirt and dragged me away from the fans and pushed me up the steps. I hadn't realised it but I was holding everything up. The Wigan team couldn't go up until I had got my medal. Bob could have lost his rag after getting beat but he didn't. We had been best mates for years, we still are.

"It was an absolutely marvellous feeling. Some of our players were back on the field wearing Town hats and scarves. Kids had grabbed all my tie-ups and taping. Looking back, I was obviously proud of playing for Cumberland, England and Great Britain but this cup win was the highlight of my career. It was in front of all our fans and with all my best mates and it felt good because we had lost the final the year before against Widnes when they had scored in the last minute.

"All the Wigan players were waiting at the bottom of the steps until I got my medal and my man-of-the-match tankard. When I got out on to the field I remember being kissed and cuddled by all our fans. By the time I got back into our dressing room I was told I had missed all the photographers taking pictures. There was loads of champagne being supped but no one had too much. It wouldn't have made any difference because all our adrenaline was still pumping so fast."

The triumphant party stayed at Wilderspool for around two hours, attending to the requirements of the sponsors, signing autographs and being snapped with various fans and dignitaries, as camera flashes popped, alongside the large trophy which had been placed at the head of the main table, looking glorious and all festooned in blue and white ribbons. The Wigan squad were understandably morose and weren't much interested in taking part in the festivities but Bob Blackwood, Boxer remembers, who everyone respected and liked, took the time to congratulate every Town player personally, one by one, shaking their hands warmly, which was a classy and a remarkably generous thing to do and so typical of his genial personality. Back in the centre of Workington, the streets were full of Town fans, some in a drink-induced state of euphoria, and strangers would wave at people standing far away, and everywhere you looked men, women and children, many wearing blue and white scarves and tri-corner hats, would burst into song, thinking life couldn't get much better than this.

The party returned to the 200 Club at Derwent Park where a big reception had been laid on and normal membership requirements were suspended which attracted an amazing crowd which probably contravened safety regulations. According to older supporters with long memories, it was the best night of celebration at the club for 25 years when Town had brought home the Challenge Cup from Wembley. The festivities did not stop there.

Three nights later, the team was invited to a reception at Workington's Town Hall where Mayor Bob Spedding, alongside Arthur Robinson, the chairman of Allerdale Council, gave their civic congratulations. The event was again covered diligently by the town's weekly newspaper which reported that the crowd, which had assembled outside the building, was causing safety concerns and the players had to be ushered in anonymously through a rear entrance. *The Times & Star* reported: 'A crowd estimated at 2,000, packed the forecourt of the old Town Hall and the streets and pavements around and they cheered wildly as the players took it in turn to hoist the cup aloft. Several encores had to be given for the chanting fans and the last of the crowd did not disperse until three hours later – and only after the cup, filled with beer, had been passed along them.'

Various prominent participants were quoted, beginning with coach Ike Southward, who was also pictured alongside Boxer posing with a toothless grin and holding his man-of-the-match tankard. "I knew we could do it," said Ike. "I was a bit worried when we were not getting the ball in the right places. If we had done, we could have put 30 points on them."

Tom Mitchell said: "This is the result of a lifetime. What the team did has made worthwhile every minute of 32 years of waiting. I was unusually calm throughout the match because we were the better side all the way through. That golden boot of Iain MacCorquodale kept our noses in front. But I won't single out any individual player because everyone was playing for the other 12."

Boxer said: "Right from the start of the final build-up in training, the lads were confident we were not coming back to Workington without that cup. We made it hard for ourselves and Wigan pressed strongly in the second half but the tries they scored were silly ones. They were a good team and it all went according to plan. We just blocked their star man Vigo."

Club president Harry Webster described the victory as "the greatest moment of my association with the club." He added: "We took a team to Wembley three times but we have never been able to lift this one in 32 years. It is a great day for the game in Cumbria."

Chairman George Graham, who led the team out at Wilderspool, said: "I said we would win it and I have sensed it from the word go, because I have watched the lads in training and I knew they were 100 per cent fit. It was a great disappointment when we lost it last year and we were determined that this year, victory was the only thing we would be content with."

There had been 12 Cumbrian-born players in Workington Town's Lancashire Cup winning team and it was, quite literally, an historic event. The competition went way back to 1905 when Wigan beat Leigh at Broughton 8-0 to win the first Lancashire Cup, a match that was watched by a crowd of 10,000. Town's win in 1977 was the first time the trophy had left the confines of the county and there was great hope in West Cumbria that the team was on the cusp of greatness.

Sadly, such optimism was misguided and this great side would be broken up and within three years, six cup final heroes had gone. The team were not thinking of such enduring matters as they packed their suitcases for the trip to Spain three weeks later, which would be the first time most of the players had travelled abroad.

CHAPTER 12

What Went on in Benidorm

Quite what Tom Mitchell was thinking when he decided to offer the players the incentive of a holiday in Spain in return for winning the Lancashire Cup is difficult to figure out. You did not need to have psychic powers to predict that the trip had a high probability of disastrous consequences. Twenty Cumbrian rugby league players celebrating their biggest sporting achievement with a third party picking up the tab, more than a thousand miles from home in a Mediterranean paradise where a pint of lager would set you back 60 pesetas (20p), well, something bad was always going to happen.

What unfolded in Benidorm's three-star Hotel Calypso, 300 yards from the Levante Beach and a five-minute walk from more than 100 drinking establishments was astonishing. There were many incidents which the laws of libel prevent recounting, probably the majority, but what remains is more than enough to give you a sense of the unbelievable. There was nothing malicious you understand, just high jinks on a level no normal person could ever comprehend – seven astonishing days where most of the squad were in a high state of inebriation which always overruled commonsense.

Their escapades would include lost passports, the threat of arrests, plumbing malfunctions, secret service agents, mass brawls, flooded rooms, threats of eviction, riding powerful motor bikes along busy town centre roads at 90 miles an hour, broken down cars, missed flights, replaced flight tickets, compensation claims from bar owners and what was probably a new world record for alcohol consumption.

It all started quietly enough as the coach left Derwent Park heading for Prestwick Airport, at the other end of the A76. As you might expect there was a jolly atmosphere enhanced by more than 100 cans of Whitbread Tankard beer. Prop forward Eddie Bowman had recently returned from Great Britain's World Cup trip to Australia where he had starred alongside Ken Gill, Len Casey, Roger Millward and Steve Nash. The team lost in the final but the experience had given Eddie great confidence in matters of world travel. So as the beer flowed, he decided to volunteer himself for service as an authority on organisation. The truth of the matter was that his expertise didn't amount to much, apart from an unshakeable and obsessive belief in the importance of keeping passports safe at all times.

A powerful thought had placed itself in his head that he should check with all the members of the party personally to make sure that they had their passports. No one was much interested in his advice as he moved through the bus dispensing his wisdom and truth be told, they were starting to believe he was a bit of a nuisance as they pulled into the airport car park, retrieved their luggage and headed for the departure lounge.

The unofficial leader of the group was Workington Town secretary, Major John Francis Fillingham MBE, who, as you might expect, conducted his relationships in an abrupt military fashion, as if he was ordering soldiers around on the parade ground. Major Fillingham wore an aristocratic moustache, dark rimmed glasses and didn't have much hair, and all this added up to make him look like he was the result of a scientific experiment which had cross-pollinated Wyatt Earp and Woody Allen. The major had been a war hero who had fought on the front line against the Nazis, in Italy. Unfortunately for the Major, taking on the might of the German Wehrmacht had not prepared him for the calamitous week in front of him. It was about to get off to a bad start when the former Intelligence Officer was told that one player was at the check-in, a long queue forming behind him, as he frantically searched for his passport until, finally accepting, with a look of absolute disbelief on his face, that he had left his passport on the mantelpiece of his Kells home, more than 140 miles away – Eddie Bowman.

The Major, to his credit, managed to pull off some kind of deal with airport authorities that would allow Eddie to board the plane though he would require a new passport from the British Consulate in Spain, before he would be permitted to return home. Poor Eddie tried to keep a low profile on the plane but he was subjected to much ridicule on the three-hour flight to Alicante airport and the party was soon picking up room keys and preparing for their first night out in Spain.

The players would arrive and remain in one group throughout the week, like a shoal of fish moving together as one entity, from one feeding ground to the next. That first night set the pattern for the week and would involve bar owners initially welcoming the large party with open arms, sensing a profitable bar bill before realising, too late, that the negative cost in broken bottles, smashed glasses, damaged bar furniture, cracked windows and injured bar staff, including several incapacitated bouncers, left them way out of pocket.

The next day, as Peter Gorley remembers it, he was the innocent victim of a plumbing malfunction which would set off a chain of events that would affect dozens of people. He was awoken sometime that morning by the sound of gushing water coming from the bathroom which was in an advanced state of flooding. The magnitude of the catastrophe began to disturb him so he decided to wake up Boxer, who was staying further down the corridor. Peter needed sensible advice, but he was unlikely to receive it from the scrum half who was not held in particularly high esteem among his friends as a problem solver. When they looked along the corridor they could see Ike Southward outside Peter's room being reprimanded by the hotel manager who seemed to be losing his temper, while several maids were already at work, mopping up the water.

"There was a long corridor and it was full of chamber maids with mops and buckets," recalls Peter. "When I looked inside the room there were two more Spanish cleaners with more mops. They couldn't speak much English but they pointed to the sink and said something like: No turn tap, no turn tap. I just turned around and walked back out again.

"Ike asked me what had been going on in the room. He said that the water had gone through the floor, and into the room below, causing lots of damage. There was water everywhere. I'd never seen so much water. All the floors were tiled and there must have been nowhere for the water to go but down below."

They decided to do a runner and were soon firmly ensconced in an English bar around the corner. The full scale of destruction would soon be revealed and it involved an elderly German couple who had travelled to Spain the night before hoping to relax but instead, found themselves in the middle of a flood alert. They woke up that morning, their first day in Spain, expecting to take a short walk along the beach but instead found their bed was surrounded by a small lake. To make matters worse, the water, which was cascading down all four walls like a waterfall, had seeped into the wardrobe and ruined all their clothes.

Peter and Boxer returned later that day with the mishap more or less resolved. The German pensioners had been moved to another room as far away as possible from the Town party after being compensated for their damaged items and they spent the rest of the week avoiding the culprits as best they could. Major Fillingham had paid for the damage but if he was thinking things couldn't get much worse he would be sadly mistaken.

The next evening, the party headed along the promenade, and settled in a nearby bar where large amounts of beer were drunk supplemented by jugs of sangria with cut lemons and ice cubes floating on the top. Someone suggested a satisfactory pastime would be an arm-wrestling contest which was won with ease by Peter Gorley, who dispatched the entire Town team, one by one, and was happy to take on all-comers, which unfortunately included a few powerful Spaniards, who couldn't quite grasp the rules. Not surprising there was some kind of misunderstanding, no one can remember the reason, and the end result was an argument, closely following by raised voices and then a few punches were thrown, as Boxer remembers it. The details are unclear but what is certain is that several young Spanish men were injured and at least two were unconscious but the party managed to escape before the Guardia Civil arrived with their truncheons and automatic pistols.

On the subject of mass brawls, this first night was by far the worst though that is not to say the rest of the week was uneventful. The following day, two large Spanish men had attached themselves to the party and were seen everywhere they went, and always furtive, occasionally scribbling unknown observations in notebooks which everyone assumed was some kind of incriminating evidence of their wild behaviour. Nothing more came of it, but the men had immediately been appointed by the group as 'members of the Spanish secret service.' They never found out why they were there or who they were but they disappeared on the final day and no one was ever charged with any offences.

Major Fillingham, when he was not attending to legal matters, compensation claims or whatever problems the players had encountered on a particular day, could be found drinking café con leche in the foyer of the hotel, with an anxious look on his face. The reception had a small section devoted to tourism and he would occasionally read through the pamphlets which revealed that there were many historic and cultural trips on offer which weren't very appealing to the players.

They included the relaxing waterfalls of Callosa d'en Sarrià, the remains of a second century Roman fort at Augusteum and an intriguing day in The Microgiant museum at Guadalest, where, according to the pamphlet, you could admire the Statue of Liberty painted in the eye of a needle or see a patterned elephant on the back of a mosquito. The pamphlet urged tourists 'to bring the whole family and be prepared to be baffled and amazed.' Unfortunately, Major Fillingham had already been baffled and amazed quite enough by the antics of the players. And they weren't finished yet.

The Major had at least resolved the issue of Eddie Bowman's passport difficulties. He thought he had anyway, following a lengthy telephone call with a government official at the British Consulate who had told him not to worry. Lost passports were a regular occurrence, he was told. All that was required was the personal attendance of Eddie and payment of the necessary fee.

Not for the first time, the Major had underestimated the players' capacity for irresponsible behaviour and their chances of a successful conclusion were not improved when Boxer joined Eddie and Paul Charlton for the short journey to the Consulate. An open-air buggy was hired and the three players set off with Eddie carrying an explanatory letter which had been written by the Major to explain their predicament. He suddenly became taken with the idea that the Major had developed an irrational dislike to him and that the letter contained derogatory descriptions of his behaviour.

"Eddie opened the letter which just had all his details in it and nothing else," remembers Boxer. "At the same time something flew out of the buggy but we thought nothing of it. Perhaps it was a bird, something like that. At the Consulate, we saw this really helpful man who read the letter and told us everything had been arranged and that all we had to do was pay the bill. Then we all realised that what had flown out of the buggy was the money the Major had put in the letter."

The trio returned to the hotel, red-faced, and the major couldn't rid himself of the idea that they had spent the money on alcohol but nevertheless, he refunded the money, and later that afternoon they were back in the reception with Eddie clutching his emergency passport. Sadly, the saga of misplaced passports had still not been concluded and would provide one final problem for the Major, who was starting to take on the persona of Herbert Lom's paranoid police officer in the *Pink Panther* films.

The party had befriended a Swedish motor cyclist, who was believed to be sleeping along the beach somewhere near the Balcon del Mediterraneo. He was a frequent visitor, mainly at meal times, where he had perfected a plan of eating without payment by pretending he was a member of the rugby team.

"He was always hanging around us," recalls Peter Gorley. "He had a huge motor bike so I asked him if he would take me for a ride and Boxer decided he wanted to come too. We set off with Boxer in the middle along the promenade which was really busy. I couldn't believe how fast we were going. I couldn't see the speedo but he was really hammering it. We must have been doing more than 90 miles an hour, he just kept zooming along.

"We only had on our shorts and sun glasses and if we had come off we would have been like strawberry jam all over the road. Boxer kept shouting: 'Slow him down. Slow him down.' I didn't think he would hear me so I just put my hands over his eyes but he just kept on going. Eventually he slowed down, thank goodness, and he dropped us off back at the bar where all the other lads were waiting."

The final day arrived and the party left the hotel mid-morning heading for the nearest bar not wanting to miss a final opportunity 'to get all tanked up' recalls Boxer. Not surprisingly, Eddie had developed a fear of misplacing his passport that was bordering on paranoia and he suddenly decided that the best course of action was to place it for safekeeping with the hotel's reception, away from harm's way and all sorts of untold chaos that was likely to take place at the bar.

Eddie took it upon himself to grab the passports of Boxer and his stand-off partner Derek McMillan but his plan soon started to go awry, beginning with a brief conversation with the receptionist who spoke reasonable English. He was just fine with the normal kind of queries such as 'what time does the bar close?' or 'can I have my room key, please?' As Boxer remembers it, Eddie thrust the three passports in the receptionist's hand saying something along the lines of: 'Eeyar Marra, put thas passports yonder to keep 'em safe. Be reet, wer gan for a bevvie,' which was Cumbrian for: Here you are, my friend, could you please keep our passports safe, we're going for a few drinks. And Eddie left to join the party in the bar feeling rather pleased with himself, leaving behind a completely bewildered receptionist holding three passports in his hands, not sure what to do.

"On our last day, I wanted to go out all spruced up," recalls Boxer. "I put on a black shirt and white jacket that I had bought in Whitehaven especially for the holiday and I felt I was Brad Pitt. In those days, everyone wore their collars on top on your jacket lapels. Eddie Bowman came to see me in my room and we had a couple of pints in the hotel before we went on our march around the town. Eddie told me my white jacket would be in a right state after our night out and that it would be ruined with beer and would probably end up with sick all over it.

"The first pub we went in was called Dane's Bar and almost right away all these Spaniards set on us. They had got snotty with one of our players and it all started because of Paul Charlton, which was so out of character from him. He leaned over and smacked this Spanish bloke right in the mouth and it all kicked off – all the Spaniards jumped on Paul. Well, all hell broke loose. The Spaniards never had a chance. A couple of them jumped on me and I was still wearing this white jacket and they ripped my vent right up to the collar - my jacket was hanging right off me.

"Sol Roper, Andy Key and Ike Southward walked in when all this was happening. One of the main Spanish troublemakers ran right past them to get away and we were running after him to flatten him. Sol was shouting to us: 'Catch him, catch him,' but we couldn't get him and he just ran off somewhere. When we got back in the bar, Sol said: 'I wanted to sign him for Town, because he was too fast for you buggers.'"

The players returned to the reception a few hours later and began loading their suitcases onto the coach which was parked just outside, waiting in the shade, and all set for the 30-minute journey to Alicante airport along the AP-7 motorway. The final calamity of the holiday which was about to unfold would leave the Major, who, it was thought, just might be on the verge of a nervous breakdown, slumped on a chair with his head in his hands, being comforted by Ike.

This all probably sounds too ludicrous to believe but the following account has all been confirmed by several eye-witnesses. To cut a very long story short, the bewildered receptionist had completed his shift after placing the passports in the hotel safe but he had, for some reason, taken the only key with him and he could not be located.

Thankfully, a resourceful holiday rep, who had seen it all before, came up with a simple plan while the players looked on from the back of the coach pressing their faces against the glass windows so they wouldn't miss anything. The three players would accompany the party to the airport, where they would have to wait until she returned the following day with the passports and three new flight tickets.

Boxer, Derek and Eddie waved off the party at the airport and set about enjoying a relaxing evening in the lounge celebrating their final night in Spain drinking beer and trying out the odd Spanish cocktail such as the Bomba Española, which is made from brandy, dry sherry, Galliano and Campari and usually served with a spiral of orange peel and a grape. They spent the night dozing in the departure lounge, occasionally woken by security staff, prodding them with truncheons. The rep returned later that day with their passports and flight tickets and they boarded the plane without incident.

As the aircraft cruised 30,000 feet somewhere above the French Pyrenees the three players realised they had spent all their money, including what they had intended using for train tickets to get them back to Cumbria. After landing safely, they set about persuading taxi drivers to take them to Cumbria with the promise of a large tip. Eventually they found a kind-hearted driver and were soon travelling along the A76, fast asleep, and nursing heavy-duty hangovers as they flashed alongside the valleys of Lowther Hills.

There was still sufficient time for one final calamity which came in the shape of an overheated engine and somewhere around Moffat, the three players were clambering along green fields looking for streams to fill up water bottles to replenish the radiator. The car had come to a halt in a lay-by, with great piles of steam rising from the bonnet. After an hour's delay, the car had cooled sufficiently and they eventually arrived safely at Derwent Park where Town director George Graham was summoned to pay the taxi driver.

They had considered making their own way from the bus station in the middle of the town but Eddie was having none of that. "Take us home, marra," he told the driver. "If you drop me off anywhere near the bus station, with all the luck I've had on this holiday, I'll probably get knocked over by a bloody bus."

The original party had arrived safely the day before, where they were met by a reporter from the *Times & Star* who had been despatched by a news editor anticipating a brief story accompanied by a photograph of the players smiling at the camera. It would be written along the lines of: Town's rugby league heroes returned home safely etc etc but the ambitious reporter, after being informed of the absence of Eddie, Boxer and Derek, wrote an altogether different intro which Boxer recalls was something about: Mystery surrounds the disappearance of three Town cup stars.

The story was published on the front page and unfounded rumours quickly began gathering momentum throughout West Cumbria with the most popular explanation involving the three players being arrested after some kind of botched robbery with the assistance of three Spanish prostitutes.

Normality was quickly resumed and as you might expect, that was the last time Workington Town would ever take a group of players to Spain.

CHAPTER 13

Sol: My Guiding Light

Boxer did not like losing but he had always been a player who did not dwell on such things for too long. It didn't take him much time before he would be circulating among his team-mates, reminding them to get such things into perspective. The following week would bring another game, another challenge, another opportunity to show their greatness and Boxer was a resourceful destroyer of gloom who was immune to self-doubt.

His capacity for optimism would be challenged on Sunday, October 1, 1978, when he was in a Cumbrian team who were destroyed by the touring Australians 47-4 at Craven Park, Barrow. Things got off to a bad start in the dressing room when Reg Parker, the former Barrow forward, who played alongside Willie Horne, informed the eight Workington players that if anyone was sent off, he would automatically miss the Lancashire Cup Final, the following week against Widnes. He was quite emphatic about it. There was a disciplinary meeting being held on Thursday evening, he told them. This understandably created a conflict of interest as a cautionary approach to taking on 17-stone Australian forwards was never going to work and was particularly inappropriate regarding Boxer whose opposite number, Tommy Raudonikis was once quoted as saying: "I hate Poms as if they had done something wrong to my family." Self-preservation quickly over-ruled Boxer's fear of missing the cup final and within five minutes, he was rolling on the ground, fighting with Raudonikis, who was a dedicated chain smoker who could get through 100 cigarettes in a single day.

"We were told that if anyone was sent off there would be an automatic two-match ban - it destroyed us," recalls Boxer. "Raudonikis was pulling my face off, so I thought to myself to hell with the Lancashire Cup, I can't take any more of this – he was writhing bits out of my face. So I had the ball and he took another swing at me and he ended up on the floor, which is summat you don't do – it is so hard to hit anyone when they are on top of you.

"So I threw the ball away, and got stuck right into him. I wasn't having it any more. The First Test against Great Britain was the following week so he got taken off. They were worried about him getting any damage or getting sent off."

The 1978 Lancashire Cup Final stands out in Boxer's memory for a pre-match altercation he had with a county official called Bob Brady. Mr Brady, who was a director at Barrow, was a tall, imposing man with receding hair, reminiscent of Jackie Gleason in *Smokey and the Bandit* and he had a powerful personality with strong opinions on just about any subject. He was a successful businessman who ran a haulage company that had been started by his father Tom in 1921 after borrowing £80 to buy a horse and cart. Bob, who was known affectionately at The Big 'Un, was proud of his working class roots and he was well known for his proficiency at profanity which came straight out of the mouths of shipwrights, welders, coppersmiths and platers, building submarines at Vickers Armstrongs. Bob, who was much admired by his employees, would address most men as Son, which was more a part of his idiosyncratic nature than a lack of respect or rudeness. It was said that Mr Brady's expertise in blasphemy had once shocked an army drill sergeant.

The teams are lined up in front of the grandstand at Central Park, Wigan, before the kick-off and Mr Brady, in his capacity as a Cumbrian representative, is part of the official party, who would normally smile and shake hands with the players and perhaps wish them good luck. Unbeknown to anyone, Mr Brady was smarting over Cumbria's embarrassing defeat by the Australians at Craven Park just six days before. He was of the opinion that the team had capitulated to the tourists without much effort and the presentation provided him with the perfect opportunity to issue a face-to-face reprimand to Town's county players.

Boxer is standing next to Peter Gorley when Mr Brady takes his turn to shake their hands before staring them both in the face and saying: "I hope you sods try a bit harder than last week." The jibe was totally unexpected but Boxer is having none it. He squeezes Mr Brady's hand, perhaps too tightly, before moving close to him, right in his face, and yelling: "Why don't you bugger off back to Barrow."

Town lost that final against Widnes 15-13 after the Cumbrians had held an eight-point lead with just 13 minutes left before player-coach Doug Laughton and Stuart Wright scored late tries. Boxer was again voted the man-of-the-match but he didn't care much. Their last appearance in the final was the following season when they were defeated, again by Widnes 11-0, and was more notable as the end of an unforgettable era of accomplishment. It was Boxer's final game for the team he loved.

§

In February, 1978, Ike Southward stood down as the coach of Workington Town. He wasn't sacked and he didn't resign, it just sort of happened that way. In matters of legendary Cumbrian players, Ike was way out there on his own and if he looked over his shoulder he might just have Douglas Clark, James Lomas, Martin Hodgson, Brian Edgar and Paul Charlton alongside him. He was a magnificent player but his popularity was based on much more than just athletic excellence. Ike may have played for Great Britain 11 times and been the world's most expensive player, but fame had left him unaffected and so, well, normal. He was the kindest, most gentle, helpful and compassionate man you could ever meet. Ike was worshipped by everybody and probably more for his sympathetic character than for his try-scoring feats which were without parallel, quite extraordinary and numbered 376.

He had been a consistent and guiding presence in the development of Boxer Walker and he would continue to be an authoritative influence at Derwent Park and available to anyone who needed him. John 'Sol' Roper took charge of the first team and, not for the first time, Boxer was about to benefit from a satisfactory set of chance circumstances that would provide him with a teacher who specialised in every aspect of scrum half play. In fact, Sol had been Boxer's hero when he was a young boy watching Haven back in the 1960s. The two scrum halves had much in common though they were from different generations – Boxer was just two-years-old when Sol made his debut for Workington Town in 1954 against Featherstone Rovers.

"I had watched Sol playing for Whitehaven when I was a kid," says Boxer. "He was a right showman and I really looked up to him. He was my idol. I remember talking to Eddie Bowman about this and he felt the same way about a great forward who took him under his wing at Whitehaven. He was called Alan Burns and he was eventually transferred to Oldham. Eddie told me that Alan would drive into the line and just turn and all the other players would be running off him and Alan taught Eddie how to play like that. It ended up being the same between me and Sol. He was my mentor.

"I had never met Sol when he took over from Ike but I know he was at all the games. I knew all about him, of course. Everyone knew Sol. I thought I would be polite so I went straight up and congratulated him. He seemed really angry. 'Never mind that, come with me into the boardroom,' he told me. He said he knew what I was on and that I was drinking too much aniseed. I didn't know what he was on about - all I knew about aniseed was that it was the scent that trail hounds ran after. Sol was a big hound man. 'Yes, that's the stuff,' he told me.

"Poor Sol has gone to his grave now and he still thinks I was drinking aniseed. Of course, he was referring to Pernod which I admit was my favourite short. I took it with a drop of water. There were two Whitehaven players who Sol had been told had gone crackers after drinking too much 'aniseed' and he told me he didn't want the same thing happening to me. 'Get off it,' he shouted at me and he just turned around and left me in the boardroom."

Sol's qualifications as a suitable scrum-half role model are explained in great detail in Robert Gate's *100 Cumberland Rugby League Greats*. The article reveals that Sol played for England Open Age amateurs at the age of 17 before signing for Workington Town in 1954, and 16 days after making his first team debut, he appeared for Cumberland against Yorkshire. He played in the 1955 Challenge Cup Final as the youngest man on the field and three years later he was back at Wembley as Town's captain, and at the age of 21, the youngest skipper in the history of the competition. He left Workington in 1966 and played for Whitehaven for five more years. Sol made more than 500 professional appearances.

"As a scrum half Sol Roper knew all the tricks of the trade," says Robert. "He fitted the stereotype – invariably the smallest man on the field but just as invariably the gutsiest. He was renowned for his low, clean tackling, his stamina and his guile. His total of 94 tries was testimony to his attacking values."

Sol had the misfortune to play in an era which was concurrent with Alex Murphy, who is generally accepted as the best number seven there has ever been. Murphy, who played for St Helens, Leigh and Warrington, became a high profile coach with a reputation for outspoken comments and controversial opinions that did not go down too well with the game's authorities but which made him much in demand as a newspaper columnist. He appeared regularly in the *Manchester Evening News* and *The Daily Mirror* under the appropriate pen-name of Murphy's Mouth alongside a ham photograph where Alex is shown poking out from the top of the page and adopting an angry pose suitable for an expert with contentious views.

So Sol's path to a Great Britain appearance was blocked by a grand master but he was more fortunate to play alongside Great Britain tourist and stand-off Harry Archer, whose nickname was The Architect. Robert Gate says they were 'telepathic,' going on to describe their ten-year partnership as 'probably the most celebrated half-back pairing in Cumbrian history,' which is quite something.

Harry was a fine player and only a fool ever tried to mess with him. He looked more like a second row forward but he had all the creative skills expected of an international stand-off. If Harry ever took exception to something, for example if a forward tried to intimidate Sol, he could not be placated and he was an uncompromising advocate of retribution.

Towards the end of his career, Harry did not take too kindly to younger players who might threaten his position. Sol had an altogether different attitude to rivalry from below. He accepted it as an inevitable part of life and would occasionally impart advice in a benevolent way. But not Harry.

When he was defending, Harry could be explosive and violent. He had an icy anger inside him. Paul Charlton tells the story of a young stand-off trialist who was once invited to train with the professionals to assess his suitability as a new signing. According to the story, a practice session had been set up which had left the young player lying on the floor, out cold, and as he stumbled to his feet with stars circling around his head, Harry was heard to say to a couple of the seasoned pros: 'He'll have to get past me if he wants to get my shirt.'

In his autobiography *The Memoirs and Sporting Life of Tom Mitchell,* Tom says: "Wakefield Trinity away. Whether his opponent deserved it or not Harry flattened him on the far side of the field but the referee saw it from 20 yards away. His forefinger beckoned. Harry sauntered towards the ref and then straight past him without waiting for the certain sending off. Harry, addressing the official, said: 'Don't bother yourself ref, I'll just keep walking.' No look of innocence, no expostulation. Harry the realist."

Boxer was a seasoned professional when Sol took over at Town, but he became a greater all-round player after he had soaked up all the information that was made available to him. Sol might occasionally become frustrated if Boxer deviated from carefully-prepared plans if the occasion presented itself, but he knew that was part of his genius and he accepted his strong belief in unpredictable patterns of play. He never reprimanded him, quite the opposite, and it was this devout belief in spontaneity that made him such a joy to play for. Sol was a player's coach.

"When we were waiting in the tunnel to go on, Sol would often shout to me: 'Walker, you're not fit to tie my laces,' " recalls Boxer. "It was all to get me going and I never answered him. He was just winding me up. He would often say to me: 'Come here, Boxer. Let me smell your breath.' When he was coach, he would get in his track suit alongside Ecky Bell and all of us, the first team and the A team, had to do 20 laps for a warm-up. One time he came up to me and said: 'Walker, I am joining in on the last lap and we're going to sprint to the try line and if you're behind me, you're going to do another 20 laps. I couldn't catch him, I had probably been on the pop the night before - I was knackered. I got close to him so I caught the back of his legs and tripped him up just in time to beat him. I denied it was me. He played war but he didn't do anything about it.

"Another time when Sol was coach, we were playing at Hunslet, and our captain Paul Charlton sent me off. I dropped the ball and after 20 minutes had gone by they scored in the other corner. Paul came across and started blaming me. I wasn't having that and he started telling me not to answer him back and that he was the captain.

"I told him that it wasn't my fault. Paul told me to get off the field - he sent me off. So I just started walking towards the changing rooms. He ran right after me and said: 'Where are you going?' I said that I was going in the bar for a few pints and he ended up begging me to come back which I obviously did. I remember we drew 15-15 which was a great result and a draw away from home was winning pay for everyone.

"When I was a youngster watching Sol play, I remember how good he was at dictating play and I tried to be like him. I was always talking to our players and Sol taught me how to play that way. He told me to be the gaffer in the middle of the field. I took over from Paul Charlton as the club skipper when he went to Blackpool. I was chuffed to bits. I am only 5ft 6ins but I felt a foot taller when Sol made me captain, especially coming from such a great player who I looked up to so much.

"There were a few coaches who told me to stop tackling so much and leave it more to the forwards. But Sol wasn't one of them. We all knew he would tell us if we weren't working hard enough but that didn't happen at Town. All those big forwards who could have buried me in the ground at any time, never answered me back, not once in all that time. Every captain makes the wrong decision sometimes but no one in my teams would ever complain. I learnt a lot from Paul Charlton too. He was the best captain I played under.

"Here is an example of how we were all mates and how we looked after each other. Say Eddie Bowman or Les Gorley missed a tackle - which didn't happen very often - as the captain I might tell them off and ask them to sort themselves out. I am just using these two as an example. Some people would be put off their game but to the lads at Town, it was just water off a duck's back, nothing ever bothered our forwards.

"If anyone ever says someone is a perfect player they are wrong. There is no such thing as a perfect player. You might be weaker in tackling but brilliant at running or the other way around. There is a weak link in everyone. The worst game I ever had for Town was when I was persuaded to play when I had flu. I told one of the coaches that I was struggling to play but he told me to just go first man and fetch the runners on - I just couldn't do it. I remember getting booed off the field and that was the only time that ever happened to me.

"I got up to all sorts back then. One night before a match, I decided to behave myself for once and to only drink a couple of shandies and just have a crack with the lads and then get off home to bed. There was a lad called Kenny Todd, who played centre for Whitehaven and it was his wedding anniversary. He made a big fuss of me and he had a big bottle of brandy with him. Apart from Pernod I never touched shorts but I had a mouthful just to please him.

"Kenny kept saying have another and I wasn't drunk but I felt bad because I wasn't used to spirits. When I got on the bus the next day, my stomach was awful and I felt really weak. We used to stop at a spot in Kendal called The Steak Bar and the smell from the kitchen was making me feel terrible. I went for a walk by the river to try and walk it off. We were playing Blackpool, and I decided that I was going to tell Sol that I couldn't play. I told Eddie but he give me a rollicking and told me not to be so stupid, and that Blackpool were a poor team. He said that I wouldn't have to do much and we were certain to get winning money.

"He told me: 'Just follow me, son,' and I did and I scored two tries and both of them were from a yard out - he could have scored them himself but he preferred to help me. I remember in the *News & Star* the next day the headlines read *Walker The Superstar*. It was all Eddie, I didn't do anything.

"I loved Sol and I loved playing for him. He taught me so much. Looking back, I owe him everything."

Hooker Alan Banks about to receive the ball with
prop forward Derek Watts in support.

Coach Ike Southward leads out Town's winning Lancashire team at Wilderspool, followed by skipper Paul Charlton. To the left, 1958 Great Britain tourist Vince Karalius, the Wigan coach.

*Boxer tackles his great friend Bob Blackwood, who would
be transferred from Wigan to Workington the following
year – Bob was a brave protector of half backs.*

Loose forward Billy Pattinson and Les Gorley combine to stop a Wigan attack.

Stand-off Ray Wilkins scores Town's second try
in the 1977 Lancashire Cup final.

Les Gorley and Derek Watts smother a Wigan attack.

John Risman, Ray Wilkins and Peter Gorley are swamped by Town fans on their way to the cup presentation. To the right, coach Ike Southward.

*Skipper Paul Charlton with the Lancashire Cup. This was the first time
the trophy had left Lancashire in the tournament's 72-year history*

*Fans celebrate at the final whistle of the Lancashire Cup
Final after Workington had defeated Wigan 16-13.*

*Loose forward Billy Pattinson salutes the crowd while
skipper Paul Charlton holds the Lancashire Cup.*

Town's Lancashire Cup Final man-of-the-match Boxer Walker.

Jubilation in the dressing room, with chairman George Graham, front left,
Tom Mitchell, Corky and Peter Gorley with former secretary Jimmy Hodgson.

Tom Mitchell with Boxer Walker. 'When I first saw him play at 16, Boxer was already directing the efforts of a mature amateur pack,' says Tom. 'I was at the corner flag when an opposition forward crossed and the dressing down he gave his team-mates behind the posts was unbelievable. I pursued his professional signature for two years – well worth the frustrating process.'

Town coach Ike Southward with Andy Key, assistant coach and masseur and chairman George Graham.

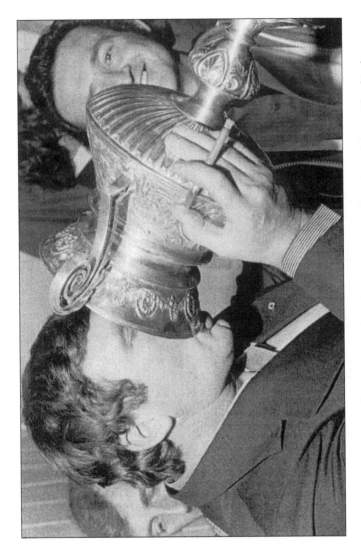

Ike Southward, who was worshipped and respected as a legendary player with a kind heart, drinks from the Lancashire Cup, while Andy Key, right, waits his turn

Workington Town with the Lancashire Cup. John Risman, Ralph Calvin, Harry Marland, Brian Lauder, Ian MacCorquodale, Ian Wright, Les Gorley, Paul Charlton, Eddie Bowman, Arnold 'Boxer' Walker, David Collister, Derek McMillan, Alan Banks.

Town's Lancashire Cup heroes earned £100 bonus each and a trip to Benidorm. Back: Ken Groves, Bill Pattinson, David Atkinson, David Collister, Paul Charlton, Alan Banks, Les Gorley, Eddie Bowman, Peter Gorley, John Risman. Front: Ray Wilkins, Ian Wright, Arnold 'Boxer' Walker, Ian Hartley.

CHAPTER 14

They've Sold All My Mates

Workington Town were known throughout the game for their tough and entertaining brand of rugby league. They had a team of stars but there is no argument that the greatest influence came from four Cumbrian-born players who had either won, or would go on to win, full Great Britain caps. They are, of course, Eddie Bowman, brothers Les and Peter Gorley and Arnold 'Boxer' Walker. They were close friends and big-game players who felt a corporate responsibility for what was necessary to get the job done. Yet, less than three years after Town's history-making Lancashire Cup win, they were all gone, much to the consternation of the club's fans, who couldn't quite figure out what was going on.

Evidence of exactly what sequence of events took place to produce their departures is hard to find, not least because these incidents happened almost 40 years ago and most of the Town board in control at that time have long gone. The exodus began in October, 1978, two weeks after the final Town appearance of Eddie Bowman, in a 13-5 defeat at home to Wakefield Trinity. The ball-playing front row forward was sold to Leigh for just £7,500 after making 199 appearances for Town. Even now, it seems a preposterously small sum, and more incredible considering it was only a year after Eddie had starred for Great Britain in the 1977 World Cup in Australia, when he had formed a formidable partnership with George Nicholls, the Saints second row forward. GB lost the final 13-12 at the Sydney Cricket Ground, in front of 25,000 fans, and his team-mates from that final are a who's who of legendary players and include Ken Gill, Len Casey, Roger Millward and Steve Nash.

Boxer says, without a moment's hesitation, that Eddie is the best ball player he played with or against. "He used to tell me, come on, follow me," recalls Boxer. "And the ball would always be there. He could run and he was one of the quickest forwards I ever played with."

In the summer of 1979, tough forward Bob Blackwood left and the exodus continued as six more players were shunted out of Derwent Park. The pessimistic mood deepened at the end of that season when winger Iain MacCorquodale, who was a cult figure because of his prodigious goal kicking, joined Reg Bowden at newly-formed Fulham. By then, Town had become a selling-club and to give the board the benefit of the doubt, there was clearly some kind of financial crisis rumbling in the background. The fans, unsurprisingly, did not see things in the same light, and there was a brooding resentment on the terraces as their heroes left the club, one by one.

When the team reported for pre-season training, there were alarming rumours about certain players 'being available if the price was right'. Normally, players just got on with things and focused themselves on building up their fitness but matters were about to take a turn for the worse.

Les Gorley would never play for Town again. No one could believe it. Les had signed for Town shortly after Boxer, in 1971, and his development from a raw amateur with Great Broughton to one of the best second row forwards in the world was no surprise to anyone. Here's what happened.

Boxer is parking his Morris Marina outside the changing rooms but he is intercepted by chairman George Graham, who invites him to the boardroom. He has something important to tell him.

"He said he wanted a private word with me," remembers Boxer. "I was captain at the time but I remember asking myself: What have I done now? I was trying to think what I had been up to so I could sort out an excuse, some sort of explanation."

Graham closes the door and says: "I thought I would get you in before anyone else could tell you. We have sold your mate, Les Gorley."

"I couldn't believe it," says Boxer. "I said to him: 'He's the backbone of the team. He's our best player.'"

"Look, Boxer," says Graham, moving closer. "The reason we sold him is that we think we have had the best out of him. Sometimes Les complains about a back injury, or a dodgy knee, so we decided to sell him to Widnes. He's gone now and he's not coming back."

"But, George," pleaded Boxer, as if there was still a way the deal could be prevented. "Who can fill his boots? No one. Why have you let him go?"

Mr Graham's qualifications as a sound judge of long-term sporting injuries are unknown but what is certain is that he was making a catastrophic error in his opinion of Les Gorley's maladies. The board felt that the forward's future was in serious doubt, so he said, and, far from regretting his departure, the prevailing view in the boardroom was that the £18,000 fee was cause for celebration. Sadly, their decision would prove calamitous, and to say they had made an error of judgement is the biggest understatement since Noah said, "it looks like rain."

Les, who had already played for England in 1977 against Wales, played 224 games for Town, scoring 50 tries. But it was his achievements, after he left Town, that provide the most compelling evidence, if any were needed, of how foolhardy the board's decision was to let him go.

Les, who appeared 16 times for Cumberland, went on to play in three Challenge Cup finals for Widnes, and won the Lancashire Cup Final in December, 1979, just 14 weeks after leaving Workington, ironically playing a leading part in the 11-0 defeat of Town. As if that wasn't enough, he won another cap for England against Wales in 1981, and played five times for Great Britain, against France, New Zealand and the Australian Invincibles in 1982, believed to be the best team of all time.

Looking back, the board's concerns about Les's physical condition, which were completely unfounded, were so far off the mark that his sale might just be the most inept decision made in the history of the club. He went on to play 162 times for Widnes, scoring 22 tries, won three Premiership titles and still had enough gas in the tank to conclude his career at Whitehaven, where he played 47 more times before finally hanging up his boots in 1986.

During the celebration evening to commemorate his inevitable induction into Town's Hall of Fame in 2011, proceedings were interrupted to enable the large crowd to view a video link to Australia, in which Workington's former full back and coach Paul Charlton was seen, flickering from a television screen, from 10,000 miles away. Paul offered his personal congratulations and began describing with great admiration and with an ex-pro's insight, what made Les so special and why he had been honoured to coach and play with him.

"When I first saw Les, I was taken by the size of the guy and his attitude," says Paul, sitting on a yellow sofa and looking cool in a red and white England shirt. "Les was one of these guys who stood out. He had a lot of character, passion and desire and a lot of height, weight and speed.

"He was one hell of a player and we would talk to each other a lot during games and he gave me a bucketful of tries, yet all I was doing was finishing off the work that he had created. As for his defence, well I certainly wouldn't have liked running at him. He was the sort of player who could pick you up with one hand - he was that big of a fella. His presence on the field might make people think, I'm not going near him, and they would run the other way.

"Les had a great attitude and will to win. I knew the first time I saw him that he had the class to become an international. He was playing with good players and all that rubbed off on him and Les became even more creative. He was a player you just couldn't hold down, he could offload the ball, and he was a big strong runner, who could create gaps – he could do anything."

The unnamed Australian interviewer asks a question pertaining to how they were both employed as carpenters away from rugby and Paul, never one to turn down an opportunity to share a joke, continued the interview, saying: "Yes, we chose the same profession. And Les still has my hammer," he says before staring straight at the camera, to conclude the interview with a direct message to Les, his family and friends, who are supping their drinks around the television set.

"Les, it has been a great honour to play with you - and against you - that was something special. I wish you all the best tonight and I hope to be with you soon."

The sale of Les, not surprisingly, did not go down too well with his brother Peter and as soon as the move was confirmed, he walked out of the club after attending a solitary training session.

"Peter became disillusioned with life at Derwent Park," reports author Peter Cropper, in his detailed biography of Peter Gorley, *From Great Broughton to Great Britain.* "He felt, with some apparent justification, that Workington were becoming a selling club, unwilling to invest in the new players needed to maintain the high standards. He made himself unavailable for selection and he asked for a transfer a week after Les's departure for Widnes and his move became inevitable."

The following day, Whitehaven and Bradford Northern contacted Town to begin negotiations. Whitehaven were in the Second Division and Peter, still ambitious, felt that such a move would not assist his hopes of playing international rugby. Bradford were a different matter. The coach, Peter Fox, was highly regarded and had an obvious talent for persuasion. A fee of £25,000 was agreed but Bradford's understandable insistence that Peter and his family must move to Yorkshire, scuppered the move.

Then St Helens came calling and a deal was brokered in a few days. Peter signed for Saints on Sunday, October 7, and he scored a try on his debut two days later against Rochdale Hornets. This is how Peter Cropper reports the move. "St Helens had been impressed by Peter's displays over the years and they were interested in signing him. They had started the season extremely poorly. Widnes had beaten them easily in the first round of the Lancashire Cup at Knowsley Road and two weeks later, again in front of their own fans, Saints were defeated by local rivals Warrington.

"Team strengthening was necessary and Workington's 27-year-old second-rower would fit the bill by providing much-needed fire power. He had acquired plenty of big-match experience, arguably he had yet to reach his peak and, all things being equal, he would serve Saints with distinction for a good few seasons to come. History shows the St Helens board made an excellent choice."

Peter was the second world-class player to be shipped out of Derwent Park in unsatisfactory circumstances. He was slightly taller than his brother Les, and perhaps a few pounds lighter, proportions which gave him the perfect requirements to be a back row forward.

Peter, who was a year younger than Les, joined Town in 1975, after an unlikely series of events involving a testimonial for Town's charismatic hooker, Howard 'Smiler' Allen. Workington had been following Peter's progress with Broughton Red Rose for some time but were unsure about his suitabilities to turn professional. He was attending a testimonial for Smiler at Derwent Park, alongside his father, and entirely as a spectator at the match, which would be watched by more than 1,000 supporters. Cumbria, skippered by Smiler, were taking on a team of All Stars which included Peter Smethurst, Eric Prescott, Geoff Fletcher and Dave Smith.

The problem was that an unspecified international had pulled out at the last minute forcing Ike Southward to quickly ask Peter, still wearing his overcoat, and standing among the crowd anonymously, if he could help out. Nothing was expected of him other than making the numbers up, Ike promised. The difficulties did not end there and Peter found himself declining the invitation on account of his right arm and hand being encased in plaster following his recent and painful acquisition of a broken thumb. Despite protestations from his father, Peter followed Ike into the visitors' dressing room, where the players were in the latter stages of preparation and looking up, wondering who Ike's friend was and what qualifications he had to join them.

A small saw was procured from somewhere and work commenced on the removal of the cast which took longer than anticipated, while other organisers searched for a pair of boots, size tens, he had told them. Five minutes later and Peter was running on the field, rubbing his still swollen wrist and wondering what he had let himself in for. He needn't have worried. Peter played a star role in the match which recorded a victory for Cumbria 34-22.

Tom Mitchell, who else, had been monitoring Peter's progress for some time and he was waiting in the dressing room to snap him up, in full view of the participants who weren't much interested and were more intent on downing bottles of beer, which were plentiful, joshing and playing juvenile pranks on Smiler. The honoured hooker, a regular attender of social get-togethers, was a lot worse for wear before he left the changing rooms to attend a dinner. Peter was not in a suitable frame of mind to contemplate his options - his thumb had begun throbbing with pain - and he managed to put Tom off, well, sort of. The Town director, always impatient and wanting to get things done, turned up that night in Peter's local, The Volunteer, in Great Broughton. It must have been quite something to have been an eye witness of the proceedings. Peter is enjoying a pint of beer with his brother Les, surrounded by friends and neighbours and it is safe to assume the atmosphere would have been relaxed as the locals knocked back a few pints together. Probably, the most famous Cumbrian alive, Tom Mitchell, walks in, and there would have been no mistaking him with his Texan hat and Old Testament beard. Peter and Tom find a corner in the pub and financial negotiations are soon concluded with perhaps 20 people watching them. Tom is gone now and he leaves holding a signed form in his hand and for certain, he is feeling rather pleased with himself. Peter buys his brother a pint which is the least he can do considering the large cheque he has in his pocket and he starts pondering the bewildering events of that unforgettable Sunday.

Peter made his debut for Town on November 2, 1975, in a 25-8 win at Blackpool Borough and over the next four years he was an ever-present, playing 124 games and scoring 13 tries. He played in three Lancashire Cup finals for Workington, including the 16-13 win in 1977. He had also become a regular for Cumberland, playing eight times for his county. Peter would go on to make 234 appearances for Saints, scoring 46 tries and becoming close friends with Australian captain Mal Meninga. In 1994, Peter was a shock guest live on Australian television when Mal was the subject of *This Is Your Life*.

"Workington were selling good players and not replacing them and I couldn't understand it," recalls Peter. "If we had signed a couple of new players we would have had a really good side yet Town were just selling players. I went to see the directors about it and there was a fella on the board called Denis Pattinson, he had shoe shops in the town and he was a nice man. I had heard that another director had called me a troublemaker which really annoyed me as and I have never caused trouble in my life. That was my parting of the ways. They put me on the list and I was never going back even if it meant playing with the amateurs again. I couldn't have picked a better team to go to than Saints."

Now all of this detail is all well and good but hardly necessary to understand the complex events that were about to unfold. But first you need to know about a chance meeting in Whitehaven town centre that got Boxer thinking and would prove prophetic. It was no secret that he was angry, upset and bewildered, following the departure of Eddie and the Gorley brothers but he was slowly recovering from his astonishment and trying his best to pull himself together for the good of the team. West Cumbria is a small place and the pubs and clubs of Workington were full of dissenting Town supporters who were watching powerlessly as a great side was being broken up without explanation.

Boxer's father is standing in front of the main bus station on Bransty Row, which is now occupied by Wetherspoons, in the centre of Whitehaven, and just 100 yards from the marina. He is waiting for a bus to take him home and a large car pulls up and the driver beckons him inside.

"I'm going your way, Duncan. Get in," he says.

The car is a black Rover 3.5 V8 and not a common sight around these parts, among the Hillman Avengers and Austin Allegros. Duncan does not recognise the car but he is certainly acquainted with its owner, who is David Wigham, the chairman of Whitehaven Rugby League Club, and who originally came from Kells. He has done rather well for himself as the chief buyer for the town's chemical factory, Marchon, which then employed around 3,000 people.

There's not much talking going on as the Rover cruises along Lowther Street and Swingpump Lane on the five-minute trip to Hensingham. The car stops and Duncan thanks him, not quite sure what to do next. He closes the door behind him, but Mr Wigham is winding down the window and leaning over gesturing for Duncan to stay put, just for a moment.

"I've heard through the grapevine that Arnold is disillusioned at Workington," he says. "I would love to sign him - he is just the kind of player we need." But he's not waiting for an answer and the car is soon disappearing along Cleator Moor Road. When Duncan appraised Boxer of the encounter, they weren't sure what to make of it, so nothing much more was said. But one thing was apparent; David lived in a large house, situated in an altogether different part of the town. Boxer wondered if the chance meeting was something else, perhaps pre-planned.

Eddie Bowman and Les and Peter Gorley had symbolised and maintained the bloodline that had been Cumberland's legacy to the sport. They were worthy additions to a long list of incomparable forwards going back to the early 20th century and include Douglas Clark, Martin Hodgson, Brian Edgar, Geoff Robinson and Les Moore and continued by Dick Huddart, Bill Martin, John Tembey, Bill Kirkbride and Bill Holliday. And now they were gone. After training that night, Boxer began considering his options, but try as he might, the only thing that was clear to him was that it was time to go.

"After we won the Lancashire Cup, if we had all stayed together we would have won everything," remembers Boxer. "We had a nucleus of a great side – all we had to do was stop together. And what happened?

They sold everyone. Honestly it would not have entered my head to leave Town if my mates had stopped.

"All the directors were usually at Derwent Park on Thursday nights - that was pay night. I went in and told them I had had enough and they banged me on the transfer list straight away. It broke my heart to leave Town. I did nearly 10 years there. I didn't want to leave and it was one of the worst days of my life.

"When I walked out of the boardroom I didn't go back. That was it. I trained with Kells. I never saw them again. They had sold almost a full pack that used to give me protection, great players like Eddie Bowman, Les and Peter Gorley and Bob Blackwood. I felt invincible with them in the team. It has always been a true saying that if your pack gets on top, it is so much easier for the backs. And our pack was one of the best. I looked around me and they were all gone."

After almost nine years, 195 appearances, 53 tries and 35 drop goals, it was time to move on. Boxer was placed on the transfer list. And it might take a world record fee to sign him.

CHAPTER 15

I'm in Haven

The northern editions of the following day's national newspapers carried banner headlines informing readers of Boxer's placement on the transfer list. There was some disagreement about the exact fee but the general consensus was settled at £32,000, and just short of the world record fee that Hull Kingston Rovers had paid Barrow the previous year for loose forward Phil Hogan. Boxer was 27-years-old and a world-class player at the peak of his powers and reporters were predicting that his match-winning capabilities would create great interest.

Boxer had taken the day off work to collect his thoughts, which was just as well, because the next 24 hours can only be described as chaotic as the game's best teams competed for his signature. It all began early in the afternoon when he had a visit from two directors from Wigan, who were fighting relegation and desperate for fresh blood - they needed someone special who could kick-start their season. They had arrived hot-foot from the family home of George Graham, on the outskirts of Workington, where advanced negotiations had been quickly concluded. The transfer fee had been agreed with a minimum of fuss, and would involve a player-cash deal with centre Keiron O'Loughlin, father of present Wigan and Great Britain captain Sean, moving to Town.

Town wanted to sell him and Wigan wanted to buy him. For the next hour, they regaled Boxer with stories of Wigan's glorious history and how much first-team coach Kel Coslett admired him and how his career would benefit from a move to Central Park. They were courteous and respectful but keen to resolve the deal as soon as possible before other rivals could get involved. The directors were most insistent on that.

"We would love you to come to Wigan," they told him. "And we're prepared to write you a cheque for £4,000 right now if you sign the forms." And the cheque was held out in front of him as they leaned forward from the sofa in his living room, showing the cheque, not too near but just close enough so Boxer would read the figure and be in no doubt that they meant business. "Just sign here," they told him. He had the presence of mind to ask for a few hours to think things over, and the directors left, leaving a contact number and a warning - they must have an answer before the end of the day.

Boxer's head was spinning. But he knew Wigan were in trouble. Coslett, a Welsh full back and forward, who had played more than 500 games for St Helens, had only recently replaced Vince Karalius at Central Park, following a poor start to the season. Nevertheless, they still had a talented team that included Dennis Boyd, George Fairbairn and Des Foy. But he had to consider all that travelling, along the winding A66 and another 90 miles down the M6.

He called his best friend Billy Starkey and they went to St Mary's Catholic Club for a few beers and to ponder recent events. Around 3pm, as Boxer remembers it, the steward called him over to the bar to receive an urgent telephone call. The Wigan directors had somehow tracked him down and were still hanging around and, they told him, after consulting other board members, they had been instructed to increase the signing-on bonus to £5,000, but they needed an immediate response and weren't prepared to wait much longer. Call this number with your answer, they told him. It was just the start of a long and confusing week. Boxer never made that call.

Warrington were the next team to come calling, and negotiations followed a similar pattern, although this time discussions only took place on the telephone. The director had agreed a transfer fee of £30,000 with Town and he had been given permission to conclude the deal with Boxer himself, which he hoped could be agreed, verbally at least, right there on the telephone.

"Our coach Billy Benyon thinks the world of you," Boxer was told. "We would love to sign you." Now Warrington were a whole new ball game. The Wire, as they were known back then, were a top side, full of Great Britain internationals including John Bevan, John Dalgreen,

Tommy Martyn and Brian Case. And if that wasn't enough, his stand-off partner would be Ken Kelly, the club captain, who was quick and brave and the kind of player who would complement Boxer's skills perfectly or so the director said. "You'll be great together," he told him.

Boxer wanted more time but Warrington weren't prepared to wait. So they told him to meet their representatives at Forton Motorway Service Station, close to Lancaster on the M6, that night.

"Billy will be there to meet you too," they told him. "And he'll bring you a cheque for £5,000 with him."

But Boxer never turned up. Wigan continued to struggle and were relegated at the end of the season despite acquiring Welsh rugby union schools' international Ness Flowers, who was a decent player but a bit of a flop, playing only 19 games before being shipped out to Huddersfield.

The following day, Boxer's brother Alan, who was his number one fan, and an electrician at the colliery, was waiting for him at Haig pit head, after his shift. He had an important message from Frank Foster, the coach of Barrow and former international forward who hailed from Flimby, had a hard man reputation and was definitely someone you didn't want to mess with. The message had come by way of Peter Hurst, another collier, who was a former front row forward for Barrow. It was Frank's telephone number and he wanted Boxer to contact him urgently.

"I knew Frank well," recalls Boxer. "We had a good chat and he told me how much he wanted me. He said the Barrow board were really keen and that they would look after me and sort me out with a good car. He promised me everything would be worked out. I was really interested as I had a few good mates there that I had played with for Cumbria and it obviously wasn't as far as Lancashire. Frank said someone would be contacting me."

The chairman of Barrow was Bill Pears, a successful businessman, who was putting together, in partnership with Frank Foster, an outstanding team. The club were reaping the benefits of a successful lottery scheme and some of Cumbria's finest players were there, along with big names from rugby union. And the mood of optimism in Barrow, which was once appointed 'the most working-class town in England' in a survey conducted by a national newspaper, was boosted by persistent rumours that Vickers Shipbuilding and Engineering Ltd were close to securing a huge order from the Conservative government, then led by Prime Minister Margaret Thatcher. VSEL, which is now called BAE Systems, and the town's leading employer and builder of quality war ships since 1871, was about to be awarded a deal to build four Trident nuclear submarines, at a cost of £1,500 million each, which would bring thousands of new jobs to the town.

Boxer's Cumbria team-mates Ralph McConnell and Malcolm Flynn were at Craven Park, alongside outstanding forwards Derek Hadley and Eddie Szymala and rugby union county players Steve Tickle and Ian Ball.

Now if you were going to write down a list of personality traits that would make absolutely sure that under no possible circumstances, Boxer would never, ever agree to a deal to join Barrow, Bill Pears would have every one of them. He was a tall, well-built man, who always dressed smartly, wore glasses and had thinning hair which he combed back in neat lines and gave him the appearance of a rather strict headmaster, an occupation that had not been particularly successful in persuading Boxer to obey authority figures, going back to his experiences as a five-year-old child at St Mary's Roman Catholic School.

The chairman, if he had any sense, should have at least been courteous and respectful, especially considering Boxer's standing in the game. But that didn't happen. Mr Pears would normally start conversations with rugby league players from the standpoint of someone who always knew he was right and that your opinion didn't amount to much. He wasn't considered much of a rugby man on account of his fondness for Manchester City - he was a regular attender of football matches at Maine Road, where he held a season ticket in a particularly fine part of the stadium and he would cheer on Joe Corrigan, Dennis Tueart, Kevin Reeves and Paul Power, wearing a blue scarf.

"I got a phone call from Bill Pears that night," says Boxer. "I was interested but he had a bit of snottiness in him, you know, the way he talked to me and it knocked me sideways.

"He said Barrow wanted me but I would have to behave myself: 'I don't want your cockiness and you won't decide when you train. We will,' he told me. I couldn't believe it. I said: 'Hey, hang on a minute, it's you who wants me to sign. Not the other way round.' So I put the phone down and that deal just fell through right there and then."

Two more weeks drifted by and nothing much was happening, though if you believe newspaper reports, as many as 10 clubs had been linked with his transfer. Messages from third parties had been passed on but nothing much had come from them. So Boxer was thinking that he was in a bit of pickle, though Peter Gorley's transfer to St Helens in October was satisfactory news, knowing his great friend was making a fresh start with a top side.

Unbeknown to him, a meeting was taking place in the boardroom of Whitehaven Rugby League Club and there was only one item on the agenda – him. The financial plight of the club had taken an upturn due to happenings 12 miles further south, along the A595, where British Nuclear Fuels was prospering and providing thousands of well-paid jobs. There were rumours of sponsorship deals and the appointment of new directors.

The exact details are unknown but what is certain is that chairman David Wigham, the man who recently had an apparently chance encounter with Boxer's father, was proposing that Haven should sign the scrum-half. The problem was not raising the money, but reservations certain directors were harbouring involving persistent rumours that had been circulating around the town for some time. There was no proof of the authenticity of these stories, but they were nevertheless being recounted in the boardroom. The majority of these claims, though not all of them, involved excessive drinking and extravagant behaviour in unnamed pubs and clubs and often carried out in the company of spectacularly beautiful women. Some directors were concerned that such behaviour was unseemly for a professional sportsman and there were other stories too, pertaining to breaching club discipline at Workington Town. Boxer would occasionally miss training, so said the stories, and might turn up late or miss the team bus or start fights or be a negative influence in the dressing room or sulk or undermine the board or refuse to sign autographs. Then there were all those unpaid fines and various motoring offences and you couldn't forget those gambling debts and other problems, so they said, that were too serious to even repeat. It was all perfectly true according to someone's friend who was told by his brother-in-law's boss who met the next door neighbour at the bus stop.

David Wigham did not believe these rumours, not for a minute, and commonsense prevailed not least because of his reputation as a thoroughly decent person. Business dealings with Mr Wigham did not carry a risk of dishonesty. He was a devout Christian who frequently attended services at the Salvation Army Church in Catherine Street which advertised a devotion to saving lost souls under banners which proclaimed they were 'church leaders committed to transforming the lives of people in their community.' Leading officers were referred to as Majors and Mr Wigham took such lofty claims seriously, in fact, the belief at the time was that the pursuit of happiness on Sundays by taking part or watching any kind of 'entertainment' was likely to have a detrimental effect on the possibilities of your entry to heaven, when the time comes. Unfortunately this prohibited Mr Wigham's attendance at the Recreation Ground and he could occasionally be spotted on afternoons, walking along High View, on the high ground to the south of the town centre, peering across the slate roofs, with the harbour to the left and the Lake District mountains to the right, where he could, if he tried really hard, just pick out the tiny shapes of players running around almost a mile away.

Mr Wigham had been instructed to consult the first-team coach Phil Kitchin, who lived in a beautiful Edwardian house, on Herbert Hill, overlooking the harbour with spectacular views of the Irish Sea and from where you can see the mountains of the Isle of Man on a clear day. They are sitting in Phil's front room in Wellington Row, and he's wondering what could be the reason for the chairman's visit and that it must be mighty important.

"Right, Phil," he says. "We have a big decision to make. We have a young team and we are going places. What do you think about signing Boxer Walker?"

Phil stands up, to give his opinion more emphasis and he can't quite prevent himself from raising his voice slightly. "What do I think of it? He'd be the best thing to happen to this club for years. Boxer is inspirational, he's fiery, he's cheeky and he's a great player."

Mr Wigham, sensing there is a long conversation unfolding, interrupts Phil. "Yes, we all know that," he says, before stopping and staring down at the floor, searching for the words before asking: "What about the other stuff?"

"Other stuff?" asks Phil, getting increasingly frustrated. "Now look, we are talking about a very, very special player here. Have you ever known

Boxer have a bad game? No. He always performs on the park. I know he's a bit of a lad - the trouble is he doesn't try to hide it. That's his problem. Ask yourself this. And I know this for certain, if you ask any of the great players, and I include Alex Murphy in this, if they like playing against Boxer, they would all say no. We can build a team around him.

"No one around here has to ask about his ability. We all know how good he is. Please, don't look at his outside life, just look at how he performs every week for Town. Well, he can do that for us."

The next morning David Wigham is knocking on the front door of Boxer's house, and he's walking in with great purpose before shaking his hand warmly, and getting straight to the point: "We want you, Boxer, you're coming to Whitehaven."

He was the fourth director to make an official approach for the scrum half and though it came out later that Mr Wigham had started negotiations at around £24,000, George Graham knew the true value of the player and after talks, which lasted less than 30 minutes, the fee, should Boxer agree personal terms, would be exactly £30,000.

"David, who I knew quite well, asked me right off what I wanted," said Boxer. "I just said £5,000 and we shook hands right away and that was it. There were a couple of loose ends to tie up but I signed the forms right there and then. If I remember rightly, my pay-out was spread over a few months but I wasn't bothered about that.

"I was able to stay in my home town and play for my home team. I think David left my house around five and I was training with Whitehaven the same night. I felt a weight had been lifted off my shoulders and I couldn't wait to start. I knew a lot of the players from the county side and from the amateur game.

"David told me how much the coach Phil Kitchin wanted me and that was great to know. I felt a bit bad about Haven's scrum half Colin Hall. We were good mates and he was a very good player from Broughton Moor. Yet he made me really welcome and never missed a training session. That was how good of a club man he was and it made things easier for me. He went on to have a testimonial and it was well deserved."

Boxer's departure was the end of an era at Derwent Park and it was not well received by supporters. Two years before there was a genuine belief that the team was on the cusp of greatness but that optimism had now been replaced by gloom and a collective fear about an unknown future. All their heroes had gone. Speaking in the *Workington Times & Star* the week before he left, Boxer spoke with great sadness to reporter Phil Cram: "Things are down at Workington but I will say no more than that," said the scrum half. "The club have some great players like Harry Beverley and Paul Charlton and I will always be grateful to Sol Roper who has taught me more about scrum-half play than I could have learned anywhere else."

The same edition of the weekly paper which carried the full story of Boxer's departure, reported elsewhere that loose forward Billy Pattinson, who had always been a fans' favourite, was 'thinking about asking for a move'. The Town fans couldn't take any more.

Chairman George Graham said: "We have lost a very good player in Boxer but he was adamant that he wanted to go and he did stress in his transfer request that he had nothing personal against anyone on the board at Workington. We did not transfer-list him because we decided we would hang on as long as we could in the hope that he would change his mind about wanting away."

The fans didn't see it quite like that. Workington Town and Whitehaven were rebuilding their teams, but all similarities ended there. Town had sold internationals Eddie Bowman, Les and Peter Gorley, loose forward Bob Blackwood and now a Cumbrian genius who would soon be recognised as the greatest scrum half in the world.

Boxer said in that week's *Whitehaven News:* "I really wanted to come to Whitehaven. I have every confidence in the club which has shown it wants success. The supporters here are a great asset. They must rank as the best for the way they get behind the team and it is important to the players."

Haven skipper Ralph Calvin said: "His flair and talent can dictate the game. I played with him and I never saw anyone get the better of him." Haven chairman David Wigham said simply: "I am absolutely delighted that we have got Arnold with us."

CHAPTER 16

Sacked on a Garage Forecourt

hil Kitchin was a coach who was as good as it gets for Boxer Walker. He was a powerful authority on what was required to become an international half back. He would be his mentor, advisor, confidante and friend and play a vital part in the latter years of his career that would see him earn a Great Britain cap that many impartial observers believed he should have been awarded many years before.

They had much in common, starting with their roots which were exactly from the same place, give or take a few hundred yards, where they had been surrounded by the same workers. Phil's family, as far back as it was possible to go, were miners, and he, himself, was a face worker, and if that wasn't enough, he grew up in Woodhouse, Kells, just along from Boxer's home at Mid Street. So they shared the same simple virtues of collective responsibility and caring for those who needed help, the kind of Christian principles that had been such an important part of Boxer's childhood and so common all around him. These values had been second nature among mining communities going back generations, and they were a vital component in the production of professional rugby league players, and though it was hard to define you can be sure that whatever it was, Phil Kitchin and Boxer Walker had plenty of it.

They were both Kells players, though not at the same time, and Boxer had known Phil, well, as far as it was possible for an eight-year-old to have an acquaintance with an 18-year-old man, especially when that man was something of a local hero and an international player. Phil knew Boxer more in the way of a caring uncle or an older brother and he would ruffle his hair on Saturday afternoons when he lit up the Welfare Ground with his athletic excellence while Boxer looked on, with his friends, wishing he could grow up and be like him.

They played in similar positions, Boxer at scrum half and Phil at stand-off, places in a team, that, among a dozen other things, linked forwards and backs, and demanded the same qualities of speed, courage and unpredictability and which gave Phil the ideal qualification to be a knowledgeable and guiding presence. And if all this wasn't enough, they had a fondness for each other, although they could not be described as good friends - their relationship was more about respect, and certainly on Boxer's part, huge helpings of admiration.

The final component of their partnership, and probably the most important, was how highly Phil rated Boxer, who he had watched with great interest many times throughout his career, from as far back as when he was a boy on the playing fields of St Mary's Catholic School and right through, from Kells Juniors, and finally his progress at Workington Town among those remarkable players.

Phil's status as a Cumbrian rugby league legend is worth investigating. He was something of a child prodigy and captained England Under-19s as a centre in an 18-8 victory over France at Wigan in 1959. He was the Cumberland captain at that age level and had already appeared for the county at open age – and he twice represented England Boys at rugby union.

All the top rugby league teams wanted him, but he preferred to remain in Cumberland and turned professional later that year with Whitehaven. Phil played 13 times for Cumberland and he had a starring role in a shock 12-7 win over the New Zealand tourists in 1965 and two years later, he was again the inspiration when the county side defeated the Kangaroos 17-15. Other representative matches followed and he was considered one of the best stand-offs around which was high praise indeed considering his era coincided with mighty half backs which included Frank Myler, Alan Hardisty, Harold Poynton, Roger Millward and Mick Shoebottom.

He earned caps for England Under-24s and won a coveted full Great Britain cap when the Brits beat New Zealand 7-2 in 1965. Phil also played for Workington Town before returning to finish his career at the

Recreation Ground. He was inaugurated into Haven's Hall of Fame and is considered to be the club's greatest stand-off half.

§

Boxer was determined to start his career at Whitehaven as soon as possible. He wasn't sure how he would be received or what his new team-mates might think of him, and he was fearful that the huge transfer fee might create hostility or resentment. He needn't have worried. Mr Wigham told him when he left his house that he was going directly to the Recreation Ground to break the good news and that he shouldn't worry about being late. He promised to tell Phil he was on his way.

He was unprepared for what was awaiting him. The warm welcome was typical of Phil's insight into how Boxer might be feeling in this unusual and stressful situation, and illustrated how important it was for him that his transfer was accepted well among the players. It was essential for Phil that the scrum-half should feel special, at least for tonight anyway, and he wanted him to know that his arrival was especially worthy of celebration among the fans, the players and the directors, everyone who mattered.

Boxer got changed quickly and one of the coaching staff took him under the stand and out onto the field where more than 40 players were standing in a neat semi-circle, the entire playing staff, all the first-teamers, the A teamers and a few more besides. A small ripple of applause broke out and Phil started speaking, the whole scene illuminated by the soft, yellow beams falling on the pitch from the floodlights, breaking through the winter gloom.

"Right lads, you all know who this is and if anybody doesn't, put your hands up and I'll shoot them off," he began. "We have been trying to sign Boxer for a while. He is a player I really wanted. Now we are going to build our team around him."

Boxer thanked Phil and the players. Public speaking did not come easily to him but on this occasion, his discomfort was taken by the players as a sign of humility. So while he stuttered his way through his nervy explanation of how he was feeling to be here, among them, there was overall approval. He told them, first and foremost, that he was one of them and didn't consider himself anything special. He was happy to be here, he said, and if he could help anyone all they had to do was ask. Boxer promised that he would do his best for the team and he hoped to help them win. He clapped his hands and Phil and the other coaches blew their whistles, and the players immediately began jogging around the field to warm up. There was no dissension - the players were optimistic and excited to be part of what was going on at The Recre. They all knew how special Boxer was and now they had witnessed first-hand that he was without arrogance and that they could all kid around with him if the right circumstances presented themselves.

Boxer would go on to become the club captain and Haven's greatest ever scrum half, and he would soon prove to them that such a reputation, although hard-earned, didn't make him any different to them. He would earn their respect by what he did and how he did it and in no time at all he was feeling right at home.

§

If anyone had any misgivings about the bountiful skills Boxer was bringing to the club they would be dispelled after his first game which was on January 20, 1980, when he starred in Haven's 16-11 victory at Dewsbury. Alan Irving, the *Whitehaven News* reporter, wrote this in a column called Sporting Jottings: 'Arnold Walker had an excellent debut, revealing some of the touches which used to scare many a First Division side. His fame has spread throughout the rugby league world and it was not surprising that he should find himself tightly marked against Dewsbury and heavily tackled on occasions.'

It was a promising start to say the least but his leadership skills, which were based primarily on the example he set, would soon persuade Phil to appoint Boxer as the club captain, in place of Ray Dutton, a former Great Britain player. Boxer was immensely likable and, perhaps a little surprisingly, not only did Ray accept his replacement with good grace, he recognised that Boxer's appointment would benefit the team. He welcomed his promotion without complaint, not for a moment.

"Ray Dutton was great with me," recalls Boxer. "I already knew him well from when he played at Widnes. Ray kept Paul Charlton out of the

Great Britain team because he was a better goalkicker. I remember Ray coming up to me on that first training night and shaking my hand. He told me how happy he was that I was there and that he was looking forward to playing with me. He said he would always be there for me.

"Everybody knew me already and we had a lot of good players. John Bulman, who played for Kells, was a flying machine. We had two brothers, Jimmy and Denis O'Neill, Dave Macko was a tough loose forward and we also had Paul Grimes, who was a very experienced prop forward. I can't forget Ralph Calvin, who played with me at Town and Ian Litt, who was a very good second row forward. The main playmaker was Gordon Cottier - we played together with the county so I knew how good he was. Looking back, after Town had sold all their best players, I honestly thought that we had a better team.

"Milton Huddart was a very clever player - he eventually ended up at Leigh. And we had a great centre called Peter Stoddart, who was a Maryport lad. Another good back was Vince Gribbin, yet another county player who went to play for Great Britain. He was a very quiet lad, and we got on very well. He listened to me.

"What was typical of Whitehaven back then was what happened when I was first introduced to a lad who had played for Moresby at rugby union and he wasn't very experienced at league. His name was Jeff Simpson and he has recently been inducted to Haven's Hall of Fame which was well deserved. He took me to one side at training and asked if he could have a word with me. I thought to myself that he was just another young lad who had done nowt but wanted to tell me how good he was. I often got them bothering me and bragging. But no, he said he wanted to learn the game and asked me if I could help him on the pitch. I really liked his attitude and I thought to myself: 'You'll do for me, son.' To think, he wasn't big-headed and he'd come to me for help.

"Jeff was a good lad who became a great player for Haven. I never stopped talking on the field and sometimes I would shout to Jeff to make a run and he would always go wherever I told him. Even if it might not seem obvious what was happening. I might miss three men out and when I told Jeff to come on to the ball, he'd always be there exactly where I wanted him. Jeff would see me coming and there would be a gap. It would click into his head."

Haven won nine of their last 10 matches in the Second Division following Boxer's arrival and the following season, the team earned promotion after finishing fourth and winning 19 matches out of 28. They were a difficult team to break down and finished with the second best defence in the league.

At the end of the season, Boxer was runner-up in the Second Division Man of Steel end-of-season awards, along with Swinton's stand-off half Danny Wilson, who had a seven-year-old son who would go on to become one of the Manchester United's greatest footballers – his name is Ryan Giggs. The winner was York's number six John Crossley, who scored 36 tries that season. The First Division Man of Steel was Ken Kelly, Warrington's Great Britain half back.

Boxer was now the captain of Cumbria, where his leadership qualities, among better players, were even more pronounced. A valued team-mate was Malcolm Flynn, the former Wath Brow forward, who was starring for Barrow, and, if truth be known, a wonderful player who was, nevertheless, in awe of his 150-pound skipper. "I remember once, playing at Derwent Park against Town for Barrow and I caught Boxer with a tackle, absolutely perfectly," recalls Malcolm, who still lives in south Cumbria today. "You know when everything is timed just right and I can remember thinking to myself, 'he'll be finished, he'll be taken off after that.' Well he just got up, played the ball, and stared right in my face and gave me a big smile. I couldn't believe it. Everyone had told me how tough he was.

"Boxer was quick off the mark and I hated trying to tackle him because he could make anyone look like a fool. Give me a 16-stone forward running right at me any time but not Boxer. He would never hide and he was always in the middle of the forwards. I don't know how he did it, but if you ran at him and tried to push him out of the way, he would just get hold of your sleeve and pull you down. He never seemed to miss.

"There were a lot of great scrum halves around then but Boxer should still have played a lot more for Great Britain. He was like my scrum half at Barrow, David Cairns, they both played way above their weights and had huge hearts. If a team had forwards like Boxer and David, it would be unbeatable.

"It was an honour to play for Cumbria, of course, and especially so when Boxer was the captain. I loved playing for him and he was really good at firing everyone up in the dressing room. Whenever he was my county captain, he would end his team-talks with a rallying cry they used at Workington – he would bang the ball on the table and ask us all: 'who are the boys that make the most noise?' and we would all shout out at the top of our voices, 'hey, hey, hey,' and when we went out, we felt we could beat anybody."

Phil was creating something special and with Boxer's help, Haven had played outstanding rugby league that no one on the terraces at the Recreation Ground had witnessed since Dick Huddart was on the rampage in the 1950s. Crowds improved and soon 4,000 people were turning up at The Recre as the team pushed for promotion. No one could quite figure the Cumbrians out.

"I really enjoyed playing for Phil," recalls Boxer. "We had a few planned moves with certain forwards but Phil just let me get on with it. He knew that I knew what I was doing. Some coaches might have set ideas of how a team should play but it wasn't like that with Phil. We were well prepared and he trusted us – everything can change when you get on that field. It might not work that way, perhaps the other team would close you down, so I had to use my brain. It's easy coaching Wigan or Warrington with all those internationals. There wasn't much money available and we had to make the best of what we had."

The gap between the two divisions was enormous and more often than not, three of the four promoted teams went straight back down again as the challenge of facing sides such as Leeds, Warrington and Widnes instead Blackpool Borough or Huyton was an impossible gap without changing most of the squad.

Haven agreed new deals with Ralph Calvin, Paul Grimes and Gordon Cottier, in the summer before their attempt at the big time. And 25-year-old front row forward John Glover was signed from Rochdale Hornets for £20,000 along with Hensingham winger Billy Fisher, who was only 18 but considered one of the brightest prospects in the county. The club tried to sign Glyn Shaw and Les Gorley from Widnes but the deal fell through and the directors even considered bringing in Paul Charlton, who was then 38. Whitehaven prepared for their opening First Division match at Leigh with a team of Cumbrians who were big on heart but lacking the guile of their opponents. Haven were thrashed 37-2 and it was soon clear they were in for a very long season. After only eight weeks, ball-playing loose forward Gordon Cottier was transferred listed for £35,000 with the team winless and written off.

On January 19, 1982, the board dismissed Phil Kitchin following a 27-3 defeat at Barrow and though his record of 13 losses and one draw could hardly be described as anything other than disastrous, the prevailing view from the terraces was that he had been let down by the board, who hadn't brought in enough quality players.

That week's *Whitehaven News* reported Phil's departure with its usual blanket coverage and he was quoted as saying: "This has come like a bolt out of the blue. There is no way I intended to resign but, after being asked to resign by the directors, I decided I wouldn't stay where I wasn't wanted. I am really sick about it and disappointed in the directors." Phil went on to point to a crippling injury list to key squad members before adding: "I don't think I have been a failure but I do feel as if I am being made a scapegoat for everything that has happened. The players have all got stuck in and done the job I have asked them to do."

Any right-minded person would be hard-pressed not to conclude that Phil got a raw deal at Haven, yet there is not a trace of bitterness in him as he reviews the events surrounding his dismissal. In fact, speaking in 2016, he prefers to talk about Boxer's courage, his flair for the unexpected and how important he was to the team.

"Boxer was a player with great style," says Phil. "Roger Millward was a superb scrum half but he wouldn't want to play against Boxer. I had watched Workington many times and I knew they had a great team full of special players and yet Boxer was the main man. He organised everyone on the field. 'Go there, go here,' he would tell everyone and if they didn't do what he wanted, he would play war with them. It was that leadership that I wanted to bring to Whitehaven.

"I know one thing for certain, if you ask any of the great players and that includes Alex Murphy, if they wanted to play against Boxer, they would all say no. He is way up with all the best in the game and if he had ever gone to a big team he would never have had to do all that tackling, but that was his game. He wanted to be in among it, especially in attack with the ball in his hands. Boxer was a pleasure to coach.

"He never gave me any trouble at all. We had a bit of banter which was expected and I enjoyed that too. He never gave me a single problem, not once. Boxer always calls me Phillip now. Nobody else calls me that. It's a sign of respect, I think. I'm sure Boxer would have won more Great Britain caps if he hadn't had his bad injury. I am good friends with Alex Murphy and Boxer reminds me of him though he was a lot smaller. And he did a lot more tackling than Alex. Boxer was in the thick of everything all the time. We have always respected each other. When he first came to Haven everything I wanted he did and I loved working with him."

The response to Phil's dismissal from the club's board came from football director Eppie Gibson, the ex-Town and Haven international, who, in public at least, had great sympathy for Phil's situation, saying: "Phil has obviously worked very hard for the club in getting the side out of the Second Division. It is just unfortunate that we haven't had any results this season. It was a disturbing decision for the directors to make but it was felt something positive had to be done to help Whitehaven onto a new course. People have been pointing fingers at the odd directors but the decision was taken unanimously and it came right from the top."

There were only 15 First Division matches remaining and they were already adrift at the foot of the table and the *Whitehaven News* hinted at Boxer's immediate promotion to player-coach which made a lot of sense and would give the club time to prepare for the following season and enable the directors to calmly put together a recovery plan.

"Phil was very unfortunate when he got the sack," remembers Boxer. "Luck just didn't go our way but we never got hammered by any team. And the main reason for that was guts - we might not have had the most skilful team but we had one of the bravest. They should never have got rid of him. Looking back they should have signed better players and that didn't help Phil. I blame myself in a way. We should have beaten Bradford but I dropped the ball over the line and that win might have given Phil more time. I messed up and it was my fault. Looking back now I should have apologised to Phil and all the players after that game but I was just feeling too down. I remember that I didn't go into the club which wasn't like me. I let Phil, the players and all the fans down.

"The same week Phil got sacked, I got a phone call from David Wigham saying that the directors wanted to see me in the boardroom. That was when they told me they wanted me to be the player coach. I was chuffed to bits but when my career finished and I look back now I don't think I should have taken it. They were in no hurry because they were already relegated and they just wanted a fall guy and that was me. I got a couple wins for them but it wasn't worth it. I think we were on around £50 for a win and I got an extra £70 a week for being the coach but it was only for a few weeks anyway."

Boxer was an immensely likeable person who played up to his reputation, which was well-founded, as a kind of maverick who thought the rules of normal behaviour often did not apply to him. And as a result of his ownership of the most famous nickname in Cumbria, his transgressions - often involving excessive drinking - were forever being passed around and they grew with the telling. What tales were repeated about him, being thrown out of this bar at a particular time or being arrested for some irresponsible prank. Most of them weren't true but that didn't stop them from being repeated. You might forget a Bill or a John or a David but you were never going to forget a Boxer.

He didn't do much to deny these allegations and he would be the first to admit that there weren't many pubs in Whitehaven with bar staff who were unfamiliar to him. To Boxer, it was as if his genius with a rugby ball had granted him a few extra years of adolescence, a way of behaving immaturely that was harmless and would be broadly forgiven. Yet beneath all that generosity and extravagant behaviour he was an intelligent young man who had a sharp mind. And he knew rugby league as well as any living man, no one could argue against that.

So he set about an impossible task with great enthusiasm and anyway, he always held the view that the most important people were not the players, and certainly not the directors but the fans, who all loved him. Within the first week, he had introduced a whole raft of new policies and team changes, which took the directors by surprise. They were brave and meticulously planned and analysed by Alan Irving, in that weekend's *Whitehaven News*, the reporter who had diligently reported his rise to the top and, much later in his life would own up to Boxer being one of his favourite players.

The scrum half had almost pulled off a winning start as his team narrowly lost 15-12 at Wakefield Trinity. Alan Irving reported: "Haven still haven't won this season but new player-coach Boxer Walker told me: 'I am really proud of the lads. I asked for 100 per cent but what they gave me was 200 per cent.' I was among those who felt Phil Kitchin should have had longer to prove his admirers' claim that he was one of the best coaches in the game. But already I am impressed by the approach and attitude of his successor to what I described last week as a job and a half.

"Boxer Walker has tackled it positively and imaginatively by selecting a team which was different, interesting and effective for most of Sunday's game and, by all accounts, Whitehaven were the better team. He also dropped John Glover, the £20,000 prop who so far had not lived up to the club's second biggest transfer fee either in performance or fitness. Walker has also asked former skipper and player-coach Ray Dutton to bring together all of Haven's out-of-town players for once a week training sessions in Lancashire. He has also taken immediate steps to iron out any lingering sore points and telling all the players in no uncertain terms what he and the supporters expect from them.

"Walker has been on the warpath all right, leaving no one in any doubt that he is the Recreation Ground chief in word and deed. Doubts have been expressed about Arnold's wisdom in taking on such a demanding managerial role at the age of 29. But I have been struck not only by his characteristic enthusiasm for the job but also his courage in making difficult decisions, introducing new ideas and having the confidence to be his own man."

Alan Irving, struggling to maintain his impartiality, finished by quoting Boxer, who said: "You could see the determination in the lads' faces at Wakefield. I think that not only did they want winning pay for the first time but they also wanted to help me get back at some of my critics. It will come. I just know it will and when it does I think some team is in for a hammering."

Inevitably, Whitehaven were relegated at the end of the season, but Boxer had conducted his duties with great enthusiasm and there were signs of improvement. The team had defeated Wigan and Barrow and had only conceded 565 league points in the season which was an average of only 19 points a game which gives statistical evidence of the spirit in the side, began by Phil Kitchin and continued by Boxer Walker.

"At the end of the season I got a phone call and I knew something was up," recalls Boxer. "Our last game was at home to Leigh who were coached by Alex Murphy. They had to beat us at the Recre to win the league championship and we almost beat them. If we had, Hull would have been the champions. It was the top club against the bottom club and Alex said after the game how frightened he was about getting beat. There was a hell of a crowd there – they put the kick-off back for 15 minutes.

"I remember Alan Irving interviewing me after the game for the *Whitehaven News* and he told me that performance would keep me in the job. I still don't believe it but I got the sack on the forecourt of Batty's Garage down in the Whitehaven town centre. It is a car wash now. David Wigham just pulled up alongside me and said they wouldn't be renewing my contract. I couldn't do nowt about it so I just accepted it. From what I heard, some of the board thought I might take the pet lip and not play the following season but I wouldn't do that. I told David that I accepted it and that I would turn up the next season and do my best."

Once again there was a comment piece from Alan Irving in the *Whitehaven News* that was sympathetic to Boxer's situation and overtly critical of the board. He reported: "The directors are not above censure. The club has not been altogether fair with Boxer Walker who was asked to try and get them out of this mess four months ago. Alex Murphy was full of admiration, not only for the way Walker motivated makeshift Haven's stirring performance against his Leigh league champions in the last match of the season but also for Boxer's own international-class show. Full of enthusiasm and plans, Arnold was looking forward to coaching the side next season and he had every justification for expecting the directors to give him a fair crack of the whip. I think the view is shared by quite a few Whitehaven players that he deserved the chance of continuing next season. Boxer is still one of the best scrum-halves in the game and he was so keen to install professional pride into the players, that he was busy, when the sack came, trying to attract sponsorship to kit them out in club suits."

Haven didn't waste much time appointing Boxer's successor, Tommy Dawes, a Barrovian with a county-wide reputation for a tough, no nonsense approach to discipline and an aversion to familiarity with players. Within a few weeks, Boxer, who had played for Great Britain 14 months earlier, would suffer the indignity of playing for the A team. Though, as things worked out, he didn't quite see it like that.

CHAPTER 17

Upset Tommy

Boxer Walker and Tommy Dawes were never going to get along. They were too different. The scrum half would admit that most of his previous coaches had indulged him, and recognised his genius for what it was and the incredible things he could do for the team. As long as he performed on the field, they were prepared to turn a blind eye to his misdemeanours. He had always been a subtle manipulator of his position as a star player which had occasionally flared up in disciplinary procedures but for the most part, his talent spoke for itself and coaches were happy to go along with it.

His knowledge had been acquired from Cumbrian rugby league royalty and the list of his mentors is worth reviewing, beginning with Les Herbert, the Kells hero who had played twice for England amateurs. His tuition continued with contributions from Billy Garratt, Eppie Gibson, Sol Roper and Phil Kitchin and you couldn't forget Ike Southward and Paul Charlton who, whatever way you look at it, were two of the greatest players the game has ever seen.

Tommy had been a brave and reliable full back for Barrow but he wasn't a star and in Boxer's eyes he certainly didn't amount to much as a player in comparison with his other, more high profile mentors. He was better known as a touch-judge who was often seen running up and down the touchline at Derwent Park or the Recreation Ground, a fit and athletic looking man, with blonde hair and a thorough understanding of the laws of the game.

What was without question was his suitability as Haven's coach. Tommy brought with him an impressive reputation for getting the job done and despite his perpetual disagreements with his star player, Haven won promotion to the First Division. Boxer made just 11 first-team starts as their relationship deteriorated from distant to non-existent. Quite whose fault it was is a matter of opinion.

Boxer could be a player in the mode of a flawed genius and he had always prospered by gentle handling and an arm around his shoulder. Tommy, for all his knowledge and respect within the game, liked everything done his way. He was a harsh disciplinarian and a meticulous planner who was always going to struggle to get the best out of a great player such as Boxer. The scrum half was of the opinion that if Tommy were an actor he could have easily slipped into the pompous persona of Captain Mainwaring without making too much of an effort. The coach had a clergyman's dislike for blasphemy and gambling and on the first trip from Whitehaven, and with the bus still climbing along Wellington Row and the harbour still visible behind them, he was troubled to discover a card school already underway. He immediately banned gambling to the bewilderment of the players and returned to the front of the bus carrying the offending pack of cards with a frown on his face, as if he was a strict teacher, confiscating contraband from naughty children. He considered any form of enjoyment as a distraction from what the players should be focusing on – preparing for the game.

"Tommy hated me and I hated him," remembers Boxer. "He didn't like me from when I was at Workington Town. Tommy was a touch-judge and whenever I was playing, he was running on the pitch every five minutes, waving his flag in the air, and telling the ref what I was supposed to have done. When I heard he had got the Haven job I remember thinking it wasn't going to go well for me. I felt he had it in for me. We just didn't get on right away.

"I didn't play for him - I played for my mates and the fans. I never got on with Tommy. To be honest I am not putting all the blame on him though. I admit I didn't make it easy for him in training. Sometimes, if we were passing the ball between the players, perhaps practising moves, I would deliberately drop it just to wind him up. Another time it kicked off was when Tommy told us to get ready for sprint training. There was a cinder track behind the Popular side at the Recre so I put on my running spikes. But instead we went onto the farmer's field and it had been raining all week and it was full of sludge. Tommy had us doing tackling practice on each other.

"I was partnering another scrum-half called John Milburn and I told him that I didn't want to end up on the ground rolling around in all that mud, so we agreed to tackle high, properly but so we wouldn't finish all messed up. Tommy saw how clean we both were and all the rest of the lads were as black as the ace of spades and he didn't like it. I think he thought we weren't doing what he wanted.

"He didn't say anything but I just knew he wasn't very happy. That all happened on a Thursday night which was when the team was announced. Tommy picked the side and then someone would pin it up in the dressing room. When I looked at the team, I realised he had dropped me and put Colin Hall in. I went straight in to see Dawes and he told me I had been messing about in training and that he was putting me in the A team. I couldn't believe it. I wasn't being big-headed but I said to him: 'I am the captain of the county side and you're putting me in the A team.' He just said he had no choice and that he had to discipline me. As I was leaving he told me that if I had a good game he would put me on the bench for the first team."

Tommy's authority was absolute and without question and Boxer's reluctance to follow his meticulously planned instructions was another impediment to his selection. Before he came, it was said Tommy was the kind of stickler for detail who might demand that the players walked onto the field with exact conformity which might include the players' socks pulled up to their knees at exactly the same length. If nothing else, Boxer had always been an expert at exploiting situations that might, on the face of it, appear to be disadvantageous to him. So he figured out a devious plan and went about putting it into action. Tommy was a serious man who didn't laugh a lot, and the word was that when he got wind of Boxer's deception he couldn't prevent a smile from appearing on his face, though it was gone quickly enough.

"After playing county rugby, it was a doddle playing in the A team," Boxer recalls. "I cruised through it and I hardly remember getting a really hard tackle, so every week the same thing happened. In the first team I was just sitting on my bum and coming on in the last five minutes and hardly getting touched. I thought to myself that it was great. I was getting winning first team pay and also winning A team pay most weeks. I think back then the winning pay for the first team was around £60 and for the A team it was something like £25.

"So I started messing around in training all the time. He knew I was doing it on purpose. I know he was thinking he was the gaffer and I was thinking I was. I think this went on for at least 10 weeks. The trouble was I had told one or two of my pals in the first team and it got back to Tommy what I was up to. I heard later that he kept saying: 'The crafty little bugger'. After that, all of a sudden, he stopped picking me in the A team and I was still on the bench for the first team. A couple of weeks later I guess it all blew over and I was starting in the first team again."

Whatever Boxer thought of Tommy as a charmless authority figure he had to admit that he was a successful coach. Whitehaven were promoted to the First Division that season after winning 20 of their 32 matches and Dawes returned to his home-town team of Barrow. His success at Craven Park was extraordinary. In his first season, Barrow won the Second Division championship by 14 points and set 17 records, some of which still stand today and include most tries scored in a season at 209, the highest points total at 1,126 and the highest winning away margin which was 72 points. All these statistics are incredible but they weren't Tommy's greatest achievement. On October 1, 1983, Barrow defeated Widnes at Central Park, Wigan, live on the BBC, to become the first club from the Second Division to win the Lancashire Cup in the tournament's 78-year history. As if that wasn't enough, Widnes had played 10 full Great Britain internationals.

That season was a throwback to the glory years of Willie Horne in the 1950s, when Barrow had a team of internationals. In fact, their unparalleled Lancashire Cup victory became such an important achievement that the entire Barrow team was inducted into the club's Hall of Fame in 2003. Tommy Dawes, despite his initial success, was sacked in 1985. His replacement at Haven was Frank Foster who had long been a big fan of Boxer and though he recognised the importance of discipline, he was, as far as it was possible, a player's coach who everybody loved playing for.

"Frank coming to Whitehaven was great for me," remembers Boxer. "Frank and me were big mates. He was an excellent coach and trainer. He made a big difference to us all. Frank used to pick on me all the time in training because I was one of the senior players and the rest of the lads, especially all the young ones, knew we were good pals and it made them think that if he was giving me the works they had better get stuck in themselves and they all did. I knew what was going on and it didn't bother me one bit. We ended up really fit. Frank loved me and he still does. We got on really well."

Frank, who coached Barrow for 10 years, following his own distinguished career with Town, Hull KR, Bradford Northern, Barrow and Oldham, quickly created an atmosphere of harmony and Boxer looked forward to the new season with great optimism.

He was still only 31 but a few weeks later, and after only two league games, he would be assaulted one last time. His neck was broken and he would never play or work again. But first, his 19-game career for Cumbria as a scrum-half and captain without equal and the inside story on the Great Britain call-up everyone had been saying he deserved for years.

CHAPTER 18

Band of Brothers

The record attendance for a County Championship match is more than 12,000, a figure reached several times in the late 1940s. But 30 years later the competition had become less important and, occasionally at least, certain players would not go out of their way to make themselves available, especially in the heartlands of game, where selectors had 14 teams to choose from. That never happened in Cumbria, where players took their roots more seriously and selection for the county was talked of with great passion.

Cumbria travelled to Central Park, Wigan, to face Lancashire, on September 16, 1981, and they were not expected to win. And to make matters worse, there were four late withdrawals - two on the day before and two on the same day of the game, with the kick-off less than 10 hours away. This unexpected development severely depleted the side and as late as 6pm, there were fears that they might be unable to raise a side. The coach carrying most of the team from Cumbria had to take several detours to service stations along the M6 to enable anxious officials to grab hold of handfuls of change and use public telephones where they opened their contact books and commenced contacting eligible Cumbrians, who were based within range of the stadium.

Johnny Jones and Joe Stewart stepped in from West Cumbria plus the Lancashire-based pair, Harold Henney and Bob Blackwood. The full Cumbria team was: Steve Tickle, Ralph McConnell, Peter Stoddart, Johnny Jones, David Beck, Mel Mason, Arnold 'Boxer' Walker (captain), Harold Henney, Alan McCurrie, Malcolm Flynn, Les Gorley, Peter Gorley, Gordon Cottier. Subs: Joe Stewart and Bob Blackwood.

Perhaps it was the drama of the situation that helped the players dig deep down inside them for inspiration. Defeat was a possibility they were not going to entertain and they pulled off an unexpected 27-15 win. Boxer, who was skippering the side for the fifth time, scored two tries and kicked a goal with most of the headlines referring to the early dismissals of hookers Alan McCurrie for Cumbria and Nicky Kiss.

Bob Blackwood, who is often referred to as Spanner Man, was a back row forward who would conjure up images of mayhem in the minds of rival fans. He was a fine player who excelled mostly in his role as a violent protector of half backs. Boxer loved playing with Bob, who took any attempt to intimidate his team-mates as an affront to his sensibilities and it always ignited his retributive inclinations. Bob was never ever someone to take liberties with and, as you might expect, he was a key motivator and committed manufacturer of fearlessness among his team-mates. His acumen for havoc provided him with the perfect requirements for an alternative occupation as a night club bouncer and he was a regular and much-feared doorman at Jim Mills' night club in Widnes town centre. The club, which had opened in 1979, was a popular venue where Bernard Manning, Roy Walker and Engelbert Humperdinck often appeared. Two hours after the final whistle at Central Park and 15 triumphant Cumbrians were celebrating and knocking back a few beers while Big Jim is assisting the waiters to bring out large platters of scampi and chips.

The county selectors met the following weekend to pick the side for the second game which would take place at the Recreation Ground on Wednesday evening. The players assumed that they would have no choice but to give their display a glowing assessment and that their defeat of Lancashire was so unexpected and extraordinary that the side would remain unchanged. The selectors didn't quite see it that way. Newspapers published the team on Monday and all the players who had cried off had now made themselves available and the makeshift team, which had defeated Lancashire so emphatically, had an altogether different feel to it.

Les Gorley was one of the best second row forwards in the world but he took his star status as nothing much to get excited about. He was a quiet man not given to public shows of emotion and while other more extrovert players such as Boxer were a vocal and demanding presence among the senior players, Les would just sit back and take it all in. When he spoke everyone listened and on this occasion, for once, he had plenty to say. There was a body of opinion among the senior players that believed a great injustice had been perpetrated by the selectors. So Les telephoned his brother Peter and his captain Boxer Walker to solicit their opinions, which were exactly the same as his.

The exact chain of events will probably never be known but for sure, Les telephoned Jack Atkinson, Workington Town's representative on the county selection panel, and gave him a simple message which would not be subject to negotiation and would leave them with only two choices. "Put out the same team or we ain't playing," he said. What went on behind the scenes is unclear but the following evening, the original players were all reinstated.

Boxer was always popular among his team-mates and his eagerness to fully support what many people, coming from a different viewpoint, might have considered a mutiny, strengthened his iconic status as a great leader and was enthusiastically received across the county. Justice had been achieved, but unfortunately for Boxer, within 24 hours, his reputation would take a nose-dive. And it all happened right in front of the players who loved him – in the middle of Derwent Park dressing room.

§

It is sometime around 6.10pm on Tuesday, September 22, 1981. Fifteen brave men are sitting in the dressing room at Derwent Park preparing for their final training session before facing the might of Yorkshire at the Recreation Ground the next evening. Following their unexpected victory over Lancashire the previous week, Cumbria were close to making history. If they could win they would lift the county championship two years in succession, only the third time that had ever happened.

Most of the team were Cumbrian-based and had only travelled a few miles to the stadium while hooker Alan McCurrie had driven three hours from central Yorkshire where he was a star for Wakefield Trinity. Everyone was changed and ready to start but one important player was missing - skipper Boxer Walker and coach Sol Roper was pacing up and down, staring at his watch and wondering if they should start without him.

There was a bang on the door and Boxer was among them wearing a stupid grin and just standing, unsteadily, right next to Sol. There was complete silence as the players stared in his direction, their mouths slightly open, not sure what to make of it. Nothing was said for several seconds. It was as if someone had told an absolutely disgusting and rude joke that was not in the slightest bit funny. Boxer was as drunk as it is possible to get without being unconscious, following an eventful pub crawl around Whitehaven town centre, where he began with the best of intentions at the Shakespeare, in Roper Street, sometime around 2pm. Unfortunately, his celebrity status and sensitive feelings quickly got the better of him. Following a few drinks in the Ship Inn, his father's favourite bar, and a couple more in the Vine Hotel, he dropped in on The Central, in Duke Street, where he telephoned for a taxi to take him to Workington, but not before a few more beers. And here he was, making a fool of himself, and looking like Lee Marvin in a scene from *Cat Ballou*. Then, suddenly, without warning, he fell over, right at the feet of Sol – crash – and he was on the floor, struggling to get up.

Sol was familiar with Boxer's irresponsible behaviour and he had developed a certain skill in controlling him yet still allowing the scrum half to express himself, unhindered on the field. He had given up trying to moderate his behaviour or interfering. Sol just let him get on with it. But this, well, what could he do about this car crash in front of him?

"Oh my God, you're going to get me sacked," said Sol, helping Boxer to stand up and pushing him towards the door and ordering someone to telephone for a taxi. "Get this silly sod out of here."

Boxer stumbled out of the dressing room and was contemplating a right turn which would have taken him into the 200 Club lounge, now known as The Tom Mitchell Bar, where further alcoholic attractions awaited him. Fortunately for him, Town's front row forward Harry Beverley was barring his way. Harry was known for his fearless play on the field but, like most tough men, away from the ritual confrontation, he had a gentle and kindly personality. He literally carried Boxer along the corridor and into the car park where a taxi was pulling up. Harry grabbed him by the throat with those enormous hands of his and blasted into his face: "Get yourself home or I'll rip your bloody head off," he said before throwing the scrum half into the back of the taxi, perhaps more violently than was necessary, but with an economy of effort, like one might swing a heavy suitcase into a luggage rack in a railway carriage, and he slammed the door and watched the car pull away in the early evening twilight.

"I had been on the drink all day," recalls Boxer. "I was in a right state and looking back I was so lucky to come across Harry who was a fantastic guy. I turned up for the match the next day and walked into the dressing room. I thought I would be dropped but no one said anything so I started getting ready. Sol just looked at me and never said a word."

Cumbria won the match 20-10 in dreadful conditions with the rain falling down in great silver sheets - large pools of water had appeared without warning on the field as gale force winds blasted across the county from the Irish Sea. The team had made history and, as unbelievable as it may sound, viewed through a prism 37 years later, in a modern world full of scientific analysis, gluten-free meals and sports psychologists, Boxer, with alcohol still coursing through his veins, was quite magnificent. He scored a vital try and, according to contemporary match reports, had a fine game against his opposite number Steve Nash, who was a Great Britain international and World Cup winner. "The Gorley brothers formed a progressive second-row pair for Cumbria with Les playing a prominent part in two of their tries. Walker led Cumbria with his usual aggressive spirit," reported Raymond Fletcher in *The Yorkshire Post*. Back in the dressing room, his transgressions were forgotten and there was much merriment but Sol was still distant with his scrum half as the beer cans popped open.

"I had come out of the bath and was getting dressed," says Boxer. "Sol just walked over to me and shook his head a few times. I couldn't figure it out. I asked him what the matter was. I always remember what he said: 'Do you know something, lad. George Best has nothing on you. You're always drinking and messing about in night clubs – you'll sup anything out of a sweaty clog. You defy medical science.'

"I just couldn't be controlled, I don't know why. There was a police chief inspector called Ted Alderson at Whitehaven. I got to know him really well. He got hold of me one day and told me what everyone was saying about me around Whitehaven. He told me that all the directors were nattering about me. He said they were getting phone calls every week saying I had been seen staggering around the town centre. He told me that if I felt like a drink I should go somewhere out of the way, like St Bees, where I might not be recognised. I told him that it wasn't as much fun drinking on your own where there were no people. I liked company and I wouldn't listen to anyone."

§

Boxer made his debut for Cumberland on October 24, 1973, when they lost to the touring Australians 28-2 at Whitehaven. He was just 21-years-old and had played less than 30 first-team matches, but even then, those who knew about such things could see he had greatness in him.

"I remember getting a phone call from one of the Town directors," recalls Boxer. "He told me that the original scrum half, who was a good Whitehaven lad called Joe Bonnar, who went to Wakefield, had pulled out injured. I was only a young pup and I was really shocked - I didn't expect it. I was really chuffed to bits, and it had honestly never crossed my mind, not for a minute. The captain was Spanky and I played really well."

Boxer would go on to play 19 times for his county, winning two championships and captaining the team eight times, including scoring the winning try in a victory over New Zealand. His appointment as skipper was inevitable. He was following a long line of leaders who had fostered a togetherness that would envelop the players in a fraternity of loyalty which was almost spiritual and could not be equalled in the dressing rooms of Lancashire and Yorkshire. Pulling on the black and white hoops of Cumbria made them feel invincible and full of self-belief and self-reliance, born of isolation – a band of brothers. When a new player joined this exclusive club, he was made to feel special and at ease, wanted, important, respected and a lot more besides. It was like being invited to a new and incredibly loyal and affectionate family rather than being in a team of professional sportsmen. Boxer's qualities of leadership were based on the example he set. He was never distant or aloof but rather one of them and always willing to take on his share of work though there were many coaches and team-mates who felt he should leave his defensive duties to other, less creative players. He would never hide or take a rest. And they all loved him for it.

"I remember being picked as captain for the first time," he says. "I took over from Paul Charlton who had retired and we beat Yorkshire 17-13. I was so proud. To be picked as county captain I must have been playing really well. But it was also important that I got on well with all the lads. I would make sure I had a crack with our experienced players and find out what they were thinking. It is no good having a captain who everyone hates – that's never going to work. And you have to keep your head, you can't just go around the field shouting or losing your temper. I had more experience then. Every captain - and I don't care who it is - makes mistakes. When I was captain I suppose the lads all respected me and my decisions. They didn't question me, ever. I had to get on not only with the players but also with the coach and all the officials. If there was a problem with the players I would have to sort it. I suppose a captain is a bit like a union leader. It is no good 12 individual players charging in to sort things out. They came to me and I had to sort it. I was the spokesman."

In his second season in charge, Cumbria won the county championship for the first time since 1966, after defeating Lancashire 19-16 at Craven Park, Barrow, before travelling to Hull Kingston Rovers the following week and getting the better of Yorkshire 17-16. Their opponents took the game very seriously and played seven full Great Britain internationals.

"I will never forget that match at Hull KR," says Boxer. "There was a lot of traffic and we arrived late. Our coach was Phil Kitchin and when I look back I can still see him giving us our team talk at the head of the coach while we tried to put on our shirts and boots. He gave a great talk, telling us that we had to put all this behind us and not look for any excuses. He told us how much faith he had in us and how talented we were and that we should go out there and show everyone how good we were. I remember having a laugh with Bill Oxley, one of Cumbria's selectors from Barrow, after the game. He told me that he was just starting to tell someone that I was not doing much and just as the words were coming out of his mouth I scored a try, right under their posts."

Winning the county championship had always been a big deal to Cumbrians and it was a tradition of the tournament that the winning captain received the trophy after the final game at a civic reception. Such social events were not Boxer's thing but even he would admit that such a public acknowledgement of his team's amazing achievement would be something to savour. There was one problem – the trophy wasn't there.

Peter Gorley has a vivid memory of what unfolded on that night in Hull. "Everybody respected Boxer and not just in our team, in every other team throughout the game," he says. "We knew when we went out on that field, playing for Cumbria, we had faith, respect and trust in every one of our players. We knew we weren't just a match for them but that we could beat them. On that night at Hull KR we arrived late but we had five minutes in the dressing room before the kick-off and there were a load of programmes on the treatment table. The first thing we did was look at their team. I was sitting next to our Les and I remember this really well, I asked him what he thought. He told me: 'Well, our pack is better than theirs.' I said I thought so too and that if our backs could hold their backs we would win.

"Just before half-time we got a penalty on their 25-yard line and Boxer tapped the ball quickly and passed it to me. Trevor Skerrett tackled me and I hit him with my shoulder and managed to squeeze past Knocker Norton, to get over for a try. It was nip and tuck all through the second half until John Cunningham dropped the winning goal late on. Trevor and Knocker were both great lads, we had some brilliant times together.

"In the after-match reception, because Lancashire had won the county championship the year before and everyone was so confident that Yorkshire were going to beat us, they didn't have the cup to present. There was a director, I think he was from Barrow, and he made this speech which must have been so embarrassing for everybody, apart from us. He told everyone that we had come down here and nobody had given us a chance and that the only people who did were the lads in our dressing room. You haven't even bothered bringing the trophy, he told them all. We all burst out laughing."

Three weeks later and the Cumbrians beat New Zealand at the Recreation Ground, wearing a new strip with a running fox sewn onto the chest. Boxer remembers: "That was one of my proudest moments. The weather was terrible and again - Phil Kitchin was a big part of that win. He gave a great speech in the dressing room that fired us all up.

He told us that we were the champions and that we had to show them what we are made of. They picked their full Test team and no-one gave us a chance. I can still remember scoring the winning try. There was a scrum on their line and I dummied their scrum half, Gordon Smith, and stepped by their loose forward and captain Mark Graham. We all jumped up in the air because there was no time left and we knew we had won. We were overwhelmed, and we started going crazy and jumping on each other's backs. What an achievement for a team from Cumbria to beat a touring side. Phil was so proud of us."

During Boxer's nine-year career, he played alongside more than 100 different team-mates including several who had played many times in Test matches for Great Britain. Yet when you ask him who are his favourite players, his answer is so surprising it can only be described as unbelievable, especially so, considering he shared dressing rooms with many legendary men. They were not the fastest, the strongest, the most creative, the most elusive, they did not kick goals and they did not score many tries. Even the most passionate county supporter would not describe them as matchwinners, no, rather they were vital, and often unseen members of Cumbria's supporting cast. But they are stars to Boxer. They are Malcolm Flynn and Tom Gainford. Malcolm was a Wath Brow forward who played with distinction for Barrow for more than 10 years and Tom was a Whitehaven loose forward who also played for Barrow. According to Boxer, they had inexhaustible supplies of what might be described in a broad sweep as courage, bottle, guts, valour, team spirit, togetherness, willingness to sacrifice yourself for the common good, and a whole host of other emotional descriptions - but whatever you want to call it, their contribution was the essence of what made Cumbrians, back then at least, special, unique and so difficult to beat.

Tom's appetite for defence was a truly remarkable thing to witness first-hand. And on top of that, if the grand title of 'best value player' existed he would be right up there, at the top of the tree. Tom inevitably came from Kells, and he was summoned to the Recreation Ground in 1967 where directors opened up negotiations which were concluded in around 20 seconds. Tom's lack of arrogance made him popular among his team-mates but it was not a particularly helpful characteristic in financial negotiations and, for sure, he underestimated his true worth. He was offered £100 signing on fee but played hard ball and signed on the dotted line for another £25.

In all matters concerning tackling, Tom was in a category all of his own. If he came off the field with a tackle count of less than 40 he would brood in the dressing room, with a guilty expression on his face. He made 284 appearances for Whitehaven, in 12 years, and at least 10,000 tackles later he was transferred to Barrow for around £12,000 – which was almost 100 times his signing on fee.

"Malcolm and Tom would always be there for the team," says Boxer. "They were a dream for a captain. If we had six tackles to clear our line and I said to one of them: 'come on, yours again' and they might perhaps take four out of those six, they would do it. I would never do that but Tom and Malcolm would always be there ready to do whatever I asked them for the good of Cumbria.

"I never had one single complaint from them, not in the dressing room, not on the field, nowhere. I think Malcom should have played for Great Britain. He would be in my side all the time. I played with the best around for England and Great Britain and Malcom was just as good. I loved him.

"As for Tom, well his work-rate was always 200 per cent. You could always guarantee he would be there knocking all the big men down time after time. He did so much defending that he kept our ball players fresh. And just like Malcolm he never complained about other players who didn't do half his work. He was the perfect player to play with for Cumbria.

"A couple of years ago I was getting in my car in the middle of Whitehaven and a woman shouted to me, asking if I knew her nephew, she told me he was called Malcolm Flynn. My eyes lit up with excitement because I hadn't seen Malcolm for years, not since we played together. He was one of the best players I had ever played with. She couldn't believe it, and I told her to make sure she told him what I had said. Malcolm was right up there with the best and almost as good as Les Gorley but Les was perhaps a bit cleverer. Tom was tall but he wasn't even two stones heavier than me. Yet he was a complete tackling machine and he hardly ever missed. No one got past him. I liked playing with people who didn't moan. Another player I want to give a mention to is Ian Wright – how he never played for Great Britain I'll never know."

Two days after Cumbria defeated New Zealand, selectors announced Great Britain's 20-man squad for the forthcoming opening Test match. All the newspaper reporters' predictions were accurate – Boxer had made it. He joined the players for a pre-match training night at Rothwell, Leeds, along with his Cumbrian friend Peter Gorley, 10 days before the First Test. But again, his dream of wearing that shirt would be broken by another thug who knocked him out cold and left him with a fractured cheekbone.

*John 'Sol' Roper, playing in the 1955 Challenge Cup final against
Barrow, about to be tackled by Reg Parker with Bill Healey in the
background. 'I had watched Sol playing for Whitehaven when I was
a kid,' says Boxer. 'He was a right showman and I really looked up to
him. He was my idol and mentor. I loved Sol and I loved playing for
him. He taught me so much. Looking back, I owe him everything.'*

By 1978, Boxer Walker was being tipped for international honours and, he says, he was a much-improved player since Sol Roper had taken over at Town. 'When we were waiting in the tunnel to go on, Sol would often shout to me: Walker, you're not fit to tie my laces,' recalls Boxer. 'It was all to get me going and I never answered him. He was just winding me up.'

Iain MacCorquodale, Town's prolific goal-kicker. Corky kicked 775 goals and 31 drop goals in his eight-year career at Derwent Park

Barrow director Bob Brady, who accused the Town players of not trying against the Australian tourists in 1978

Harry Archer was the gifted half back partner of Sol Roper. The stand-off, who was also known as the architect, is shown receiving treatment on the touchline at Wembley stadium by Bill Whalley in 1958. Town lost the Challenge Cup Final to Wigan 13-9.

Doug Laughton, the Widnes coach who tried to lure Boxer to Naughton Park

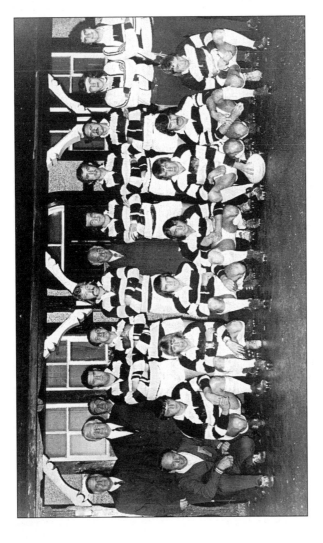

Cumbria's county side in 1973, in front of Whitehaven club house. Back: Jeff Bawden, Bob Nicholson, Miles Todd (groundsman), Spanky McFarlane, Howard 'Smiler' Allen, Steve Hogan, Harry Walker, Ralph Calvin, Harold McCourt, John Risman, Tommy Thompson, John Cunningham. Front: Masseur Raymond Thompson, Gordon Cottier, Arnold 'Boxer' Walker, Ian Wright, Keith Davies, Paul Charlton, Dennis Jackson, Bob Nicholson.

Eddie Bowman, Town's ball-playing forward, who made 361 career appearances including four for Great Britain. Boxer says: 'Eddie would run into the defensive line and two players would often be running off him, one either side – Les and Peter Gorley.'

Cumbrian Bob Blackwood, Ray Dutton, who played with Boxer at Whitehaven, Mick Adams and Jim Mills, celebrate Widnes's 1974 Lancashire Cup Final 6-2 win over Salford.

Peter Gorley is tackled by Jim Mills, who was playing for Widnes. Jim says: 'Boxer was definitely one of the best scrum halves I played with or against in my career, as good as any scrum half I have ever seen.'

Reg Bowden, the Widnes scrum half with the 1979 Challenge Cup. 'Reg was the toughest scrum half I ever played against,' says Boxer. 'How he never played for Great Britain I will never know. If you could pick 13 Reg Bowdens, you could beat any team in the world.'

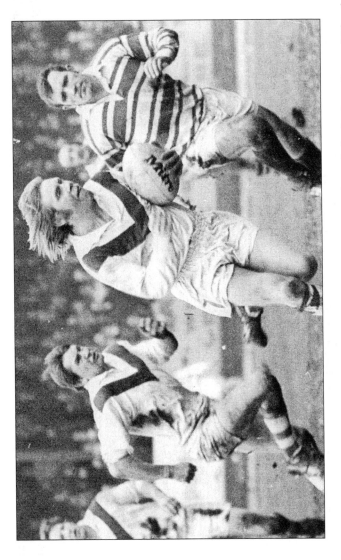

Boxer Walker makes a break with Paul Charlton backing up. 'Charlo was as fast as lightning,' says Boxer. 'When he was Town coach, in training, he never asked anyone to do anything that he couldn't do. He was a marvellous captain – he never wanted all the attention for himself – and he was a great inspiration to his players on the field and in the dressing room.'

Workington Town, 1978: Back - Ian Rudd, Billy Pattinson, David Collister, Bob Blackwood, Eddie Bowman, Harry Beverley, Peter Gorley, John Risman, Les Gorley. Front - Derek McMillan, Ray Wilkins, Paul Charlton, Arnold Walker, Alan Banks, Iain MacCorquodale.

Jim Mills played 23 games for Workington. 'Big Jim was unbelievable,'
recalls Boxer. 'He was a really clever player who would use his
loaf and he loved running at half backs or centres. Backs might
tackle Jim once, perhaps twice and then most of the time that
was enough and he would run through them. He was massive,
around 18 stones. Off the field though, Jim was a gentleman.'

*Sol Roper, the wonderful scrum
half and coach, who was such an
inspiration to Boxer.*

*Major John Fillingham MBE, the
war hero who had to deal with the
problems in Benidorm.*

*Harry Beverley, the powerful
front row forward who was signed
by Tom Mitchell from Dewsbury
for £10,000. 'I lost count of the
number of breaks and tries I made
because of Harry,' says Boxer.*

*Bill Pears, the Barrow chairman,
who could not persuade Boxer
to come to Craven Park.*

Cumbria's county champions, and the official party, who beat the Kiwis at Whitehaven in 1980: Phil Kitchin, coach, Barrow director Stan Hughes, Terry Moore, Keith Hodgson, Ian Rudd, Tommy Thompson, Steve Tickle, Ralph Calvin, John Bulman, Peter Gorley, Harry Walker (Town director), Peter Stoddart, Ken Benson (Barrow director), Ray Thompson (physio), Ken Shepherd and Jack Atkinson (Town directors). Front: Billy Pattinson, John Cunningham, Eddie Bowman, Arnold 'Boxer' Walker, Vince Fox, Les Gorley, Malcolm Flynn. Sitting: Chris Camilleri, Alan McCurrie, Ian Ball.

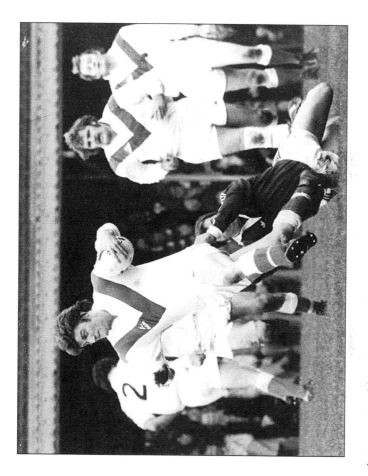

Billy Pattinson, Town's international loose forward, who played more than 300 games for the club. 'He could run, back up and tackle, all the things you want in a loose forward,' says Boxer. 'Billy was always there when you needed him and he was a really good pro.'

Phil Kitchin, the Great Britain stand-off and Haven and Cumbria coach. 'I really enjoyed playing for Phil,' says Boxer. 'We had a few planned moves with certain forwards but Phil just let me get on with it. He knew that I knew what I was doing. Some coaches might have set ideas of how a team should play but it wasn't like that with Phil. We were well prepared and he trusted us.'

CHAPTER 19

The Adams Family

It is October, 1980, and there are old men who have been standing on the terraces at the Recreation Ground since the club's formation in 1948, who will swear Boxer is the best scrum half they have ever seen. Three months earlier he had been awarded the title of the greatest number seven in the world by the respected magazine *Open Rugby*. If that wasn't enough, Alex Murphy, a scrum half himself who played 27 times for Great Britain, and was beyond comparison, had been calling for Boxer's international call-up for years. But it hadn't happened.

He was 28-years-old and at the peak of his powers. Greatness glowed in him, and Boxer was making full use of many years of authoritative instruction from influential figures who had recognised his genius and helped him along the way. It had all begun when he was a little boy collecting balls and pretending he was Billy Boston on The Welfare at Kells and continued with the guidance and care of great men such as Les Herbert, Harry Whitaker, Sol Roper and more recently, Haven coach Phil Kitchin.

By nature, Boxer was not inclined to pessimism and he had dared to wonder that the upcoming Test matches against New Zealand might provide the ultimate acknowledgement of his standing as a magnificent scrum half. According to national newspaper reports, the team would be selected with one eye on that year's county championships which Cumbria had recently won, under his captaincy, for the first time in 15 years. On top of that, Cumbria, skippered again by Boxer, had beaten the New Zealand tourists 9-3 at the Recreation Ground the week before the team would be announced. Boxer was the best player on the field and he had scored the winning try. It was inconceivable that he would miss out again. The 26-man squad was announced on the morning of Friday, October 10, and he had made it.

"I found out from all my mates in the pit who had read the story in the papers," remembers Boxer. "It was the proudest day of my whole playing career. All my mates had been telling me for weeks that I had been playing great and that I was sure to get in but I wouldn't believe them. I had heard it all before for years and years. I was prepared for the disappointment. I got used to missing out and it wasn't something I was bitter about. When I found out, I was jumping out of my skin to play for my country. To be honest I did feel I'd earned it. I had been through that many disappointments."

Two days later Boxer is lying on a bed in the casualty department of West Cumberland Hospital, still wearing his Haven kit, and a surgeon is staring at X-rays before announcing, quite casually and without much emotion, that he has dislocated his cheekbone and that it would take several weeks to heal, by which time the tourists would be back in New Zealand. His dream was over. "It was against Bramley in a league game at The Recre," remembers Boxer. "I passed the ball to one of our forwards and I got hit late, so late I wasn't expecting anything. I was out cold and I had to be carried off on a stretcher and I woke up in the dressing room.

"I realised right away how bad the injury was and I just started crying, not moaning, I was actually sobbing. Our chairman David Wigham came in and put his arms around me. He had signed me and we always got on well. David was a good man. I was so depressed because I knew that was it. My test spot that I had worked so hard for all my life had gone down the drain with one daft late tackle. I was broken-hearted.

"David took me straight to the hospital and I had to be put to sleep by the surgeon. He told me later that he had put his thumbs inside my mouth and pulled down the lower part of my jaw to get it back in place. He told me that he had clicked it back. I was in agony. It was worse than toothache and I had a massive black eye. I was told I would be out for a few weeks. I couldn't believe it. I was down and out and I thought to myself: 'Hard lines, Arnold, you have missed out again.'"

The directors were furious at what had happened and how, on the face of it, one late tackle had destroyed Boxer's international hopes. The thing is, as far as the Whitehaven board were concerned, late was not the first word that came to mind when they discussed what had happened. No, they saw it more as a violent assault which was way outside the normal parameters of what might be described as the darker side of professional rugby league. David Wigham was upset and angry. He had already contacted senior police officers at the main station in Scotch Street to discuss the feasibility of a legal case which, as far as he saw it, had the advantage of being able to call on 3,000 eye witness reports to prove what had happened. But Boxer was having none of it and immediately insisted that the club abandoned the police investigation. Mr Wigham, speaking in the *Whitehaven News* the following week said: "After discussing the situation with Arnold, the club have decided, in accordance with his wishes, not to pursue a police complaint."

One did not need to be schooled in the higher branches of orthopedic surgery to know that the prognosis was catastrophic. Under the best possible circumstances a fractured cheekbone might keep a normal, fit man incapacitated from office work for around six weeks. Boxer was many things and normal was not one of them. He withdrew from the first two Test matches but he felt he might just have a chance of playing in the third Test, which would be held at Headingley, on November 16, and just 36 days after his injury. Boxer received a message from the selectors stating that he would have to play a First Division fixture for Whitehaven to prove his fitness before he could be considered. A fractured cheekbone is a very serious injury, they told him - we are not risking you in a Test match unless you have fully recovered.

The black eye went and the swelling reduced but the pain was still there. Yet, remarkably, on Sunday, October 26, Boxer took a mouthful of painkillers and put on the number seven shirt for Whitehaven and played against Swinton, just 16 days after being knocked out and much to the consternation of medical opinion. Over the years he had fostered a practised endurance to pain but however you look at it, this had been an extraordinary recovery.

The First Test match at Wigan was drawn and Boxer made the trip to Odsal to watch the second Test with his coach Phil Kitchin, partly as a patriotic supporter and partly to provide high-profile evidence of his recovery.

"We lost the Second Test," says Boxer. "I remember giving an interview to Arthur Brooks, who wrote for the *Daily Mirror*. Back in those days, reporters had a big influence on team selection and Arthur told me to keep it to myself but that he had heard that I would be in the squad for the Third Test. I wasn't sure whether to believe him or not but the next day it was announced and he was right. I was in."

Boxer's delight was increased with the news that his close friend and former Town second rower, Peter Gorley, now starring for St Helens, was also in the 20-man squad. The two Cumbrians travelled to Leeds on Wednesday afternoon in Boxer's green 1.7 Morris Marina. The starting 13 had still not been selected and Boxer was in direct competition against Saints half back Neil Holding, who had played for England earlier that year.

"I knew all the lads from playing against them," recalls Boxer. "Pete was just as worried as me about if he was going to start or not. When we walked into the hotel lobby, the Great Britain manager Colin Hutton was waiting for us. He came straight up, shook our hands and told us we were both starting. It was a great feeling. I shared a room with Peter and we hit it off with all the players right away. We felt part of a family. I was already good mates with Trevor Skerrett from Hull and Mick Adams, Mick Burke and Keith Elwell, who all played for Widnes. When I was at Town, all our players got on really well with the Widnes lads and we wouldn't leave Naughton Park without having a few beers with them.

"We had been given a bag full of Great Britain training gear and I couldn't wait to put it on. The next day I met the coach Johnny Whiteley at Carnegie College where we did some easy training and worked through a few moves. Johnny shook my hand and told me how happy he was that I had got over the injury and that he was proud of me. That made me feel great. He was a real gent. At night we were given a few rugby league videos to watch and we were told at breakfast on the day of the match that we could do anything we wanted. Johnny had said we should just relax.

"Peter and myself had decided to mess about in the hotel pool but when we told Mick Adams he went mad and told us that was the worst thing we could do and that swimming would drain all our energy. We just stayed in our room and watched the telly - *Swap Shop* with Noel Edmonds was on while we lay on our beds. I remember Telly Savalas, the man who played *Kojak,* was the guest.

"We got on the team coach and we passed a street that we were told was where the Yorkshire Ripper had last murdered someone. He hadn't been caught back then. When we pulled into Headingley, there were fans everywhere and I was really up for it. The whole team walked on to the field and chatted for a few minutes before going to the dressing room. I remember that the Great Britain sponsors were Adidas and I always wore Puma boots. The kit man went around the dressing room with a tin of paint, trying to make all the boots look like they were made by Adidas by painting three white lines down the side.

"Everything was laid out neatly, and the Great Britain number seven shirt was hanging on a peg with all my other stuff. I stared at it and I remember thinking to myself that I was the best scum half in the country. Normally I didn't start getting stripped until 20 minutes before the kick-off but this was all so different. I couldn't wait to put it on and it fit me absolutely perfectly, just tight enough. When I looked around, all the lads were staring at me, still wearing their blazers. There was still 45 minutes to go and I was the only one changed. Colin starting teasing me and some of the players laughed but I didn't care. I was proud as punch and with about 15 minutes left to the kick-off, Johnny started talking to us. He was really calm and nobody was saying anything. We were all just listening to him, taking in every word but no one was standing still. We were moving from one foot to the other or walking around the room. It was really quiet apart from Johnny talking. It is a long time ago but I can remember very clearly Johnny telling us simple things and he kept saying over and over again: 'Treat it like a normal game, lads, just play like you have played for your club side. That's what got you here.'

"It was a really great crack and though the nerves were starting to kick in, I had my game head on. I might have been only 5 feet 6 inches but I felt 11 feet tall."

The two teams lined up in front of the North Stand, 26 brave men going to war. Various anonymous dignitaries, old men in dark blue suits mostly, were introduced to the players in order of their position in the team, beginning with the full back. Kiwi skipper Mark Graham presented the tourists, who shook hands obediently and courteously but no one was smiling and nothing much was being said. Great Britain skipper Len Casey took over the official introductions and soon the players were standing alone, jogging on the spot mainly, keeping moving to calm their nerves, occasionally looking into the crowd but unable to pick anyone out.

The tannoy crackled into life and the New Zealand players were announced one by one, accelerating the mood of anticipation with violent conflict just a few minutes away. "Let's hear it for Michael O'Donnell," he began and the full back followed his instructions obediently as he swung away right on cue with a ball in his hands and headed for the sticks in front of the Old Eastern Terrace. A small ripple of muffled applause broke out across the stadium, which had opened in 1890, and the names were read out, much faster now, and soon the entire team were huddled together, slapping each other's backs, and shouting obscenities, not wanting to waste this last opportunity to manufacture confidence and foster a collective spirit.

"Come on everybody, here's our team, put your hands together for Great Britain – here's Mick Burke at full back," the announcer said, and the whole process was repeated but the noise was louder as the crowd roared together, a great big wall of noise climbing into the Yorkshire sky, as they waved flags and clapped, the atmosphere rising, the mood celebratory, uplifting and full of excitement as the seconds ticked by inextricably towards confrontation. Des Drummond, John Joyner, Steve Evans, John Atkinson, John Woods – half the Great Britain team and then, the number seven: "Arnold 'Boxer' Walker from Whitehaven," and the roar grew louder, deafening even. More than 400 Cumbrians had made the three-hour trip, in cars, buses and trains, from Kells, Whitehaven, Workington, Maryport, Cockermouth, and some from Barrow, to see their hero get what was rightfully his, what he had earned in courage, mangled fingers and broken bones, everything that had ever happened in his sporting life, manifesting itself here, right in front of all these people. And they roared the loudest and the longest, right up into every corner of the ground. Back home, in Cumbria, 150 miles away, Boxer's sister Margaret and their father Duncan are watching proceedings on BBC Television, Eddie Waring is describing the action, assisted by Alex Murphy. Looking back now, more than 36 years ago, and Margaret can still remember the look on her father's face and what happened when his son's name was announced and he saw him wearing his Great Britain shirt in the middle of some of the world's greatest players. "Dad didn't know I had seen him but I did," recalls Margaret. "He was actually crying - he was so proud of Arnold."

Boxer recalls: "When I was standing in that line of players I looked around me. I thought to myself: 'Bloody hell, I am with some stars here,' and I am a part of it. When they read my name out I still couldn't believe it. I could hear all these cheers, just for me. I'll never forget them."

The Kiwis formed a group, in no particular order, close to the halfway line and prepared to give their haka, the traditional war cry of the Maori people. The British team are perhaps 20 yards away, standing together in a small circle, arms around each other. The New Zealanders are staring, looking their opponents square in the face as they begin foot-stamping and pointing out their tongues, their eyes wide open. *Ka mate, ka mate! ka ora! ka ora! ('Tis death! 'Tis death! 'Tis life! 'Tis life!),* they roar and the crowd falls silent as the battle cry barks across the stadium. Each word is fortifying them as they summon up support from the courage of fallen ancestors and then, as quick as it started, it's all over and the players move into position to prepare themselves for the kick-off.

The haka was a mighty fine thing to call upon to put brave men into the best frame of mind and they were, for sure, all fired up. But the British players were too strong and determined and they went on to win 10-2, with two tries from Jamaican-born wingman Des Drummond, who scored the late winner, despite being hindered by a shin injury. In fact, he was about to be substituted before he sidestepped four Kiwi defenders in a confined space, smaller than Hilda Ogden's living room, to slide over near the corner flag. Des, who would go on to play for Great Britain 28 times, was the matchwinning hero but he had a more modest interpretation of his contribution, telling reporters in the post-match press conference: "I just shut my eyes and went for the line."

Drummond rose to celebrity status following his performances in the BBC competition *Superstars,* finishing second in 1983 and clocking a competition record 10.85 seconds for 100 metres. He was an exceptional power-lifter and all-round athlete.

Boxer remembers: "The big thing was relaxing and starting to feel confident. It was hard because we all felt a massive weight on our shoulders because we were a Test down and we had to win to draw the series. I hit it off straight away with my stand-off John Woods - I already knew he was a brilliant player and now I knew him as a brilliant lad off the field. He was magnificent.

"I heard that John came up to Kells with an amateur team a few years ago and he was asking after me. That was typical of him. John Joyner, another mate from that match, came up to Cumbria recently and wanted to see me too. I thought I had played well. Alex Murphy talked to me after the match - I always call him The Greatest and I really look up to him. He was commentating for the BBC and he told me that until Des Drummond scored two late tries I was going to get the man of the match award.

"The thing I remember most is how Mick Adams was always encouraging me and talking to me. He was non-stop: 'Go on, Arnie, keep it up, son. You're hammering him. He hasn't a chance against you.' He just kept saying it, every time there was a scrum. 'You've got him in your pocket.'

"The game was so fast. You're talking about elite players. Although we won the game, the series was drawn and we were happy to win and they were happy to finish level. When the hooter went for the end of the game, all the British players hugged each other - we were so relieved.

"A few years later a question about me was asked on *Question of Sport* when Bill Beaumont was on. They showed a clip of Des Drummond scoring in the corner and then me jumping up in the air and hugging him. Willie Carson was asked who I was and from what I heard, he didn't know.

"In the dressing room we were all relieved. Johnny made a short speech and thanked us and we all started clapping. Peter had his usual game, of course, he was so dependable. He would never let you down."

The players and coaches were in a jubilant mood and there was all the usual embracing and back slapping so prevalent in British Lions documentaries. They were soaking up the warm and communal satisfaction that is prevalent when a job is completed well and in the most difficult of circumstances. There was a collective feeling of well-being. Boxer, never one to stand in the background on such occasions, got right into the swing of things, though not before staring at his number seven shirt one last time before carefully placing it in his bag. It looked beautiful to him, still mud-stained but magnificent, the unique badge with the brown face of a lion staring out between white letters standing out on a red and blue background, the words GREAT BRITAIN above the lion and below more words, RUGBY LEAGUE, N.Z. TESTS.

As the coach pulled up outside the changing rooms, Widnes back row forward Mick Adams went around the players, one by one, all 14 of them, shaking their hands individually and with great enthusiasm, staring in their faces sincerely, saying to each one: "This team will probably never play together again. It has been an honour to play with you. Thank you."

The New Zealanders had been staying at the same hotel in Leeds city centre and the two teams mixed together in the bar, sharing jokes and there was lots of laughter and celebration. Two guitars were acquired from somewhere and the players began singing Maori folk songs made famous by Prince Tui Teka. There was much affection and mutual respect as the Brits sang along as best they could. Boxer and Peter headed back towards Cumbria sometime around 8 and they stopped off in Kendal, where they were immediately recognised and a small crowd formed around them cheering before queuing up for autographs.

"Johnny Whiteley was a really good guy," remembers Peter. "He was one of the nicest people I have ever met in rugby league - a real gentleman. Johnny and Eric Ashton were the two nicest blokes I have ever met through rugby. They had no airs and graces and were just two lovely people. I was in awe of people like that."

The following day, Boxer led Whitehaven out at the Recreation Ground, in a First Division fixture against Batley. The Cumbrians gave him a standing ovation - he kicked a drop goal and was named man-of-the-match. The following week Boxer received a small parcel which arrived by recorded delivery and contained his Great Britain badge and a brief congratulatory letter. The badge contains a beautiful embroidered circle on a black background with an intricate golden band around capital letters stating BRITISH RUGBY LEAGUE INTERNATIONAL. Inside there is a silver, braided circle surrounded by four emblems – a thistle, a red lion, a shamrock and a Prince of Wales feather.

"I kept the Great Britain shirt in my drawer for a few months," says Boxer. "I never took it out to show anyone. I wouldn't do that. Then I took it to the cleaners and got it all spruced up and took it to Kells. I gave it to the treasurer Ian Gainford, who is a great lad and a good friend - that was where it was always going to end up. I thought it is better donating it to Kells where lots of people could see it. As soon as I got the shirt it was always going to Kells. I started with them and they made me – I would never have amounted to anything as a player without them. I suppose it is my way of repaying them. Kells rugby league is in my blood. I am proud playing for Great Britain and that shirt is my pride and joy.

"A couple of weeks later when I went in for a pint, it was on the wall among all the others. I never really look at the shirt. That's just me. I am not one for showing off."

§

Three months later Boxer played for England against France at Headingley. The French won the game 5-1 and contemporaneous reports from every newspaper agreed on one thing – the referee was biased. Guy Cattaneo, from Perpignan, awarded the French 11 first half penalties and the English only two. The French try, which was scored in the 60th minute by Hervé Guiraud, followed a blatant knock-on, Town loose forward Billy Pattinson was kicked in the face by Gine and George Fairbairn scored a late try which was ruled out in mysterious circumstances.

It was the Frenchmen's first win in England since 1949. When the game finished, one of the team's most important duties was protecting Mr Cattaneo from the rioting crowd, assisted by several police officers.

Raymond Fletcher, the respected rugby league correspondent of *The Yorkshire Post*, who was not a reporter who could ever be accused of getting carried away, described the game as 'a ludicrous farce and a joke.' Arthur Brooks, writing in *The Daily Mirror*, called for England to refuse to play France again and Wigan full back George Fairbairn described the referee as 'diabolical.'

Boxer says: "We needn't have gone onto the park. It was shocking. My stand-off was Ken Kelly and he was a great player and I was looking forward to playing with him but the referee ruined everything. I don't like blaming refs but this really was an exception. I got the blame and I got dropped. I remember my mate Knocker Norton contacted a national paper and a story appeared saying it wasn't fair to drop me."

Boxer never played international rugby again.

CHAPTER 20

Is He Dead?

It is difficult to imagine an activity more hazardous to the neck and back than professional rugby league. The spine, or backbone, is made up of a column of 33 bones and tissue extending from the skull to the pelvis. These bones, or vertebrae, enclose and protect a cylinder of nerve tissues known as the spinal cord. Between each one of the vertebra is an intervertebral disk, or band of cartilage serving as a shock absorber between the vertebrae. At least that is what it says on a website run by some of the country's leading orthopedic surgeons.

The neck and back are a complex part of the human anatomy and when subjected to the normal extreme forces of violence that are ever-present in rugby, very susceptible to long term injuries. Players never consider any of this, of course - it just comes with the territory and they are equal to it.

"I never thought about injuries," says Boxer. "If you are not in the right frame of mind or you are frightened, you should go to the pub and play darts or dominoes. Rugby league is the hardest game in the world. There are no helmets, like in American Football. I don't know why there haven't been any more fatalities or more people ending up in wheelchairs."

Boxer, as far as he can recall, had four serious injuries in his career and three of them involve his back or neck – the other required major knee surgery and kept him sidelined for almost a year. He refers to them as 'bad 'uns' and you have to push him very hard to persuade him to talk about other maladies which include, among other things, broken noses, two dislocated collar bones, pulled and torn hamstrings, dodgy knees, sprained ankles, seven broken ribs, numerous black eyes, swollen eyes, cut eyes, torn ankle ligaments, two fractured cheek bones, various dislocations and unspecified numbers of lost teeth. He is particularly dismissive of broken fingers, of which he has had many, and he describes such mishaps as: "Nowt worth mentioning. You just got them taped up and played on. We all got broken fingers nearly every week. Dislocated collar bones were nowt either - we had a good physio and he would just turn my head away and give it a yank and if I was lucky it just popped back in."

To any normal person, such disdain for pain is quite something, and Boxer's descriptions are a reminder of the super human qualities required to play rugby league. Take the case of Alan Prescott, the St Helens forward who is best remembered for a spectacular feat of courage playing in a Test match for Great Britain against Australia at Brisbane in 1958. Alan, who would go on to coach Workington Town, broke his arm after only three minutes and as substitutes were not permitted, he waved away pleas to leave the field and carried on for the rest of the match, which the Lions hung on to win 25-18. Two weeks later, with one arm in a sling and the other holding aloft the Ashes trophy, he was carried shoulder-high around the ground in Sydney after the Lions won the third and deciding Test 40-17.

"He gathered the ball, he ran, he dictated the pattern of play and he tackled well with his good arm," Tour Manager Tom Mitchell told journalists. "Only those present at the game had any idea of the man's naked courage."

Most of the Aussies were unaware of the extent of the injury, as Prescott's arm hung limply from his shoulder. "Alan swapped places in the scrum to try to protect his broken right arm, but otherwise tried to carry on as though nothing had happened," says Tom Mitchell. The match became known as The Battle of Brisbane and Prescott took his place at the top of a long list of remarkable achievements from rugby league players facing adversity.

Boxer's first career-threatening injury occurred when he was making his debut for Cumberland against Australia at Whitehaven in 1973. The tourists won 28-2 but the county players considered their performance almost Herculean and there was much celebration in the dressing room after the match. Australia had fielded their full Test side, which included Arthur Beetson, Bob Fulton, Steve Rogers, Graeme Langlands and Mick Cronin.

Boxer limped off at the end of the game clutching his right knee although there were plenty of other areas of his battered body that required medical attention. He was aching all over after a series of particularly violent exchanges with Australian scrum half Tommy Raudonikis, who went on to become a fully-fledged legend.

Raudonikis, the son of a Lithuanian immigrant father and a Swiss immigrant mother, starred for the Western Suburbs, played for New South Wales 24 times and made 20 appearances for Australia. He presently works as a commentator for Channel 9 in Australia and was named in the list of Australia's 100 Greatest Players in 2007. Of course, statistics aren't the only measure of greatness and what they definitely don't say here is that Raudonikis's other reputation, which ran concurrently with his prowess as a great player, and was perhaps his greatest claim to fame, involved his toughness, or, put another way, how proficient he was at circumventing the laws of the game, depending on your point of view.

Raudonikis's legendary status continued long after he retired in 1982, and his standing as someone you absolutely didn't want to get on the wrong side of, under any circumstances whatsoever, continued to grow. He was awarded the Medal of the Order of Australia in 1982, selected in the team of the century for Wests, voted Newtown's greatest import for 100 years and was named as one of the 12 Toughest Rugby League players in the sport's history. So you can be sure of one thing – he was a tough son of a bitch.

None of this was of much interest to Boxer back in 1973, as Raudonikis ploughed into him at every opportunity. But he was never one to back down from such confrontations and the two halfbacks were seen walking off the field arm in arm at the final whistle though quite how they could communicate with each other considering Boxer's Cumberland accent, and the indecipherable New South Wales drawl of Raudonikis, is another matter.

"We had a few beers after," recalls Boxer. "Then, later on, some of the Aussie players came with us for a night out in a club called The Zodiac in Whitehaven. It was great and when the drink got down my neck I couldn't feel my knee and I forgot all about it. Me and Tommy had a good night together."

They stumbled and staggered out of the club on the wrong side of 2am after finding themselves the centre of attention. It had been a night of heavy drinking, which is saying quite something, considering the Australians' reputation for extraordinary alcohol consumption – but you couldn't blame them for taking advantage of their star status.

"I could hardly walk the next day," says Boxer. "The beer had worn off and it was obvious it was a serious injury. My knee was badly messed up. Tom Mitchell fixed me up with a specialist and he told me as soon as he pressed on my leg that my cartilage had gone and there was a lot of other damage – my ligaments had all gone too. I ended up having a big operation in the Princess Margaret Rose Orthopedic Hospital in Edinburgh. I was out for the best part of a year.

"I remember being in plaster for months and I never felt welcome at Derwent Park. I bet a lot of pros would back me up on this. Hardly anyone wanted to know me. That's what it was like when you are not performing. When I was knackered and limping about I was no use to the club. It's just not right to be treated like that."

Boxer's last three stories of orthopedic maladies belong to an altogether different category of injury. They are as bad as it gets and involve the risk of permanent disability, the possibility of spending the rest of his life in a wheelchair and are so bad, that a powerful rumour, which quickly became fact, was once circulating Cumbria claiming that Boxer, at the age of 29, had actually died.

The first incident occurred in an A team match when Whitehaven were playing against St Helens. As we have heard, Boxer, all 150 pounds of him, had figured out a unique style of tackling big men which no one could quite fathom. It had been a part of him, this carefully worked out system and he adhered to it all the time – he went high and he never went low – that was his way. And most of the time, forwards would end up on the ground with a baffled expression on their faces, wondering what had happened. But during this match, when he brought down a prop forward, something wasn't quite right. He wasn't sure what was going on and he carried on playing.

"I could hardly move after the game," Boxer remembers. "No one knew what it was. I knew something wasn't right but I just carried on playing for a few more weeks even though it was killing me – it was getting worse and worse."

Eventually Haven sent Boxer to see a back specialist called Mr Mossop who was a respected surgeon at Warrington and Halton Hospital. A range of lengthy, medical investigations were undertaken which eventually revealed the exact nature of the injury which, the surgeon told him, was severe damage to his coccyx, which is more commonly known as the tailbone.

The National Health Service website carries a detailed explanation of a range of disabilities associated with his symptoms and it finishes off with the worrying conclusion that: 'it can severely affect a patient's ability to carry out every day activities.' It is safe to assume that this explanation had duties such as brushing your teeth or tying your shoe laces in mind and would not include weekly participation in a professional rugby league match. The website concludes that 'it is a fairly rare and relatively poorly understood condition.' Mr Mossop might have written those words and his prognosis of Boxer's condition did not provide much evidence to be optimistic about a full recovery.

The specialist suggested Boxer might consider retiring from rugby league and though there was a procedure that might provide an improvement in the condition, it was extremely perilous and carried with it an unacceptable risk of permanent disability. So that was the end of that, and not for the first time, he left with their best wishes and the largest bottle of painkillers you had ever seen in your life.

The next two events happened within less than two years of each other and there are a lot of similarities, so much so that in the minds of many Cumbrians, the two events have somehow got mixed up and when supporters recount them, they will dip in to each incident and take a fact from one and mix it with the other, as one might take a sweet from a box of chocolates.

The first injury happened during a First Division fixture against Hull Kingston Rovers at the Recreation Ground around 4.22pm on Sunday, October 11, 1981. The first thing you need to know is that he should not have even been playing - he had ignored specific and detailed instructions from doctors who know all about these matters. The day before, in an A team game at Workington, Boxer had picked up an unusual and especially painful injury that involved a long wound in his tongue. It had required 14 stitches that he had received sometime that evening at the Accident and Emergency unit of West Cumberland Hospital. Doctors had warned him how painful it would be and had discharged him with powerful painkillers and explicit instructions that Boxer must confine himself to bed for a few days. Take the rest of the week off they told him - the laceration was so deep he would only be able to eat soup, sucked through his swollen lips with a straw. Be careful eating though, they told him, the stitches could be opened if you chew too hard. Less than 20 hours later he would be tackling mighty forwards such as Len Casey, 16 stones of Yorkshire beef, who was known in the game as 'Cast Iron' Casey. Boxer had always been indifferent to the consequences of pain but this was a whole new ball game. As if that wasn't enough, he had still not fully recovered from the effects of a dislocated jaw he had picked up just three weeks before.

The score was 5-5, and Boxer had kicked two penalties and a drop goal for his team. Haven were attacking the Kells end and lining up a drop goal which would probably be the end of the match. As we have already heard, drop goals were Boxer's forte - the previous season he had kicked 22, which was more than anybody else.

So everyone knew what was coming as the forwards lined up the attempt, midway in the Rovers half. The visiting pack, which contained several international forwards, alongside 'Cast Iron' Casey were tackling desperately as time slipped by. On top of that, Boxer had long been a cherished target for a belligerent forward. Something wasn't quite right as Haven played the ball, and in an instant Boxer was tackled by Rovers forward Chris Burton, who was not known for a benevolent attitude towards half backs who specialised in depriving him of his winning bonus. Normally, Boxer could feel danger, he had a kind of sixth sense of impending doom that would frustrate an opponent's worst intentions. But for once this had failed him and he was left lying on the pitch, out cold, as if he had been run over by an articulated truck.

"People often ask me if I hate players who did this type of thing to me," says Boxer, speaking many years later, without a hint of bitterness in his voice. "I always answer the same way. Not at all. Chris never wanted that to happen to me. It's all just part and parcel of the game and I don't hold him accountable for anything, not for a second. I don't blame anyone for what happened. I would have tackled someone the same and you just have to accept it as part of rugby league."

It was evident that it was a serious injury and two St John Ambulance cadets had the presence of mind to leave well alone before the club doctor Michael Gourlay took control. A plastic stretcher, more commonly used in mountain rescues and specially designed for use when there is danger of spinal injury, appeared and a rigid neck brace was applied as a small crowd gathered around him.

As well as players and coaching staff from both teams, including Phil Kitchin and his assistant Spanky McFarlane, who had known Boxer since he was four-years-old, a few fans were milling about in the background, keen to know what was happening to their hero who was still unconscious.

Among them was best friend Billy Starkey, and Boxer's stand-off half at Workington Town, Derek McMillan. The three men had been close all their lives and as soon as the severity of the injury was apparent, they pushed their way through the crowd, on the Popular side, climbed over the concrete wall, and sprinted across the field. It wasn't that they thought they could do anything – it was all done without any kind of plan, as if they felt instinctively that it was the right thing to do, to be right there, next to their friend, close to him.

"He was just lying on the ground motionless," remembers Billy. "I felt sick. I watched them putting on the brace and he still wasn't moving. I knew it was serious. We just didn't think - we knew we had to be there with him. I've always loved Boxer and we are very close. We've always been like that. If there was ever anything wrong in his life he would always come and tell me and if I had to get anything off my chest, I knew he would always be there for me. He was one of those special lads who would never leave anyone short if they couldn't afford a pint or they needed to borrow a bit of money. Nine times out of ten, he wouldn't get it back but things like that never worried him."

Now at the same time all this was going on, simultaneous discussions were taking place between the Huddersfield referee Mick Beaumont, and representatives from both clubs about what should be done about the match. There is a lot of confusion about what was exactly said and to whom, about what and when, but either way, what is certain is that the doctor became extremely insistent that under no circumstances could Boxer be moved.

The referee abandoned the game but still, no one was leaving, not until there was an update on his condition, and more than 3,000 fans stood on the terraces, as a gloomy mood descended on the stadium. "Some fans on the Recreation Ground terraces wept openly. Some thought Boxer was dead when the referee abandoned the game - the Whitehaven players were too upset to continue," said a newspaper report the next day. The rumour about the scrum-half's death quickly gathered momentum around the stadium and his alleged passing soon reached the press box where reporter Alan Irving was overcome with emotion. Boxer was his captain, his friend and his hero. So he found himself climbing onto the field to get closer to what was happening and to his great relief discovered that the player was awake and answering questions. "When I woke up on the pitch I couldn't feel anything," Boxer remembers. "I couldn't move my neck and I was in so much pain. It was really odd. I felt dizzy yet I could hear everything being said around me."

An ambulance arrived, and the crowd around Boxer, which numbered perhaps 30, parted as the vehicle reversed onto the field, its light flashing intermittently, bathing the scene in an eerie blue wash before pulling away, slowly at first, its wheels spinning violently in the mud, then moving out through the entrance and down Coach Road, passing the railway station before turning on to Corkicle. The siren was operating at full capacity as the ambulance accelerated along Inkerman Terrace at speeds approaching 65 miles an hour, the traffic pulling to the side of the road obediently while pedestrians, out for a late afternoon walk, stopped and stared, wondering what was going on.

Boxer knew where he was and what had happened. The paramedic tried to assure him that he was in safe hands but the fact that he was suffering from the mother of all headaches, couldn't move his legs and felt pins and needles in his arms, all combined in his mind to give him a pessimistic view of his situation. He was frightened.

While the ambulance was hurtling towards the hospital there was a nasty turn of events at the Recreation Ground. The crowd had turned on the referee and there was a broad weight of opinion among them that Mr Beaumont had been too lenient with some of the Rovers forwards. Apart from Boxer, Whitehaven full back Graeme Johns had also been knocked out in the first half. The threat of violence was hanging in the air and the referee had to be escorted to safety by police officers in what *The Whitehaven News* reported as 'an unparalleled tirade of abuse from the hostile crowd.' As if that wasn't enough, the Rovers dressing room had been ransacked and £330 in cash and valuables had been stolen.

The West Cumberland Hospital had been alerted to the imminent arrival of the ambulance and everyone who needed to be there, were waiting for him - porters and nursing staff and a doctor, just in case. He was taken straight to the Intensive Care Unit and placed on the danger list. A strong anaesthetic was administered and many tests were undertaken throughout the night. While all this was going on, Boxer's sister Margaret was in her Hensingham home, less than two miles away. She had been listening to the match commentary on Radio Cumbria. When the news broke she immediately went to their father's flat, just around the corner where they spent the night, holding hands and monitoring the radio for medical updates.

"I remember listening to it all on the wireless," says Margaret. "Our dad was on his own, so I went straight around there. It said on the radio that Arnold might have died. We couldn't believe it. We really thought he was dead."

The following morning, the situation took a turn for the better. Boxer was off the danger list but he was still in great pain. He was under orders to stay still at all times, instructions he found incredibly easy to follow as the slightest movement made him feel as if someone had plugged in an electric drill and was driving it into his back. Doctors soon arrived with good news. There were no broken bones in his back or neck, they told him, that was certain, and his condition was diagnosed as 'severely torn back muscles' and, God willing, he had a high probability of a full recovery.

"I couldn't move for five days," says Boxer. "I couldn't get out of bed and I was knocked out with painkillers most of the time. I remember having to use bed pans."

Later that morning he was cleared to receive visitors and Margaret and Duncan were the first to arrive, closely followed by best friend Billy, after a request from Boxer that he needed him there.

"I got a call to say he wanted to see me," says Billy. "I shot up right away. I remember how frightened he was, we gave each other a big hug and I just said to him: 'Are you OK, marra? I think you are going to be all right.' I knew he would be. Boxer had such a strong character. To think, he had asked for me. That just shows how close we are."

He was eventually moved into a general ward among patients recovering from more common disorders such as hip replacements and hernias and his presence, as something of a local hero, produced an improvement in the atmosphere that bordered on celebratory. He enjoyed their good wishes, benefitting from their concern and interest, which improved his mood no end and he would just lie there, horizontally on his bed, signing the odd autograph as best he could and just as coolly as anyone could have asked for.

There was a steady stream of visitors throughout that day, and among them was Alan Irving, the rugby league correspondent of *The Whitehaven News*, who was a dedicated Boxer fan. They had become friends and Alan was finding it difficult to report the event accurately and without emotion. He had felt the same despair when that first rumour was filtering around the stadium that the scrum half's life might have been in danger. The next week's edition carried full coverage of the event and Alan was delighted to publish a positive account which he brought his readers straight from Boxer's bedside including a photograph of Boxer, wearing a large surgical collar alongside Haven centre Brian Rose.

"I know I have had a lucky escape and it is all part of the game," Boxer said in *The Whitehaven News*. "I accept it and there is no way I will give this game up. All I want to do is get out of hospital and get back playing for Whitehaven again as soon as possible. I will probably have to wear the collar for a few weeks but once it comes off, I hope I will get the all-clear to play. I went to acting half back and I was ready to jink away when one of the tackles came in high. Something caught me and I heard three clicks in my neck. As far as I am concerned it goes down as accidental.

"I have no hard feelings towards the player concerned or the referee. I can remember exactly what went on around me while I was lying on the field waiting for the ambulance to come. I understand some of the fans thought I might be dead. I suppose that was because of all of the blankets they were bringing on. I am told that all the crowd refused to leave the stand and terraces even though the match was over. I want to thank them all for staying on and for the ovation they gave me when I was put in the ambulance. Now I only hope they will continue to get behind the team. The lads gave 120 per cent effort to get behind the team against Hull KR and showed what they are really capable of against one of the top teams."

Coach Phil Kitchin, who had been at Boxer's bedside on Sunday night said: "It is a great relief that Boxer's neck isn't broken. He was cheerful but never mentioned the injury. He didn't know the game had been abandoned but he said he thought we had beaten them. That was typical of Boxer. He is a great character as well as a great player."

Robins coach Roger Millward, the former Great Britain stand-off said: "I have always loved Boxer as a player. I did not see the incident but I thought he had just gone down to try to win a penalty, the kind of thing we have all done."

Six days later he was back at home and feeling a whole lot better, in fact, he was feeling well enough to attend the First Division fixture against Salford the following weekend at the Recreation Ground. He was introduced to the crowd, holding a walking stick and still wearing a surgical collar. It was an emotional moment as he made a brief rallying call from somewhere high up in the grandstand, thanking everyone for their support and prayers. Everyone, including a few hundred Salford fans stood and applauded for what seemed like a very long time.

He was soon up and about and then he started walking, slowly at first, but his improvement was rapid and not long after that, he was running and before anyone had expected it, he was back in training and a few weeks later he was playing full practice sessions and then, just 56 days after he was lying on the Recre pitch, thinking he might never walk again, Boxer was playing for Haven against St Helens, and it was just like nothing had happened. He had missed just five matches and medical staff at West Cumberland Hospital discussed his recovery with awe and bewilderment, shaking their heads, as if it was the most astonishing thing they had ever seen.

CHAPTER 21

The Surgeon Who Saved My Life

From time to time Boxer's neck would flare up. The discomfort was often so debilitating that he would find it difficult to get out of a car. The abuse that had been inflicted on his neck and back had accumulated for more than 20 years since he was a small boy playing on the fields of Kells. And now he was paying the price. But he was never one to dwell on or worry about medical difficulties, which is just as well considering what was just around the corner. He just took handfuls of industrial strength paracetamol and got on with his life.

Moreover, he viewed injuries, back pain and headaches as consequences that came in tandem with his gifts for playing rugby which were plentiful, as if a divine source was making him pay for his genius. So every Sunday afternoon, if a large forward, perhaps 80 pounds heavier, punched him, gouged him or tackled him late or subjected him to lots of other subtleties of violence often unseen by fans, Boxer would just pick himself up, stare him in the face, and shout: "Is that all you've got? You'll have to do better than that, big man."

And he would wipe his fingers on his white Haven shirt and take his place in the defensive line or back into position at first receiver, where he would take centre stage as the orchestrator of attacks as if none of it was such a big deal, not to him. You had the impression he was indestructible. But he wasn't, of course, and around 3.20 in the afternoon of August 28, 1983, in a First Division match against Widnes at Naughton Park, he got hit one last time, and his life changed for ever, in an instant. Boxer would never play again, he would never work again and he might face the rest of his life in a wheelchair.

"I wasn't knocked out, but I knew right away it was really serious," he says. "I felt pins and needles in both my arms. I got back to the line and I remember Eric Prescott, who was a really good player, running at me, and I just stepped out of his way. Eric didn't know my neck had gone. If he had trampled all over the top of me, God only knows what would have happened. Normally I would have dropped him, no bother, but I just couldn't lift my arms up.

"Our coach was Frank Foster and he couldn't believe it. I knew, right then, I was finished. That was it. I walked straight down the middle of the park and straight into the dressing room. I remember lying in the bath knowing I would never be able to play again. I was examined and it was decided that it wasn't anything serious but I was still feeling pins and needles down my arms and I just knew something was wrong. As I left the dressing room I told all the lads that I was finished."

Boxer, and hardly for the first time, was reacquainting himself with his old friend called paracetamol but it wasn't working too well. The following week, he was presenting himself to the orthopedic department of West Cumberland Hospital where he was quickly assessed. It was serious, doctors told him. He wasn't surprised. Boxer had become a connoisseur of pain and accurate self-diagnosis was a skill he excelled in. Unfortunately, the root cause of his injury would prove difficult to locate, but surgeons finally recommended a course of traction treatment, which involves the use of weights, ropes and pulleys to apply force to tissues surrounding malfunctioning bones which in Boxer's case was something called the thoracic vertebrae. Some of the weights used were extremely heavy, as much as 25 pounds. It was known as a painful procedure and it has since been largely discredited and rarely used in the National Health Service. But they didn't know that back then, more than 30 years ago.

"I was in the hospital getting this traction every day for five weeks," he recalls. "It was horrible. They put these special weights all over me and I had to wear a kind of scrum cap on my head with more weights. The idea was that the weights would gradually open up your spine and when they started reducing the amount, everything would go back together as it is supposed to."

When Boxer tells the story, he puts his two hands together, interlocking them as one might prepare to take a catch in a cricket match and the thought springs to mind of a dovetail joint often seen in the corners of mahogany drawers. He had plenty of visitors, including most of his team-mates and plenty of Town's ex-players and other county men and his overall mood of gloom was lifted with the arrival of a personal letter from Trevor Skerrett, Hull's international front row forward.

"It was a fantastic feeling to get that letter - it really lifted my spirits," recalls Boxer. "From what I understand, Trevor had called the hospital to find out what ward I was on. He was a great player who was as hard as nails. When I played with Trevor for Great Britain, we supped together, along with Peter Gorley, Knocker Norton, Mick Adams and Len Casey. Nothing much, just a couple of beers at night to relax. We hit it right off as mates and then on the field too. One of the Kiwis tried to clout me and Trevor was right there in the middle of it, sorting him out. I knew he would look after me. Running at Trevor was like hitting a brick wall - he was so solid and even the Aussies didn't affect him. You know when you have a big player like him on your side it is really encouraging. In the match against the Kiwis, he was always saying to me: 'Come on, son, you're doing great.' He was a dream to play with.

"Workington Town's physio was a lovely lady called Judy Hampson. She was also the physio at West Cumberland Hospital and she was really helpful. We spent a lot of time in a swimming pool together, trying to get my back moving but nothing seemed to be working and they eventually sent me home. The pain was so bad I couldn't sleep and though they kept giving me stronger and stronger painkillers, nothing changed. Eventually they sent me to see a spine specialist at Furness General at Barrow. His name was Mr Campbell."

The introduction of Mr Campbell into the rehabilitation of Boxer was incredibly important to his possibilities of recovery. He was highly regarded in the medical profession and his title of Mister had been well earned. It takes more than 10 years to train as a GP, including medical school, and four more years to qualify as a surgeon. To be referred to as Mister is a tradition that goes back to the Middle Ages when a barber's access to indispensable tools such as sharp-bladed razors, permitted them to conduct amputations and apply leeches when they could fit in a patient between a short back and sides – hence the red and white pole that was a common sight outside men's hairdressers until the latter half of the 20th century. The title of Mr, when used today, is normally reserved for senior surgeons following their membership of the Royal College of Surgeons. So if a doctor is Wayne Rooney, a surgeon referred to as Mr is Lionel Messi, probably with elements of Pele and George Best thrown in.

Mr Campbell, who once had a practice in Harley Street, was one of the leading spine specialists in the country and his powers were indisputable. Everyone who knew him, worked with him or, more importantly, were treated by him, shared the view that he was, indeed, a gifted surgeon. And some of his patients' recoveries were so successful and occasionally unexpected, there was a body of opinion that held the unshakable belief that his expertise was more than scientific knowledge, experience and a thorough understanding of medical science. There was a hint of sorcery involved, it was thought, as if he might be stirring up a cauldron of magic spells before putting on his white coat and entering the operating theatre.

Boxer travelled to Askam to spend the morning with county half back Dennis Jackson, who took him to Ulverston, eight miles away, where Mr Campbell had his practice. "He examined me and recommended something I had never heard of called a myelogram, which would mean injecting dye into my neck and back.

"I came back a couple of weeks later with my mate Derek McMillan and I was kept in overnight. The myelogram was horrendous and the most pain I have ever felt in my life. I had to drink jugs and jugs of water to clear out the die and the pain was that bad, I was actually crying. I could take things that happened to me on the rugby field but I had never experienced anything like this before."

Derek returned to Furness General to pick up his friend and take him back to Cumbria where he spent the next couple of days in bed recovering. Two weeks later and Boxer is sitting in front of Mr Campbell in his Ulverston surgery, waiting to hear the results and even now, more than 30 years later he can remember his explanation almost word for word.

"Arnold, I have some bad news for you. You have broken your fifth and sixth vertebrae in your neck and it is very, very serious," he told him. "You are probably never going to be able to work again and you will need a major operation and I can't guarantee it will be a success."

Boxer's recollections of the next few months, which would involve complicated and painful medical procedures, are patchy. As he remembers it, he returned to Furness General a few weeks later, to undergo a major and hazardous operation that involved surgically removing a piece of bone, that was surplus to requirements, from his hip and fusing it onto the offending area in his neck as a welder might fuse together two pieces of metal. Mr Campbell was explicit that there were no guarantees that the operation would be successful. The balance of probability made it a worthwhile risk, but, he told him, there was a genuine chance he might wake up paralysed, if at all.

The operation, which took almost seven hours, involved gaining access to the spinal column by inserting an eight-inch cut in Boxer's neck. Mr Campbell fused the bone, which was located just above the thorax, with incredible skill and all kinds of precise surgical tools, knowing throughout the process that permanent paralysis was the likely outcome if he erred by a single millimetre.

The procedure was designed to limit movement, to reduce pain and, most importantly, to lessen the probability of further and more lasting deterioration that might possibly, in the worst case scenario, involve the use of a wheelchair.

"I owe Mr Campbell my life," says Boxer. "He was an excellent man, just one of the lads. He was just a small man but I had loads of confidence in him, I don't know why, he always made me feel like that."

Mr Campbell's operation appeared to be successful but only up to a point and depending on your interpretation of what Boxer was told might be, if everything went absolutely perfectly, a 'normal life.' Worse still, he would have to withstand pain in the truest sense of the word, which would be more or less constant, sometimes 24 hours a day and difficult for normal people to comprehend. And in case you need a more accurate and easily understood description of the word 'fused' then here it is and straight from the mouth of one of the world's leading orthopedic spine surgeons.

"A spinal fusion surgery is designed to stop the motion at a painful vertebral segment, which in turn should decrease pain generated from the joint," says Peter F. Ullrich, Jr., MD, a 54-year-old board-certified orthopedic spine surgeon, who should know a thing or two about such matters, as he holds a Doctor of Medicine degree from the University of

Wisconsin Medical School and earned a spine fellowship at the University of Utah. "There are many approaches to lumbar spinal fusion surgery, and all involve the following process: adding bone graft to a segment of the spine, setting up a biological response that causes the bone graft to grow between the two vertebral elements to create a bone fusion which results in one fixed bone replacing a mobile joint and stops the motion at that joint segment."

That explanation is quite a mouthful but it might be easier to think of it like this. For fused, read strait jacket – of the kind made famous by Harry Houdini, hanging from a rope 20 stories up from a New York skyscraper more than 100 years ago. Movement is severely restricted. So try to picture this in your mind - you are standing in the supermarket queue with your weekly shopping. Your trolley is facing ahead of you and you turn to pay with your credit card. Sounds simple enough but Boxer can't do it. He hasn't been able to do it since 1984 and he never will. He would have to push the trolley ahead of him to make sufficient room to turn his entire body before facing the cashier head on and presenting his card to the machine.

Boxer also remembers the exact date he left Furness General Hospital because it coincided with the official opening of the facility by Queen Elizabeth – October 14, 1984. He headed back to Whitehaven to begin a new life and soon he would be officially certified as permanently disabled and his painkillers would be upgraded from paracetamol to morphine, 30 milligrams, twice a day, every day, every month, every year for the rest of his life.

CHAPTER 22

Back from the Dead

Halfbacks and forwards are natural enemies – and a player like Boxer Walker was a frequent victim of brutal assaults from large men who knew winning pay was more likely if he could be hurt or intimidated – or, better still, flattened with sufficient force to take him out of the game altogether. Back then, violence was part of the game and Boxer was equal to it. To make matters worse, he loved tackling forwards and the bigger the better, some 100 pounds heavier, and he embraced this part of the game with great enthusiasm. He would never hide in the threequarters, not for a moment – you might as well give him a knife and ask him to cut his throat. And his own forwards loved him for it.

This admiration was not shared by opponents and it is easy to picture international forwards, a volcanic anger rising inside them, huddled together in a dressing room as the kick-off looms, discussing plans to intimidate him, to hurt him – anything that would stop him. Boxer often made more tackles than anyone else so when you add all this together – perhaps 35 tackles a game, at least 30 games a year, for more than 20 years, it is no wonder that now, as he is approaching old age, his body is in a permanent state of disrepair. It is hard not to wince when you think of his long-term accumulation of chiropractic and medical maladies – which recently included the need, sometime soon, for a knee replacement, more than 40 years after it was crushed by three Australian forwards.

In 2017, Boxer is 65, and pain is with him every day. Although frequent appointments with specialists, and all the constant medical assessments he has to endure, are tedious and a bit of a nuisance, his optimistic nature and mischievous character, that wound up all those big forwards more than three decades ago, are back at full force.

He was in a much darker place back in October, 1984, after he had been released from Furness General Hospital, following all those operations, with his back fused, knowing his disabilities were so severe he would never work again. Now all of these orthopedic misfortunes are bad enough but they weren't the worst thing as Boxer began to contemplate what kind of life lay ahead of him.

"One day I was a superstar and the next day I was nothing," recalls Boxer, who made plenty of money in his 12-year professional career, but none of it stuck to his fingers. "They told me I would never work again and I was going to be an invalid for the rest of my life. I had no bitterness towards anybody but sometimes I didn't want to wake up. Every now and then it just hit me, that this was what I faced for the rest of my life. I thought to myself, what the hell am I going to do? I cried a lot, sometimes every day. I just couldn't get over it. To think that a few months before, I was still running around that rugby field as a hero and one of the best players in the world. And now I was thinking I was nearly a cabbage.

"I always had plenty of cash in my pocket and I could go anywhere and buy anything. Money was never a problem. The most hurtful thing was when I realised how daft I was, spending all that money because I didn't think it was ever going to end. There were always hangers-on. It's my own stupid fault and I've nobody else to blame. People who I thought were my friends were only hanging on to get drink money. There was the time I had played for Haven and I went up to the bar for a pint after a bath. Betty Haile, who was a director at Whitehaven, was helping out behind the bar. I asked for a pint and she said: 'That will be £40 please, Arnold. All your mates over there have been drinking like fishes all afternoon and they said that you would pay the bill.' To think, they were supposed to be my friends. I had to pay but I never supped with them again.

"I had come all the way from the top to rock bottom. It was like being hit by a 14-pound sledge hammer. I remember the worst time was over Christmas and only a few weeks after I had come back to Whitehaven from the Barrow hospital. I started going through things in my mind and I realised how stupid I had been. I started to get really low and depressed.

"When I was sent home from the hospital, I was just looking at four walls. I had been on top of the world and now I was on £25 a week dole money. I had no job, I was never going to work again, and I might end up in a wheelchair. Then something incredible happened that gave me a big boost just when I only had £10 left in my pocket. I went in the bookies and there was a horse called Ragafan and the only reason that I backed it was because it was owned by my favourite comedian, Freddie Starr. I put my last tenner on the horse and I had nowt left - I didn't even have any bus money so I would have to walk home from town which would have been a right struggle.

"Ragafan won at 12/1 and I got £130 back and that was a real help to get me over Christmas. But I was still down because I couldn't get out of my head that the year before, I had hundreds of pounds in my pocket and now I had nothing. It was like hitting a brick wall."

Boxer was in the middle of a deep depression but things were about to take a turn for the worse. All professional rugby league players had to be insured under strictly adhered to regulations but for some reason his neck injury had been medically assessed as 'an aggravation of an old neck injury' and this had a detrimental effect on his compensation payment which was eventually settled at £150 a month and would cease when he reached the age of 60. Even allowing for inflation, he was facing the rest of his life as near to the poverty line as makes no difference.

Later that season, Warrington, who were coached by Alex Murphy, came to the Recreation Ground for a First Division fixture and the legendary scrum-half, who was a well-known supporter of charitable causes, had got wind of Boxer's predicament. A meeting was arranged and Alex suggested a testimonial match and promised to return with a string of international players and a busload of memorabilia that could be auctioned off. Haven director Sol Roper, who loved Boxer like a son, supported the idea but for some reason the plan just never got off the ground.

"I lost a lot of weight and I wasn't sleeping," says Boxer. "The doctor put me on really strong anti-depressants and they just zonked me out. You wouldn't think that a bubbly, cheerful person and decent rugby player like me could end up being such a down and out. I couldn't afford to run a car and often I would bump into friends or old team-mates and they would ask me to have a pint with them. I couldn't afford to go and I had to tell lies and say I had something on but the real reason was that I hadn't a penny in my pocket.

"I remember having a pint once with Bill Francis, who was a Great Britain player, and he told me that when he finished, no directors wanted to know him. He told me that is what it is like for players who retire. No one wants to know you, he said. The directors only want to know you when you are putting your boots on and when you are finished, that's it. No long after that, somehow I pulled myself together, picked myself up and started getting myself out of it.

"It took a few months but slowly, bit by bit, I started to feel better. The two Gorley brothers saved me too. I will always remember that. I phoned them both from hospital to tell them what had happened and each time it was the same – the telephone just went dead and I thought I had lost the connection. Then, 20 minutes later, they were both standing by my bed asking me if there was anything they could do and that they would always be there for me. And they were too, just like they did on the field. I love the Gorleys to bits. They are not just friends - they are something very special to me, they are my brothers.

"I have to admit, I was asking myself sometimes, is there really a God? Does He still love me? I know that happens to a lot of people. I never lost my faith though and I know I will always believe in God. I pray every night. My father hardly ever saw the inside of a church but he would kneel down every night and say a few words. He used to say: 'Thank you for the day you have given me and my family,' and then that was it, he would bless himself and jump into bed.

"I believe that God helped me. I always say that. The Big Lad up there pulled me out of the depression. I prayed to Him every night and I still do. This will sound funny but there was a voice somewhere inside my head saying: 'Come on, Boxer. Pull yourself together. You are not a lad to give in. Don't just sit back and sulk.'

"I started to feel better and my character began coming back. It took a long time though, years and years. My memory of what happened with my second neck injury will always be hurtful. I'll never change that. Now, I think I have been very blessed in my life. I have had a few struggles along the way but I have had the best mates anyone could ever want. I have had a lot of fun. They say you should put things away for a rainy day and I didn't. I was daft with money but even now, I can't see anybody short. If I see anyone who is struggling, I would always try and help them out. I enjoyed my life day by day and I never gave my future a second thought. It never crossed my mind that something bad was going to happen to me."

§

It is early spring, 2010, and Boxer is walking down the gentle slope along Ravenhill Lane, with the great blue wheels of the pit head winding gear of Haig Colliery, rising up ahead of him. He worked here more than 30 years ago when thousands of miners would descend 1,000 feet before heading five miles out and deep below the Irish Sea to mine the black gold.

Dick Harvey, Chip Ross and Nat Lofthouse are waiting for him and the friends, all former miners, begin walking along the path, which was once a railway track called The Corkickle Brake and was built in 1881 by the Earl of Lonsdale. Powerful steam trains would be loaded with coal before heading along the cliff edge a few hundred yards where it would be washed and graded and stored in triangular black mountains, and then along to Howgill Brake. The coal would eventually end up at the town's harbour and railway stations. There is a lot of reminiscing going on, and in the main, their discussions inevitably return to their time 'down below' together and the incredible characters who worked among them. Speaking of the good old days, the friends are as wistful as it is possible to get, as they chat comfortably together and there is much laughter among them, as they pass by walkers, many accompanied by dogs and small children, out for an afternoon stroll. Sometimes, blue language might drift across the footpath, but it is never heard by other walkers and is always harmless and used only for emphasise and to give their recollections more authority.

They walk slowly towards St Bees, before returning to the pit head where, on a clear day, it is possible to see the mountain peak of Snaefell, way out west, more than 2,000 feet high and often shrouded in mist, on the Isle of Man, less than 40 miles away. Boxer is struggling to catch his breath and it is not the first time he has fallen behind his friends who are all much older than him. He feels a sharp pain in his heart, dizziness overwhelms him, his right arm shakes and tingles and his friends start telling him, with raised voices and anger inside them, as they have many times before, that he must get checked by a doctor.

"I was getting breathless on my walks and when I went up any stairs," Boxer recalls. "Sometimes I felt like someone was choking me and I kept getting pain down my right arm. My doctor sent me to the West Cumberland Hospital and they put me on a treadmill and found out I had angina. It was getting worse and worse. I was under a heart specialist called Doctor Wilma and she was great with me. She suggested I had an angiogram which would show if my arteries were blocked. I didn't tell anybody about any of this apart from my best mate Billy Starkey.

"Doctor Wilma said I must have the angiogram. She told me that there was a woman who was there recently who refused to have it and not long after that she died. While I was waiting to go in, I collapsed in my car but I managed to slow down and stop. My heart was racing and I was told later it was going at 190 beats a minute and I was close to dying. In the hospital they tried stopping my heart and starting it again but that didn't work. Eventually my heart settled down and I went back to the hospital for the angiogram a couple of weeks later. I got all wired up and I will never forget what happened. The results were right there on the television screen in front of Doctor Wilma and she said: 'Mr Walker, I am sorry to tell you that you have severe problems. You must have a bypass operation as soon as possible.' She recommended James Cook Hospital in Middlesbrough so I obviously did what she told me. I think the way she was talking I would have been dead in a few months.

"I was admitted really quickly and after the operation I was in hospital for around three weeks. I was in a right state. I found out later that there were major complications when I was in intensive care and they couldn't get me off the ventilator. My heart just kept stopping – they told me I kept dying and they had to keep bringing me back to life again.

"The surgeon who did the operation was called Mr Goodwin and he warned me that it would be a long time before I would be OK. I remember taking my first steps which was about four yards and I was shattered – I had to be helped back to my bed. Then the next day I tried again and I went a couple of yards further but it was taking ages to improve. You just can't rush it. I had no strength and I think it took me six months to walk 100 yards.

"The trouble was I was still getting problems and I ended up being taken back in James Cook Hospital again. I had had a triple bypass and two of them had collapsed and I ended up in the Cumberland Infirmary in Carlisle Hospital. They put a stent in one of them which is like a small inflated balloon in my artery, which is supposed to help the blood flow, so I guess I have one and a half working. I just live from day to day now."

§

It is around nine in the morning on a typical day in Boxer's life sometime in March, 2017, and he is making careful plans to make sure his medication is administered in the right order and at the right time of day. He starts by opening a box marked Zomorph, and placing two pills on the table in front of him. The tablets provide a sustained-release of morphine, which is a key ingredient of street heroin, and the most powerful legal painkiller available on the National Health Service. He takes two pills a day which is the maximum amount permitted without the risk of addiction and a very long list of unpleasant side effects which include dizziness, confusion, vomiting, drowsiness, constipation, a dry mouth, hot flushes, rashes, mood swings, hallucinations, blurred vision, double vision, insomnia, headaches, loss of appetite, abdominal pain, breathing difficulties and low blood pressure. His life depends on a daily intake of powerful pharmaceuticals and he opens one box after another with great dexterity. There are lots of different coloured pills, some small, some large, and in not much time, they are arranged neatly on the table in front of him, with an organised purpose borne of necessity.

The names are unpronounceable – amitriptyline, glyceryl trinitrate, ranexa, lansoprazole, atorvastatin, bisoprolol and ranolazine – there are anti-cholesterol pills, blood pressure pills, pills to control stomach acid, anti-depressants and so many more he can't remember their exact function.

He lives with pain most of the time and sometimes it gets the better of him. Morphine works, up to a point, and he would be lost without it, but occasionally he heads for Kells Rugby League Club for a different kind of painkiller. He will pull up a chair, not far away from his Great Britain shirt, among his friends, and knock back perhaps half a dozen pints of John Smith's Extra Smooth bitter, which comes in at 3.8 abv, and is just fine for deadening the senses. Beer also has the pleasant side effect of being consumed among people who know and love him. Boxer might go 10 weeks without alcohol – he does not have a drink problem, he has a pain problem. In the club, he still enjoys celebrity status on a minor scale and he is pointed out to visitors as a Great Britain scrum half who captained Kells, Workington Town, Whitehaven and Cumbria and who was held in such high esteem by his team-mates, his instructions were carried out with the force of commandments. Being well-known, had not always been a good thing when he was a young man and it had its own hazards and trials and Boxer had not been very proficient at keeping a low profile. But no one cares much anymore.

Sure, alcohol numbs the pain and it enhances the more agreeable aspects of Boxer's personality which are many and varied. He laughs a lot and his friends enjoy spending time with him. He greets strangers with a warm handshake and an infectious smile and when the subject is rugby league, they hang on his every word.

"When I look back in my life I have had lots of ups and downs but I am thankful for all the special friends I have made who have helped me. I couldn't have battled through it without them – you just can't do it on your own. When I look back to when I was a little kid pretending to be Billy Boston on the Welfare, and I think about playing for Great Britain, well, I couldn't have imagined anything like that. I have played with and against some of the greatest players of all time and had a few bob in my pocket.

"I am not trying to say that I am the only man on Earth to face a crisis and I am certainly not moaning about it. There are a lot of people who have faced worse things than me. I would hate anyone to feel sorry for me. I pulled myself together and now, I might be living with a bit of pain but when I look back and review my life I have been so lucky. I grew up watching my heroes at Kells, played for the team and Workington, Whitehaven and Cumbria and alongside some fantastic players. I went on to play for Great Britain and my shirt is on the wall in the Kells club alongside all my heroes - I still can't believe I have been so blessed. I could never, in my wildest dreams, think I could have achieved what I have. When I go in for a pint, I sometimes look up at that shirt, and it reminds me how lucky and blessed in life I have been.

"When I pop my clogs, and I often think about this, I want my ashes scattered on the field at The Welfare where I kicked off. When I am in the club, having a few pints, one of my older mates might point me out to a younger person and say: 'See this lad here, he was once voted the best scrum half in the world.' They never believe them. They always say: 'Him, that la'al lad. No way.' I suppose that is because I am so laid back and I don't like to brag. That's just me."

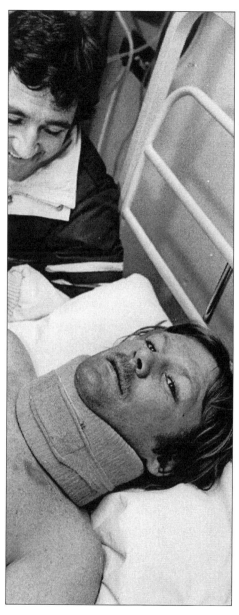

Mr Campbell, who fused a bone in Boxer's back.

Boxer recovering from his first neck injury - he played 56 days later.

Brian Rose, the Whitehaven centre, visits Boxer at West Cumberland Hospital, after his first neck injury that he suffered against Hull KR at the Recreation Ground in October, 1981.

David Wigham, who brought Boxer to Whitehaven.

*Captain Boxer Walker with Cumbria in 1981: Lyn Hopkins, David
Beck, Johnny Jones, Ralph McConnell, Mel Mason, Malcolm Flynn, Bobby
Blackwood, Alan McCurrie, Peter Gorley, Peter Stoddart and Joe Stewart.*

*Frank Foster, the Cumbrian
forward, who coached Boxer at
Whitehaven. 'Frank and me were
big mates,' says Boxer. 'He was
an excellent coach and trainer.'*

*Tommy Dawes, who had taken
over at Haven and struggled
to get the best out of Boxer
Walker. 'Tommy hated me and I
hated him," remembers Boxer.*

Mick Adams, Widnes's superb back row forward, who played
alongside Boxer for Great Britain. 'Mick was always encouraging
me,' remembers Boxer. 'He was non-stop: Go on, Arnie, keep it
up, son. You're hammering him, he kept on telling me.'

David Cairns, the Barrow and Salford scrum-half is in Boxer's team of stars. 'David was a lot different to me as regards playing clean,' says Boxer. 'I admit I could be dirty sometimes but you never got that kind of stuff from David – he was always hard and fair – and he was known for that throughout the game.' Right: Ralph McConnell, who just missed out for a place in Boxer's team. 'Dirty play didn't affect David and Ralph,' says Boxer. 'They were so fast they didn't need any of that.'

Trevor Skerrett, Hull's international front row forward, who played with Boxer for Great Britain. 'He was a great player who was as hard as nails,' says Boxer. 'We hit it right off as mates and then on the field for Great Britain too. One of the Kiwis tried to clout me and Trevor was right there in the middle of it, sorting him out. I knew he would look after me. He was a dream to play with.'

Whitehaven at Craven Park, Barrow in 1983: Back - Vince Gribbin, Bob Mackie, Ray Fiddler, Steve Pithion, John Glover, Billy Fisher, Neil Frazer, Alan Banks, Robert Weir. Front - Arnold 'Boxer' Walker, Ian Litt, Graeme Cameron, David Barnes, Gordon Cottier, Peter Stoddart, Colin Hall.

Back row county forward Malcolm Flynn, left. 'I think Malcolm should have played for Great Britain,' says Boxer. 'He would be in my side all the time. I played with the best around for England and Great Britain and Malcolm was just as good. I loved him.'

Tom Gainford, right, the loose forward who joined Whitehaven from Kells in 1967, for a signing-on fee of £125. 'Tom's work-rate was always 200 per cent,' says Boxer. 'You could always guarantee he would be there knocking all the big men down time after time. He did so much defending that he kept our ball players fresh. He was the perfect player to play with for Cumbria.'

Great Britain squad for the 1981 Test series against New Zealand: Back – Keith Elwell, Len Casey, John Joyner, Steve Evans, Roy Holdstock, Mike Smith, Harry Pinner. Centre – Jeff Grayshon, Peter Smith, Steve Hartley, Trevor Skerrett, Mick Burke, Les Gorley. Front – Arnie Walker, David Watkinson, George Fairbairn, Johnny Whiteley (coach), Keith Bentley, Chris Camilleri, Kevin Dick

Boxer Walker tackles Kiwi skipper Mark Graham in the Third Test in 1981. Great Britain won 10-2 to level the series. 'When I was standing in that line of players I looked around me,' recalls Boxer. 'I thought to myself: Bloody hell, I am with some stars here, and I am a part of it. When they read my name out I still couldn't believe it. I could hear all these cheers, just for me. I'll never forget them.'

Haven's championship team - back: Tommy Dawes (coach), Billy McCracken (assistant coach), Ian Litt, Billy Fisher, Bob Mackie, Vince Gribbin, Brian Rose, Milton Huddart, Alan Thompson, John Glover, Tony Delaney, John Bulman, Michael Taylor, David Barnes, Steve Pithion and Gordon Cottier. Front: David Ritson, John Doran, John Milburn, Michael Barwise, Joe Stewart, Colin Hall, Arnold 'Boxer' Walker, Steve Lane and Alan Pearson

136

Boxer Walker played his last game of rugby league on August 28, 1983. 'Boxer was easily the best scrum half I ever played with,' says Great Britain forward Peter Gorley. 'I have played against the very best scrum halves including top Aussies such as Peter Sterling when he played at Hull but Boxer was a match for anyone.'

CHAPTER 23

My Team of Stars to Take on the World

Boxer took some persuading to include this chapter. At times he seemed almost overwhelmed by the challenge he faced before settling on his final 13 – there were so many incredible internationals he shared his career with, too many to separate, he thought. He changed his mind often, and his team was constantly subject to review. Boxer would write his latest selections on the back of lottery tickets, and some players would be discarded and others added so that the names would be criss-crossed with black lines and his team would be illegible. He would just pick up another blank ticket – he seemed to have an inexhaustible supply he kept in a secret place – and commence further contemplation and you were left with the impression that it was all too much for him.

Many of the players were so evenly matched, he said, that a final decision might not be forthcoming and he might be sitting in his chair for some time, perhaps years, writing perpetually on blank lottery tickets and there would be no end in sight, the literary equivalent of painting the Forth Road Bridge. It wasn't so much who he selected but the guilt he felt at leaving others out. His team is a formidable one, and chosen with a simple criteria – players are selected from the professional teams he played for - Workington Town and Whitehaven and, of course, Cumbria. After much deliberation, here, in his own words, is Boxer's team of heroes.

§

The full back is easy. It has to be **PAUL CHARLTON.** I've never come across a player like him. He should have been playing for Great Britain years and years before he was selected. His big problem was that he couldn't kick goals and most of the full backs he was in competition with could do that, players like Colin Tyrer and Ray Dutton. They were nowhere near as good as him. Charlo was as fast as lightening and when he was our coach at Town, in training, he never asked anyone to do anything that he couldn't do. His training sessions were so interesting and never the same, a lot more than just sprinting. There was lots of variety. He was a very clever player. Paul would link up in the line from the scrum and just fit in, no problem.

When he was defending, Paul had the knack of making the runner go where he wanted him to and, more often than not, stop him from coming inside. And what a marvellous captain he was – he never wanted all the attention for himself. He had everything planned and Paul was a great inspiration to his players on the field and in the dressing room. I remember how he never felt he was beaten. There was one game for Cumbria against Australia and we were getting hammered so there we are, behind the posts, towards the end of the game - my nose is all beat up and my ears are hanging off. Come on, lads, we can get back in, he said to us all. Do you know what the score was – we were getting beat 47-4 - and there was only five minutes left.

On the right wing I am going for **JOHN BULMAN** who just edges out David Collister. John was another Kells player who I played with for Whitehaven and Cumbria. He was really fast. John didn't have much of a sidestep or a body swerve but give him the ball and no one could catch him. I remember one game we played against Hull KR at the Recreation Ground and John got the ball in our 25 and broke through the line and he only had George Fairbairn to beat. Now George was the Great Britain full back at the time and he was a great defender. John just ran away from him and made George look like a la'al lad. John came out of the Royal Marines and you could see right away what a great winger he was going to be. He could tackle too and he was happy to clear his line and do some of the hard work. John was really brave in defence. Alongside Ian Wright, he was the fastest player I ever played with. David Collister was completely different. He wasn't a prolific try scorer but he could really smash them with his defence. Whoever he was marking, we all knew that player would never get past David. No chance. I also thought about Keith Davies, who was very, very fast too, in fact, he was a professional sprinter at Powderhall. But we didn't play together a lot. David was in the Lancashire Cup winning team for Workington and when he hit them, well, they knew about it. He was a clean player but if I was close to David when he was making one of those crunching tackles it was as if I could feel the bones shattering in the player's body when he took them down. He was a big lad - well over six feet - and David was the quietest man in our team. He signed from Broughton Red Rose and he still lives there now. I remember a Welsh player who was with Barrow called Chris Camilleri. Now he was very fast. We played together for Great Britain and we used to travel together for training. But it has to be John Bulman.

Picking my two centres was so hard and I have narrowed it down to three. My right centre to play with John is **PETER STODDART** who was a tough and very reliable player for Whitehaven and Cumbria. He never seemed to have a bad game. Like me, Peter could get a bit fiery but I loved playing with him. He was tall and very brave. He loved tackling big men and he would always help to clear our line or run from acting half back to give the forwards a rest. I know wingers all liked to play with Peter – he would only give them the ball if there was something on. If the winger might get hammered, Peter would hold onto the ball and take the battering himself. He scored a fair number of tries and he was a big part of the Whitehaven team that was promoted when Phil Kitchin was the coach. Peter was like having another forward on the field and he was a clever support player who would follow myself or Gordon Cottier if we made a half break. If we looked around, odds were he would be there shouting for the ball.

Another great centre was John Risman who played with me for Town and he had a great game in the Lancashire Cup Final. John wasn't an exceptional try scorer but he was just like David Collister - no one would ever get past him. He was what we call a crash tackler. How it worked was this, an opposing player would get the ball in his hand and John would hit him at just the right time and the player would have no chance of getting rid of the ball and the move would just break down every time. No one got past John.

IAN WRIGHT was the Golden Man of Workington Town. He should have been an international but for some reason he just got snubbed. He was always the fastest man on the field, whoever we were playing. John Woods and David Topliss were international players who were really quick but they weren't as fast as Ian. Once he got a yard in front, he was gone and no one would catch him. Ian was one of those players who could hit top speed in a couple of steps. It didn't take him 20 yards to get going. By the time the opposition has turned around, he was away. What a marvellous player. And if he got an interception, well, that was it - you knew he would score every time. We were playing at Leeds once and Ian got an interception on our own line and they had no chance of catching him. Their winger was a Great Britain player called John Atkinson and he tried to chase him and he gave up at the halfway line. Ian was the fastest player I played with or against in my entire career. He was a good defender too, not as strong as John Risman but that was the thing – we had such a good balance. Ian was a good lad, very quiet – he never went out on the beer. It is a really tough call but Peter and Ian would make a great partnership at three and four.

The number five just has to be **IAIN MacCORQUODALE**, our great goalkicker who won so many matches for Town. What a man. He wasn't the bravest of players and he knew that himself. I remember saying to him after one game: "Corky, I am really sore here doing all your tackling for you."

He admitted it but he just answered: "Look Boxer, you do all that tackling for me and I'll put money in your pocket by kicking all the goals." He was right too. Corky was the best goal kicker I have ever seen. He could kick them from all over the field, whatever the situation and no matter how much pressure he was under. He kicked one in the Lancashire Cup Final from seven yards in our own half and it was still rising when it went over.

He could run too and he scored plenty of tries. Corky wasn't that far behind Ian Wright. Tom Mitchell signed him from Salford's A team and I remember when we first signed Corky talking with the lads at training and none of us had heard of him. He went straight into the first team and we all knew how good he was right away. What a character off the field too. When we found out he was a schoolteacher we all thought he would be a bit posh. But he wasn't, not at all. He knew how to have a good time all right. He was always great fun. One time there was a lot of talk that an American Football team wanted to sign him just to kick goals. He would have been a great success at that.

I remember the first time I met Corky, he came in the dressing rooms all smart with a tie on and everything. Well, we all thought to ourselves: "What kind of rugby player have we got here." He proved us all wrong.

The stand-off is easy – **DEREK McMILLAN**. I knew that if I missed my opposing scrum half, Derek would get him, every time. Say the scrum half ducked under my arms, and he was getting away, I didn't have to look around worrying because Mac would have nailed him. He was pretty fast himself too. All the time we played together I can only remember one time someone getting the better of him and that was Eric Hughes from Widnes - he could really run. Eric sometimes played in the centre too. When me and Derek are having a pint together in St Mary's Club, in Kells, he will admit that himself. He says: "I just couldn't get near him."

Derek was a good all-rounder, perhaps not a ball player but he made plenty of breaks. Derek's greatest talent was defence - he never missed a tackle. We went to Salford in the Lancashire Cup semi-final and Derek got the winning try. And they had all the top players then. It was a great try, straight from the scrum. I passed him the ball and Charlo pretended he was coming into the line. Derek played a dummy and all the defence took it and he just waltzed through and Corky kicked the goal and then I got a drop goal late on.

I have picked **DAVID CAIRNS** from Barrow, at scrum half. He was the man-of-the-match in Barrow's 12-8 Lancashire Cup Final win over Widnes in 1983. David was a few years younger than me and we played against each other quite often. He was always difficult to play against. I think he played a couple of times for Great Britain but he should have played more. There were so many good scrum halves around then – Steve Nash, Reggie Bowden and Gary Stephens were all knocking about. I wasn't surprised when he moved to Salford for £35,000 which was a lot of money back then. David was very quick and for sure quicker than me – you always had to watch him at the play-the-balls. He was a great tackler and I think he was actually smaller than me. He loved defending, just like me. David was a really deceptive runner who was always likely to make a break – you had to keep your eye on him all the time – he was through a gap and away before you knew it. He was a lot different to me as regards playing clean. I admit I could be dirty sometimes but you never got that kind of stuff from David – he was always hard and fair – and he was known for that throughout the game. David's long-time stand-off was Ralph McConnell who played for Wath Brow and they formed a very good partnership. I knew Ralph very well and he was a top-notcher who could do everything – make breaks, set up play and tackle. They were always hard to play against. Ralph was another clean player and if anyone smacked him or David in the face, they would just accept it. Dirty play didn't affect them one way or the other. To be honest, David and Ralph were so fast they didn't need any of that. I remember whenever I played against them, and I got past them, they could both turn around and catch me – that's how fast they were. Those two gave me as tough a game as any of the top internationals I played against.

Number eight was a really tough decision but it has to be **BIG JIM MILLS** - he just edges it from Harry Beverley. You could rely on Harry every time, taking the ball in and doing all the hard work some fans never saw. I played against Harry when he went to Fulham. Tom Mitchell signed him from Dewsbury for £10,000. I remember him coming in the dressing room the day after he had played for England against Wales with a massive black eye. He had been belted by Big Jim. Jim wrote in his autobiography that Harry was the hardest man he ever played against. I remember he was one of the most awkward forwards to tackle I had ever come across. He would run holding the ball very high and he would lift his knees right up in the air. At Town, he was always there, near the play-the-ball, demanding the ball. I would ask him: Take this ball in Harry, and there he was in just the right place at just the right time. Some forwards might say, no way, I have just taken the ball in but not Harry. One man couldn't tackle him - it always took at least two. And he had this way of turning in the tackle where there would be another one of our forwards, like as not, the Gorleys and Harry would put them through the line. Of course, it might have even have been me. I lost count of the number of breaks and tries I made because of Harry.

Now as for Jim, well, I played against him a few times when he played for Widnes before Town signed him. He was unbelievable. Jim was a really clever player who would use his loaf and he loved running at half backs or centres. Backs might tackle Jim once, perhaps twice and then most of the time that was enough and he would run through them. He was massive, around 18 stones. Off the field though, Jim was a gentleman.

He was quick for a big man. His appearance on the field was worth five points and when you had him and the two Gorleys in your team you felt you could beat anybody. I think out of all the teams we played against, Widnes players always enjoyed a crack after the game better than anyone. So Jim knew us all before he signed. He was a good talker on the field and very encouraging in the dressing room. I used to love backing him up.

Another tough decision was at hooker. I've chosen **ALAN BANKS** just ahead of Smiler Allen. Alan was so reliable. They reckon the hooker, the scrum half and the open side prop were always the main people in the scrum. Our open side prop used to hold up the other prop so Alan could see everything easily or if it was the other team's put-in, pull him down so that their hooker couldn't see the ball. Alan and me, we had a bit of trick - when it was our feed, I clicked my feet and put the ball in the scrum right away and he would strike at exactly the right moment. Alan and Smiler were on a par for winning the ball. But Alan really put himself about, he was a great tackler. I don't think he would get away with it now because every tackle was high on the chest. And he was always there backing up, looking for a break. Alan played a heap of games for Cumbria too.

One time we were playing against Widnes, and they had this prop called Bill Ramsey, who played for Leeds with Phil Cookson and Ray Batten. Well, we had a free kick and I tapped it, and Ramsey broke the line which you should never do. You must always move up together and then there are no gaps. Well, I sidestepped him and there was a big gap and Banksy was there on my shoulder, I knew he would be and he went on and scored an easy try. He was always backing everyone up, following. And Alan was so fit, he could sprint as fast as some half backs. Although he was a great tackler, I can't remember him ever getting sent off all the times we played together. Alan was a quiet lad, not big-headed at all.

At number 10 it's obviously **EDDIE BOWMAN**. The best ball player I have ever seen from all the players I have played with and against. I obviously can't judge him against Brian Edgar - that was a different era. Eddie was a Great Britain player and a tourist too, that was how good he was. You never see players like him in the Super League - there just aren't the ball players in the game today, no one in the modern game is anywhere near as good as Eddie. He was so clever with his hands. He used to tell me, come on Boxer, follow me and the ball would always be there. He was always fit and he was one of the quickest forwards I ever played with. If it wasn't for Eddie, I wouldn't have been half the player I was. If he was playing today he would be priceless and the best player in the Super League. Just think of this, Eddie would run into the defensive line and two players would often be running off him, one either side – Les and Peter Gorley. No wonder everyone respected the Town pack so much.

In the second row it has to be the Gorley brothers. What can I say about my mates. I actually think **LES GORLEY** is one of the best second row forwards of my era, I really do, he was fantastic. When he said to me: Boxer I want it, I had to give the ball to him. He took some stopping and he could gallop for a forward. His brother **PETER GORLEY** was a grafter and I don't mean that in any bad way, quite the opposite. He would tackle all day. They were two totally different players and very big lads too. They were so laid back. If you asked Les: What was it like playing at Wembley, he would just say that it was no different to walking out at Derwent Park and that would be the end of the crack. He never bragged about anything. A lot of Town lads I played with, if they were in a pub, wouldn't talk about rugby. No. If someone brought it up they would be happy to talk but they would never show off. Les and Peter really complemented each other. I remember going to a forum with Les and a guy from rugby union and the organisers brought this great big jug of beer for our table. They did that a lot in union. I like a top on my pint and as soon as they poured the beer out of the jug, it was flat. I said to Les: I can't drink this. He said to me: What's the matter, it's wet isn't it. Get it down your neck.

We signed about the same time, me and Les, and Peter came about a year later. I remember Peter signing on after he played as a guest in Smiler Allen's testimonial. The All Stars, who had folk like John Bevan playing, were a player short and Peter was asked to play. He didn't even have any boots with him. He had a blinder even though he had a broken thumb and Tom Mitchell signed him on almost as soon as he came off the field.

I remember one match we played at Leeds and we hammered them. They had a big pack with some great players like David Ward and Phil Cookson. One of their forwards clouted me and both packs started battling each other, all 12 of them. There was only one winner – the two Gorleys were killing them. A couple of their players were lying on the floor spark out. Not one of their forwards touched me after that. That is what it was like knowing they were looking after me. All the big teams came to Derwent Park worrying about taking on that pack. We were like a big family.

GORDON COTTIER just edges out Billy Pattinson at loose forward and this was one of my hardest decisions. It really is a toss of the coin between these two great players. Gordon was a skilful ball player who was very brainy with good hands. He had plenty of stamina and he was very fit, probably Haven's fittest player - he was a great trainer too. Gordon was a very good cross country runner when he was younger and you could see how he carried that onto the rugby field. He would keep running and tackling right up to the end of a match. Another part of Gordon's game that fans won't know about is how good he was in the dressing room - he was great at geeing people up and keeping good morale in the team. Of course, I knew Gordon very well before I signed for Whitehaven – he was a Kells lad who lived in the next street to me in Solway Road. Gordon didn't play for Kells though, his amateur team was Hensingham. And though he is a couple of years older than me, we played against each other and I knew how good he was as an amateur. He was a senior and experienced player when I signed for Haven and I remember how good he was at helping the younger lads along and keeping his eye on them. Gordon had a bit of pace over the first 15 yards and he was always looking around for support - he did more than his fair share of tackling too. I suppose we shared the ball playing and it was good to know he was always there to give me a break from being in the game all the time.

I still want to tell you how good Billy Pattinson was. He was a showman who used to play to the crowd. He could run, back up and tackle, all the things you want in a loose forward. He was always there when you needed him and Billy was a really good pro. I remember when we played the Lancashire Cup Final against Wigan. They had Bill Ashurst, the Great Britain forward in their team. He was a big man. Well, he nutted Billy and he won us a free kick. Corky kicked it up the field to relieve the pressure just when we needed it. You could always rely on Patty. He had a good side step and he was a really hard man. Patty scored a few good tries and usually, he had a knack of scoring a try just when we needed one. I have to say I also considered a Whitehaven player called Tom Gainford - he was a tackling machine - tackle, tackle, tackle, one after another. I've never seen anyone like Tom. He could tackle for six of us and he never complained about anyone else not doing the same work or if he was playing with injuries. Tommy was like a pole, he wasn't a big-built man. Tom was a good mate of mine, he used to live just around the corner. I would have loved to have picked Malcolm Flynn, Billy Pattinson and Tom Gainford but my back three are so good, the Gorley brothers have to be in. I loved playing with Malcolm and Tom for Cumbria – I know they would have died for the team.

Other players I considered are forward Spanky McFarlane who played for Kells Under-19s before turning pro, an unbelievable team that included my brother-in-law Les Herbert and lots of amateur internationals. And a stand-off called Ian Rudd who was deceptive, he didn't look quick but he was. He played for Workington Town and Cumbria and he didn't get the respect he deserved.

That is my team and I am certain we would be more than a match for any Super League side playing today.

John 'Spanky' McFarlane: The legendary forward who once lifted nine-year-old Boxer onto a bus luggage rack after Kells had won an Under-19 cup final against Wath Brow in 1963. 'Before I knew it, he had punched me on my nose - there was blood all over the place,' says Spanky. 'And I played the whole game and there wasn't a mark on us - the bus was in uproar.'

CHAPTER 24

The Legendary Spanky McFarlane

John 'Spanky' McFarlane is 74, though he would pass for 65, perhaps even younger, and he still looks like he could pull on the red and white shirt of Kells and burst through a defensive line, knocking big men out of the way just like he did so many times, more than 50 years ago.

His playing weight back then, when he was 25-years-old, was listed at 14 stones and it doesn't look like it has changed much. Spanky still has an impressive width of shoulder and a narrow waist and a smile is never far from his face.

He is outgoing to the point of hearty, and he laughs often and with great enthusiasm. Spanky is friendly and engaging and spectacularly good company. He is a Cumbrian rugby league legend. Many newspapers ban the use of words like legend to describe well-known sporting celebrities with the idea being that it is a legitimate adjective if you are talking about Bobby Moore, say, or Lester Piggott or Sir Steve Redgrave, but definitely not permissible to describe someone like Spanky.

That all depends, of course, on how you define legend. Spanky, like so many wonderful players before him, was born to a family of coal miners, and you can be sure he came from a background where shyness was not encouraged. He made 437 appearances for four clubs and a further 17 for Cumberland, and if you are using legend to describe a local hero who is revered in his own community, then Spanky is astonishingly well qualified. He had all the virtues any right-minded person would believe are right at the heart of things for a legend – courage to ignore mangled fingers and fractured cheekbones, sporting excellence and something indefinable but nevertheless real and which makes them the object of affection. Spanky has all this and a lot more besides.

He spent his teenage years in the late 50s and early 60s socialising in the clubs of Whitehaven listening to local bands such as Rue and the Rockets and singers Frankie Pritt and Joe Delin. Spanky would begin the evening in The Central Bar before moving on to the town's main venue, The Empress Ballroom with best friends, all Kells rugby league players, Raymond Douglas, Jeff Sewell and Tom Wren. Admission was half a crown (13p).

Chuck Berry, Eddie Cochran and Jerry Lee Lewis were the big stars of the day and the prevailing fashion at that time was loosely known as 'The Teddy Boy look' and included the wearing of drainpipe trousers and crepe shoes, fondly known as brothel creepers. Spanky, never one to follow the crowd, preferred to wear a smart suit, shirt and tie and his only concession to the expected dress code was the cultivation of long sideburns which would be seen a few years later on John Travolta in *Grease.* His most spectacular accessory was the best quiff you will ever see this side of Shakin' Stevens. The dance floor of The Empress Ballroom would be full of young girls with truckloads of attitude, looking cool with long hair flowing loosely over their shoulders and holding clutch bags and tailored jackets with velvet collars. Spanky was only interested in one girl. She was called Brenda. She was 18. And they are still together today, more than 56 years later.

The average person's mental image of someone who is 74 is not quite what you see when you are in company with Spanky. He looks so strong and healthy and there is something extraordinary about it. There is only one noticeable difference from the kind of pictures that were taken in his prime - in black and white, of course - while he was performing incredible feats in the packs of Workington, Whitehaven, Barrow and Cumberland - his hair. It is not the style, which is exactly the same and is how Elvis Presley might look today, no, it is the colour, which is the purest white you have ever seen, whiter than the snow on the Lake District's highest mountains in the grip of a dark winter.

Spanky and Boxer go way back and the older man's affection shines through every word. He responds to questions with great enthusiasm, utterly absorbed in his assignment which is to pass on his opinions which are absolutely and definitely not unbiased - as a friend, work colleague and team-mate.

"We grew up in the same street, me and Boxer," says Spanky, talking quickly. "But I'm ten years older. I remember his dad Duncan really well. He was a collier all his life and a very popular fella, a really nice old man, a quiet man until he got a few drinks, like the rest of us. I never heard him call anyone in his whole life, dear me, never.

"I remember Duncan bringing this little fella along to Kells - what a genius Boxer was. You could see it even then. Here's a funny story for you. Boxer was our mascot and we were playing at Wath Brow in an under-19 cup final. Well, can you remember those single decker buses? The ones that had those roof racks above the seats.

"On the way home, I picked Boxer up and put him on the roof rack. I think he was about eight or nine, and he started crying his eyes out. So his father shouted from the back to me: 'You silly bugger, Spanky, get him down from there.' So I picked him up and put him on my knee. And before I knew it he had punched me on my nose - there was blood all over the place. And to think I played the whole game and there wasn't a mark on us. Well, the bus was in uproar.

"I had left Workington for Barrow when Boxer signed but I played with him in the county matches for Cumbria. He was the Alex Murphy of his day. If Boxer had been playing for Wigan or St Helens, he would have played for Great Britain many, many times. You could say the same thing about a lot of Cumbrians – Phil Kitchin for sure. That was such a shame. To be honest, it was disgraceful. Boxer was something special and as for his defence - he would always find a way of tackling them. He would never let go. He was a terrier. Boxer played a couple of stone above his self, flying around everywhere. He was a brilliant wee player.

"Boxer was awesome for his size. It is a wonder he never got killed. There was nothing of him," and Spanky holds up his little finger and stares at it intently before smiling with a sense of accomplishment, as if he has just realised how clever he was, to make such an appropriate comparison. "He was like that, honestly, like that," staring again at his finger. "I know Boxer used to dish it out a bit but in those days you had to, just to survive. Just look at Alex Murphy, well he could look after himself - he was a nasty wee bugger and he was the best scrum half I have ever seen. Yet for all his dirty stuff, when Boxer came off the field he would be friends with all the opposing team. He would buy a drink for anybody."

Spanky is right into the swing of things now and the stories are plentiful. You have the feeling he might have told these tales before and that there is an abundance of them just waiting for a sympathetic audience.

"I moved to blind side prop later in my career and I went up to around 14 stone," he says. "What sickens me now about the modern game are the scrums. There's nothing happening. They don't push or anything. There will be no cauliflower ears with these lads today. Then they all get a rest after 20 minutes when they bring the subs on and they have done nothing. In our day, when the ball went in you had to fight for it. That part of rugby today - it's rubbish. You know who is going to get the ball every time. Scrummaging is just a farce. It is not as good to watch now.

"I remember once, we got left behind somewhere and we ended up in Knocker Norton's pub and Knocker and Boxer were singing and standing on the tables. Knocker thought a lot of Boxer.

"Mind you, I played against some great loose forwards – Vince Karalius, Johnny Whiteley and Rocky Turner. They were all tough players but I remember Johnny was such a gentleman. But the other two, well they were buggers really," Spanky says, rubbing his chin as if just the thought of them is all it needs to bring back painful memories.

"The first time I played against Karalius at Workington I was shaking like a leaf. He was a few years older than me - The Wild Bull of the Pampas, they called him. Well, Billy Ivison was the coach at Workington. Billy told me: 'Now then, Spanky, when Vince first started playing, I was the top of my tree and don't worry, I've had a word with him. I have told Vince that you were only a kid. Vince has promised me he won't go over the top but he'll tackle you hard.' I can still see it now, like it was yesterday. Billy then said to me: 'Spanky, you've got Norman Herbert, Bill Martin, Frank Foster and Brian Edgar in our pack. Saints will be more frightened of us.'

"We also had Harry Archer, what a player he was. I'll tell you something about Harry. Whoever it was, it could be me or Sol Roper or Brian Edgar, whenever he shouted 'mine', we had to give him the ball right away, because there would be summat on. If we even took another step forward he would play hell with you, he would be seeing something that you couldn't. That's how clever he was.

"Here's another story for you. It is about religion in them days. It didn't really matter, of course, but at Workington we were roughly half and half - Catholics and Protestants. Well, back then, Catholics couldn't eat meat on Fridays. This one time, we had a game on Good Friday, when Billy Ivison was the coach. So we set off on the bus and Billy was going around making a list for dinner – you had a choice - steak or fish. Anyway Bill Martin, who was a Catholic, asked for steak. But you're a Catholic, Bill, says Ivison. Aye, Bill said, just throw a fish's head on it. Now what a player Bill Martin was. Oh God, Big Bill was a handful."

There is overwhelming evidence in Spanky's career which provides irrefutable proof of his status in the game and his standing as an extraordinary player. "He acquired a kind of heroic status in West Cumbria as a player who never gave in," says Robert Gate, who has written more than 20 books on the subject including highly-acclaimed biographies of Neil Fox and Brian Bevan, who scored 796 tries. "He covered every inch of the pitch in attack and defence and was the archetypal all-action Cumbrian forward. He had a neat line in dropping goals and although he was not a try-scorer of any note (37 in his career), some of his scores were genuine matchwinners.

"When he was sold by Barrow to Haven for a club record fee of £3,000, he immediately became an icon at The Recreation Ground and in 1972/3 he captained them in a campaign which brought First Division status. A splendid 17-cap career for Cumberland began at Blackpool, in 1964, where a famous 13-11 victory over Lancashire was recorded. He played loose forward, second row and blind side prop for his county and in his last two games for Cumberland, he was the captain against Lancashire and Other Nationalities in 1975."

Spanky inherited his powerful physique from his father, also called John, and a face worker and front row forward, who was respected and feared throughout Kells and in the pubs and clubs of Whitehaven. When very old miners get together and the stories start to flow of long-lost characters, John is prominent among them and they will point to a stool next to the bar in the Kells Club where he would sit, holding court and chatting amiably and only a brave or very stupid man would disagree with him. There is a story that usually goes along with such recollections which everyone swears is accurate and even if it isn't true, it should be. John is walking home from Whitehaven somewhere along Harbour View late one night, so the story goes, and a large German Shepherd escapes from a nearby house and attacks him. He picks up the dog, puts those great big hands of his around its neck and strangles it just like that, killing it, stone dead, before throwing it on the ground and walking home without giving the matter much thought.

Spanky's stories are coming thick and fast now and he is enjoying the memories. He is in a high state of relaxation as he rolls back the years, his Kells accent enhancing the experience and making them all seem so real and so recent.

"I loved playing at Barrow," he says. "Frank Foster was the coach. Well he was summat special. He was so strong. He was the coach at Whitehaven for a couple of seasons. Well, listen to what the bloody cowards did. We were at the end of the season do at the Civic Hall at Whitehaven presentation night. And the next day there was a letter at his house sacking him. They hadn't the guts to tell him on the night, he'd have cleaned the lot of 'em out. Frank was the hardest player I played with, without a doubt.

"I bumped into Paul Charlton the other day, what a bloody shock I got, we went right through school together in the same class in Kells. Paul looks so well. I still keep in touch with a lot of the older players. A few of us meet every Monday. We call it the Monday club - we are all retired now. It's a good day. When I was working, Monday was the worst day of the week, I hated Mondays but once I got retired, well it's the best day of the week, you know, when all the lads meet.

"When Paul first played for Kells Under-19, gospel truth, he was slow as a snail but when he signed for Town well, almost overnight, he put yards on in a matter of months, he became a flying machine. It was unbelievable. When I was playing loose forward, we had this move and by the time I was getting my head out of the scrum, Paul was putting the ball down under the sticks. I would look up and see his arse putting the ball down.

"Paul had that much pace. And you couldn't meet a nicer fella - a lovely man. He deserved everything he achieved in rugby league. Back in them days, the Sixties, it was nothing to be proud of but there was a lot of drinking going on. But Paul never took a drink. I remember when he came back from Salford he might have a bottle of brown ale and that was all he ever had. I admired him for it.

"He was rugby mad and you would never see him without a ball in Kells when he was a kid. I've done well to not put on weight because I have drunk heavy all my life. I keep good health, I am so lucky. When we meet on Monday I can knock back a few pints, well, my two sons play hell, I am not proud of it. You are too old to drink that many pints they keep telling me. I am not in bad fettle for my age.

"Oh, the times I've had with Boxer - I call him the wee fella. Mind you every time you see him, Boxer is dressed immaculate. I think he may have got that from his father Duncan. He always had a collar and tie on. I remember Duncan now, on Sunday afternoons, coming down from the Legion and he was always so smart.

"I have been really lucky with my career – apart from this," and he stands and pulls up his shirt and holds his left arm under the light so there can be no misunderstanding of the severity of his injury. He reveals a white scar, perhaps 10 inches long, meandering from his wrist. "This is Frank Foster's fault, can you see it? Barrow were playing York and they had this good full back, who had scored two tries against Whitehaven the week before. Well, Frank was our coach, and he told me: Spanky, get shot of him early on and we can beat these buggers.

"After about 10 minutes, I kicked the ball through to this full back so I could have a great chance of getting him. Remember, I played as a pro for 14 years and I knew all about stiff-arming people, I did it all the time. I had always got away with it, and never got any bad injuries. I had the stiff arm off to a fine art. Our winger was closing in on the full back but I told him to get out of the way, he's mine, I shouted. I caught this full back right on top of his head, the ball went up in the bloody air and this full back went down. The referee was Fred Lindop and we knew each other really well - he gave me a right telling off.

"The trouble was, the full back was OK but I was in agony - I could hardly do anything. I was just a bit of a nuisance and after a couple of minutes, there was a scrum. So I went down at blindside prop and I couldn't get my arm around our hooker, Smiler Allen. He said: 'Lift it up, you useless old bugger.' He played hell with us but I just walked off. Barrow had a really good doctor called Dr Todd – he was a really nice fella. He said right away: 'Oh my God, you're going to hospital.' The bone was sticking right out. I was put in an ambulance straight away and I ended up in York Hospital and they kept me in overnight. I went to West Cumberland Hospital the next day and I had a compound fracture and had to have a big operation to have a plate put in my arm. I never played again, that was my last match. That was it. But the good thing was, I was past my best and it was my last season."

Spanky's memory was remarkably accurate. His final game was actually a Challenge Cup match at York which Barrow won 15-9 on February 13, 1977. The full back he stiff-armed was Barry Banks, who was then only 19 and not long after he was transferred to Hull for £20,000. Banks, who often played at stand-off, went on to have an outstanding career and played for England. Even though the injury occurred in the 12th minute, Spanky stayed on the pitch until close to half-time and only left the field when his team-mates, realising the full extent of the injury, insisted he went off. It was Smiler Allen's second game for Barrow after his transfer from Blackpool Borough.

"When Frank Foster first played in Town's first team he was so strong and, to me, he was on a par with Brian McTigue and that's really saying something. In those days every team had a couple of hard men, but Frank would just go out and level them. Brian McTigue - what a player."

Spanky, never one to worry too much about sudden changes of subject, stops talking, just briefly, as if he's gathering his thoughts. He looks at his watch, before making his final comments, complete with substantial visual dramatics, and there's a hint of violence in the air.

"When you stiff arm someone, it goes like this," and he swings his left arm up with great speed, once, then twice, his huge arm almost a blur, quickly and with a minimum of fuss to illustrate his talent for intimidation and just for a moment, you imagine what it must be like to feel his arm smashing into your face. He was an outstanding player and you know, because many others have told you, that he was also an expert practitioner in the violence that goes unseen from the terraces. Then Spanky laughs and he is back in the role of everyone's favourite grandfather and somehow you just don't believe them.

Howard 'Smiler' Allen was sent off 14 times in his 16-year career as a hooker for Town, Barrow, Blackpool and Cumbria. 'I would tell Boxer to throw the ball straight into the other hooker's face, says Smiler. 'Hit him right in the nose with the point of the ball as hard as you can, I would tell him.'

CHAPTER 25

Howard's Way

If you knew nothing more than the simple statistics of Howard 'Smiler' Allen's career, just empty, soul-less numbers, you would be hard-pressed to escape the conclusion that he was a special player. The hooker, who played his first professional game more than 53 years ago against Salford, made 384 appearances, scored 71 tries and kicked 41 goals. Statistics say everything and they say nothing. And what they definitely don't reveal is his expertise as one of the greatest manipulator of rules, particularly in the scrum, in the history of the sport. Statistics don't reveal his disciplinary record, which involved 14 dismissals including two sending-offs in less than 48 hours and they say nothing about various misdemeanors such as large fines, rows with directors and his separate, secret and probably illegal employment as a newspaper snitch.

Smiler, who was born in Moresby, before moving to Lowca at the age of 10, played for Hensingham before joining the all-conquering stars at Kells. He signed for Workington Town when he was 18 after turning down offers from Barrow and Leeds. He is a link with Town's golden era and played as a teenager alongside some of the club's greatest players, including Brian Edgar, Ike Southward, Harry Archer, Ike Southward, Syd Lowdon and Frank Foster. He was the incumbent hooker when Boxer joined Town as a raw teenager in 1971 and was added to a long list of benevolent instructors that began with games' master Kevin McIlroy and continued, among others, with Les Herbert, Harry Whitaker, Sol Roper and Phil Kitchin.

Rugby league historian Robert Gate says: "No matter how rough the going got, and Howard was usually in the thick of things, there would be the grinning face of Smiler, infuriating his opponents, geeing up his colleagues and either endearing himself to or provoking the fans. In popular parlance he was 'a right character.' As he got older, he got craftier and he knew all the tricks and became extremely adept at winning crucial games, either through his chicanery at the play-the-ball or through his penchant for dropping goals."

Back then, the game did not remotely resemble Sky TV's slick presentation of the Super League with its action replays and plentiful use of cameras, broadcast into our homes to be viewed on large, widescreen televisions in full High Definition. In the 60s and 70s, it was rife with hidden violence, watched over by optically-challenged officials, and Smiler was as good as it gets as a master exploiter of inconsistent refereeing. He provided expert tutelage for Boxer Walker.

"I was lucky at Town because there were a lot of injuries," remembers Smiler. "Malcolm Moss had a problem with his shoulder and then they signed old Walt Tabern, who lived in Leigh, to replace Malcolm. Then he got injured too and I got in right away. Town had some great forwards back then.

"Billy Garratt, the Kells coach, took me and my dad Bob to Derwent Park to see Jim Kitchin, Town's director, who was known as Wacko. The contract finished up maybe at around £5,000 but I had to play so many first team games in chunks of six matches and I got perhaps £50 each time I hit one of them targets. If I remember correctly my lump sum was maybe £2,500 and I got extra if I went on to play for Cumberland. I had bonuses until I had played 46 first-team matches so it was all about incentives to do well. That was a lot of money in them days.

"I played a few games in the A team then stepped up through all these injuries. At my first match at Salford, Walter came to the game and talked to me, giving me a few tips. When the ball went into the scrum in them days it went in the middle and then you would strike. If your feet were too far into the tunnel entrance, you would be penalised, or perhaps the ref would pick you up for a loose arm or putting your feet up. Then they changed the rules but that made a mockery of everything and everyone was getting injured.

"Boxer was the mascot when I played for Kells. He was always there at training or at the matches. After I left, the next time I saw him was when he started as an apprentice electrician which was part of the deal when he signed for Town. I remember we got this big job in an old people's home in Sale, near Manchester, and with Boxer being a young boy, he got a bit homesick. We had to stay there all week. His dad used to drink in a pub in Whitehaven called the Ship Inn in Duke Street. Boxer would phone his dad there most nights and as soon as he had done that he would settle down. Once he had spoken to Duncan he was happy.

"I think he would be on about £5 a week and he had to pay his bus fares from that. He was often threatening to finish and I kept telling him to hang on and that he would have a trade to fall back on. But he left and went taxi driving and after that he ended up at Haig Pit.

"We sometimes played in the A team together and I used to tell him how I wanted the ball put in. If it was our head I wanted him to put it in the bottom because I was nearer than the other hooker and I had more chance of getting it. Against the head I wanted it up in the air and the ball would be all over the place and it would be a free for all.

"If things were going bad and we weren't winning much possession, I would tell Boxer to throw the ball straight into the other hooker's face. Of course they didn't like that but I didn't worry about Boxer - that was up to him. 'Hit him right in the nose with the point of the ball as hard as you can,' I would tell him.

"It came back to haunt me because when I was at Barrow, we played Town in a Lancashire Cup semi-final at Craven Park, in a night match. It was very tight and we were right under Town's sticks, maybe 10 yards off their line and time was running out. There was a scrum and all we needed was a penalty or to win the ball and I am sure we would have scored, no bother. I couldn't believe it - Boxer threw the ball right at my nose, just as I had taught him all those years before. Whack, right in my face. It was a cold winter's night and the ref couldn't see what was going on. It really hurt. Town won the ball and as the scrum broke up I was right after him and he knew that but I couldn't get hold of him. Not long after that the ref blew his whistle and the match was over. If we had got the ball from that scrum, Barrow would have won but we lost 6-4. There wasn't a try scored and the little bugger kicked two drop goals too."

Smiler was an opportunist, occasionally for tries, and sometimes in creative ways of earning additional income. He was employed by several leading newspapers as a revealer of secrets. And throughout his career, he contributed exclusive stories to national tabloids under the pseudonym 'an insider'. Back then, no one knew and today Smiler is more than happy to reveal his role as a paid informer.

Two leaks he is particularly proud of involve a lengthy wages row by the Town players and an exclusive story reporting on the imminent arrival to Cumbria of Great Britain front row forward Jim Mills. He talks of them without a hint of guilt, in fact he puffs up his chest as he recounts the proceedings with a kind of journalistic pride.

"The players wouldn't accept what Town were prepared to give us," recalls Smiler. "I think the directors were offering us £40 a win and £14 a loss. It was in my benefit year, in 1975, and as one of the senior players I went into the boardroom with Harold McCourt and Eddie Bowman. The problem was that the two directors were Bill Whalley, who was looking after my benefit, and George Graham who was my boss. They blamed me for the unrest which just wasn't true. I think Tom Mitchell was away on business. I was in regular contact with Arthur Brooks, who wrote in the *Daily Mirror.*

"Another time, Jim Mills was on the transfer list at Widnes and all the papers were full of stories saying that Warrington were going to sign him. Town were never mentioned. George Graham used to give us our work every morning and this particular day he had only got back to Workington at two in the morning after signing Jim from Widnes. He told us everything and swore us to secrecy. I couldn't wait until I got to the telephone box to call Arthur Brooks and the story was all over the paper the next day.

"Every time I tipped off a paper I would get a £20 cheque in the post. George accused me of blabbing and told me I was the only person he had told. I kept a straight face and just denied it. I told him someone at Widnes must have leaked the story.

"I used to give stories to Jack Bentley, at the *Daily Express* too. When Tom Mitchell got back he read everything in the papers and he was furious. He came storming into the dressing room and started shouting: 'There's a rotten apple in this club and I'm going to find out who he is. Who's the rotten apple? I want to know.' I wasn't worried as I hadn't told anybody. None of the players knew. I kept it all to myself. Tom took me to one side and asked me to find out who it was and I told him I was really angry too.

'Wait until I get my hands on him,' Tom said. He never found out and I was getting £20 every time I called a newspaper.

"Tom was very cross with me for something else. I was sent off 14 times in my career. Usually for second tackles and stiff arm tackles, things like that. I was once out of the game for three months after being banned for 14 matches playing for Town. I had two hearings in one weekend. I had been sent off in a match against Swinton on Good Friday and then again at Salford playing on Easter Monday – twice in three days.

"Swinton used to have this full back who would do four or five side steps before he got to you so I thought to myself, you're not getting past me and he ended up on the floor. I went to Headingley with a bad record already. Town had an awful disciplinary record and it was really hurting us. On Easter Monday on our way to Salford, Tom Mitchell told the driver to pull into a layby and he walked up and down the bus banging on all the headrests saying: 'Now look, this has to stop. If anyone else gets sent off I will personally fine them.'

"I hadn't even been on the field for 15 minutes when the ref sent me off. Tom was waiting in the tunnel and he really laid in to me. When I came back, the secretary of Town back then was JJ Hodgson. Tom had fined me £250, which was a lot of money back then, and JJ told me to pay it off at £50 a week. Remember I wasn't playing rugby either so I had lost that too. After paying the first one, JJ would say to me: 'You're all right, Smiler I'll pay it for you.' So he paid it all and no one ever found out.

"Me and Boxer found ways of winning scrums legally and sometimes illegally but we wanted that ball and usually we got it. We gave some penalties away but we were cute about it and didn't do it in front of our own sticks. Most of the time, we got away with it. As a young lad Boxer would listen to everything I said and I liked that. After a match he was a joker. He liked a laugh and a crack. I remember breaking my arm once after I had stiff-armed someone. I had a really smart long sleeved white shirt which was expensive but when the plaster was put on I had to cut the sleeve off right at the top of my arm.

"When the plaster was taken off I didn't throw the shirt away. It was my favourite shirt and it was still really smart. So I carried on wearing it. And when I took my jumper off in the dressing room there was one sleeve missing. Boxer thought that was really funny. We had a lot of laughs about that.

"Boxer was one of the best scrum halves I played with or against. I would compare him to Roger Millward. They were similar players but Roger was a bit bigger. Boxer was a live wire and it was very hard to tackle him. He was nimble and could weave in and out of people and he was a good passer of the ball. He was a great tackler and to be honest, he could do everything. Town had a great team back then with a big pack. He should have won a lot more Great Britain caps. We played the odd time together for Cumbria and we always got our fair share of the ball.

"Boxer is held in the highest esteem throughout the game. Whitehaven built their team around him. I knew right away what a good player he was going to be. Boxer was very nippy and you had to follow him because we all knew he would make lots of breaks and then he would be looking around to offload the ball. With him being so small he was very hard to get hold of. Boxer was a very good player who tackled well above his weight."

Spending an afternoon with Smiler is an agreeable experience involving lots of laughter and some bewilderment as he recounts unlikely adventures which one might think contain a hint of exaggeration and give you a feeling of what it might have been like to have lived a life like Oliver Reed. His repertoire of tales seem unlimited and even more extensive than those of his old team-mate Spanky McFarlane, though he would probably argue the point. Smiler laughs before making brief and tantalising references to his career as a boxing champion, his acquaintance with a reigning Miss World, a £10 incentive to knock an opponent unconscious, a match at St Helens, where 22,000 watched befuddled and wondering where the ball was before it turned up under a prop forward's shirt and the day he picked up £501 for winning a single match. The tales are neverending.

"I remember watching Smiler playing with Brian Edgar and Ike Southward for Cumberland," recalls Boxer. "I was graced when I went to Town because a lot of the players were Kells lads from off my street. I was walking into Derwent Park to play with people I knew. Smiler took me under his wing. He was a back of the bus man who was a seasoned professional but he put his arms around me and greeted me into the team. If I got into any bother on the pitch, he was the first one to run in and help me out. Smiler showed me a few moves that would help us to win the ball in the scrum and he would warn me before matches who to look out for. I was spoilt for hookers because when Smiler left for Barrow, Alan Banks took over and he was a great player too. I had all the lads to protect me. It was a privilege to play with Smiler and I really looked up to him."

Peter Gorley, the Great Britain back row forward, who was transferred from Workington Town to St Helens for £22,000 in 1979. 'When Boxer was my captain for Workington or Cumbria, he commanded respect and he got that from every single player. He is without doubt the best scrum half I ever played with or against in my career.'

CHAPTER 26

My brother, Boxer

By Peter Gorley
Second row forward - Workington Town, St Helens, Cumbria, England
and Great Britain

I respect Boxer and I always have done. On the field he was a winner – he would do anything to win and sometimes he might bend the rules but so did everybody. He is a great lad and I can't speak too highly of him. We played against each other a few times when we were amateurs and I knew him as a good player back then but we weren't friends. Even then you could see all the potential he had – Boxer was just a kid and he wasn't that big but it was obvious that he could do things. He was very quick, I remember that.

When you first sign professional, if you have potential, like Boxer had, all the other players and the coaches bring it out of you. My philosophy has always been that if you can't play with better players then you probably aren't as good as you think you are. When I first went to St Helens, I got stripped in the dressing room, ready to go out and I looked around me and I was surrounded by household names. I thought I could play, you have to think that, and I said to myself, if I can't play here, what do I do? Go back to Workington? It was a big hurdle and I just had to fit in and hit the ground running and fortunately I did, though it could have turned the other way.

Boxer had the chance to go to Wigan and Warrington and myself and my brother Les phoned him, telling him to go. He would have been a big success but I guess he didn't want to leave Cumbria.

Everybody respected Boxer and not just in our team, in every other team throughout the game. We knew when we went out on that field playing for Town or Cumbria we had faith, respect and trust in every one of our players. We knew we weren't just a match for every other team - we knew we could beat them.

When Boxer was my captain for Workington or Cumbria, he commanded respect and he got that from every single player. We all knew he would give 110 per cent in every game - he was that kind of player. Boxer never backed off anyone. The bigger they were, the better he liked it. Tackling, well he tackled Jim Mills and Phil Lowe, two of the biggest men in the game many a time. As soon as they got the ball he was right at them, just like a Yorkshire Terrier, snapping away. Once he got hold of someone he would never let go. No team liked to come to Workington and it didn't matter who they were, Leeds or Wigan or St Helens, anyone.

I am not just saying this because he is my mate but he is without doubt the best scrum half I ever played with or against in my career. I played with Andy Gregory for Great Britain and he was one of the best but if you put Boxer in the great Widnes or Wigan sides he played for, he would have been just as good. They were different players and Andy was a bit chunkier but he wasn't as quick as Boxer and don't forget, he played with teams of internationals.

I missed Alex Murphy but I played against Roger Millward who was an all-time great and coming to the end of his career. It is difficult to compare different players but Boxer was more creative than Roger. He could do things without thinking, either on his own or with other players in the team. Boxer would just work out an opening that no one else had seen and just go himself or he could bring someone with him in a planned move just like the try he set up when I put in Ray Wilkins to score in the Lancashire Cup Final when we beat Wigan.

Boxer was his own player and he could do anything he wanted. For example, he could put a chip over the top and go and catch it, no one ever does that now. He often did that – he was so sharp. And Boxer was a great thinker on the field - he could see things other players didn't. In the Lancashire Cup final, Boxer was the best player on the park yet everyone contributed, it was a great team performance. We were all so focused that day although no one else thought we could ever win.

Boxer could make a try out of nothing. There are not many players around with the ability to do that. He was never cocky or big-headed but I am sure in his mind he thought he was number one and that's the right way to think. In all my career I never played with or against a better scrum half. He was the best. Just ask anybody - on his day he was peerless, a class player who could do anything. You could have a tight match and just like that, he was away and making something happen. At Town he was part of a good side and we all knew how great he was. All our team felt the same way.

Wherever we went, it didn't matter where, everybody knew and respected Boxer. You couldn't forget him, the way he played and with his trademark long blonde hair and that name – Boxer. He was a complete one-off.

He is a good lad too and I just can't speak highly enough of him, not just as a wonderful player but as a person. Boxer is the kind of man who you will never forget and anyone who knows him is lucky. I was fortunate to have played rugby with him so that is even better for me.

He is a friend but more like a brother and that's it. That is the way we will always feel about each other, for as long as we are alive, and I am sure he will say the same about me and Les. He is just that type of guy and that was what we were like on the field – we looked after each other and we had a bit of banter. He often calls me and gives me a load of abuse and, of course, it's all in good fun.

He wasn't a reckless player though he has very diminutive and he certainly put himself about and in situations where he could get really hurt. He was an easy target. As I have said before, Andy Gregory was much stockier, he was like a miniature prop forward but if Boxer had had that build he probably wouldn't have been the same player.

He is easily the best scrum half I ever played with. I have played against the very best scrum halves including top Aussies such as Peter Sterling when he played at Hull but Boxer was a match for anyone. He had such a will to win. Don't forget, a lot of these other scrum halves played with a team of world-beaters from 1 to 13. If you look at the Australian team Sterling played for and think to yourself, what would he have been like playing for Whitehaven, for example, like Boxer did. That is where you find the depth of them. Some Australians were world-beaters when they played in Test matches but when they came here and played for club sides they just blended in and didn't look anything special. Mal Meninga, who I played with at Saints, was an exception. He had everything – pace, power and skill and he was such a good person, a real gentleman.

Boxer is a good lad and I love him like a brother. I have spent some of the best times of my life with Boxer Walker. As a player we all loved him. When we went away for matches on the back of the bus there would be me, Boxer, our Les, Eddie Bowman, Derek McMillan and Ralph Calvin in a group. We were always together, home, away or at training, there was always plenty of banter between us and no bad words or animosity - we never fell out. I will never forget the player he was and the person he is. He would do anything for anyone. We are great mates. He is not just my friend, I love him - he is my brother.

Postscript

Boxer is a writer's dream and spending time with him is always a pleasant experience. His memory is amazing - he has a quick wit and he never takes anything too seriously. A smile is never far from his face and, often, in common with most great sportsmen, he is of the opinion that his rugby league career wasn't anything special and hasn't had much to do with him. I was in the right place at the right time he claims, and if you saw him play you know, for sure, that it is nonsense.

Sharing his life and listening to his amazing memories has been a great privilege. Boxer's modesty is bordering on the absurd and you have to keep prodding him, pushing him and giving him no place to go other than give his personal and first-hand accounts of his life which are always fascinating and full of honesty.

Occasionally, and mostly when he is giving credit to other people, he might get carried away with his reminiscences which would usually result in spectacular changes of subject as a thought crosses his mind that he is eager to get out in case it might slip away and never be remembered again. Order and organisation are paramount to any writer. You start at the beginning, where he was born, his family and his early influences, carrying on to playing with his friends at Kells, and continuing through all those glorious memories, full of great triumphs and frequent examples of bad decisions and excessive drinking followed by mortal hangovers when he still performed like a champion. There is no doubt that he was once a highly-qualified expert in all matters pertaining to irresponsible behaviour. No matter how hard you might try it is impossible not to like him. He is charming, modest and you have the feeling that looking ahead longer than five minutes into the future might be too long for him.

So his recollections can be haphazard so Boxer might be talking about his friendship with Billy Starkey and you are taken right back to a classroom at St Mary's where he is being caned by a teacher, six of the best, and his description is so real you can almost feel the pain on your own fingers. Then without warning, he might pause, before leaping into the future and you find yourself sitting alongside him in Great Britain's dressing room and right at the heart of things and surrounded by legendary players. It has all been quite wonderful. Now the trouble is, when you transcribe all those memories, you are left with more than 20 hours of interviews and a charitable way of describing them would be disorganised.

So here is what happened. This book is finished and the printer tells me I am past the deadline and he needs the completed manuscript by yesterday - I am having one last look at the interviews, one final read and I keep coming across throw-away comments made by Boxer, often isolated observations, that didn't find their way into the book, yet they should be. But where can I put them? I haven't got time to rewrite anything but it's a shame not to share them with you, so here they are, mostly in Boxer's own words, and in no particular order, random thoughts and observations all mixed up together just as he shared them with me last winter, one last insight into his incredible life. This chapter includes a contribution from the Wales and Great Britain forward Jim Mills and is concluded by a personal tribute from former *Whitehaven News* sports editor Alan Irving who diligently recorded Boxer's career going right back to his days as a youngster at Kells and concluding with his international appearances.

§

I was good friends with a rugby league writer called John Robinson, who worked for the *Sunday People.* He called me when it was our close season to tell me that an Australian team were interested in signing me for the summer. He said that it wasn't one of the big teams like Manly, just a district side somewhere in the outback. I was only a county player and John told me I would do well and that all the fans would love me.

It was all expenses paid, all the flights and everything, they even had a job lined up for me. Everything would have been taken care of. I knew I would have got permission from the bosses at the pit. The pit manager was a rugby fanatic and he would have approved it and given me leave of absence and my job would be safe if it hadn't worked out. Looking back, I often wonder what would have happened if I had gone. That is one of my big regrets in life. I should have tried it. Now later on in life it is hitting me. What would it have been like?

§

I remember once when Geoff Fletcher was playing for Workington Town. He was a fantastic fella and a great player who ended up being the coach and manager of Huyton and kept them going almost single-handed. He wore a wig off the field so me and some of the other younger players decided we were going to pinch it. Well, Geoff came into the dressing room and he had got wind of it - he just stopped, steadied himself and took off his wig right there in front of us and threw it and it landed perfectly on one of the pegs.

§

My favourite referee was Billy Thompson. You could always have a crack with Billy. If I felt he wasn't giving us much, I would say to him: 'Come on, Billy, give us the crack, you're giving us nothing.' Billy would just take no notice and tell me to get on with my own game. I remember one time there was a break in play and I asked him: 'Billy, if I call you an idiot would you send me off.' He said: 'Yes, I would, Boxer. There is no room in our game for that especially to a referee.' I said: 'What if I just think you are an idiot, would that be all right?'

He thought about it and told me: 'Well, I suppose there's not much I could do about that, if you're only thinking it.' I said to him: 'OK, Billy, I think you're an idiot.' Billy just started laughing his head off. That was the sort of man he was.

I had a great rapport with Billy Thompson. He was a player's referee. Everybody liked him. He was always very fair but I am sure he had a soft spot for Town, not in his decisions of course. If we were defending a small lead and time was running out against a top side full of internationals, and they were pressing our line, he would be saying to us: 'Come on, lads, there's not long to go, don't let the buggers score now. Keep them out.' That was typical of Billy.

Sometimes, if someone had belted me and I was getting angry he would whisper to me: 'Don't worry, Boxer, I've seen that. Get him back and I'll let it go but after that, no more or you will both be in trouble.' I remember another time, Billy blew up when we had a scrum and I couldn't understand why. I said under my breath: 'Billy, are you bloody blind?' and I walked away but he started blowing his whistle. Billy was fuming so I guess he must have heard me. He shouted to me: 'Hey you, get over here. What did you say to me?'

I said, really loudly, so all the players could hear: 'Bloody hell, Billy, are you deaf as well as blind.'

Everyone was laughing and though Billy went crackers with me, he couldn't stop laughing himself.

§

Reg Bowden, speaking in February, 2017, said: "Boxer was one of the best scrum halves in the history of the game. He was an unbelievable player and if I was picking a team he would be the first name down. He was so fearless and such a good tackler - when you played against him you would think he was 6ft 6in not 5ft 6in.

"On top of that, he had a great footballing brain. Boxer was the playmaker of everything Workington Town and Whitehaven did and he would always be there, leading from the front. He was a dirty little bugger, he would admit that himself. He wouldn't back down from anyone, no matter how big they were. We were very similar players and I think we put an extra 2,000 on the gate. Lots of fans would turn up to watch us knock seven bells out of each other.

"When Les Gorley came to Widnes, he was always telling us what it was like playing in the same team as Boxer and what an inspiration he was. That was why he was such a good captain. He was an expert in every part of the game. The best thing about Boxer is what a great person he is. After every game that we played against each other, when I went to the bar, he was always there waiting to buy me a pint. I know Warrington were desperate to sign him and if they had, Boxer would have been a huge success and won lots of caps for Great Britain."

§

I remember when I first began working at Haig Pit. I started on the screens on the surface for a couple of weeks before doing a 20-day course on safety and stuff like that. Because I was a rugby player I got away with murder – they used to have my picture up on the wall. I was always falling asleep at work or getting up to things and fooling about. The bosses were always threatening to sack me but they never did. All the managers were rugby daft and there were a lot of Town and Haven players there, including my best mate and stand-off at Town, Derek McMillan – we used to supply them with season tickets and they would help us get off early to get to training. I was always getting caught asleep. I just used to get my head down.

§

It makes me laugh all this talk about special diets. I remember once travelling with the county team to play Yorkshire at Hull KR. We had already beaten Lancashire at Barrow and if we won this game we would win the championship. We stopped at Forton service station, on the M6, near Lancaster, for a bite to eat. Everyone was having scrambled eggs – they didn't want anything heavy on their stomachs but me and Les Gorley ate a pile of chips and a steak and kidney pie each.

Well, we went on the field and played great and we won that match and Cumbria were the champions. Some of the older players used to say sherry and eggs were best before a game but I am a big believer that if you're in the right frame of mind, that is more important.

In the teams I played in, a lot of the players were sick before they went on the field. So having a decent meal was doing your stomach a bit of good because there was something there to come up easily. You wouldn't be retching. It was just nerves before you went out.

§

When I was at Whitehaven we played Fulham at the Recre and Iain MacCorquodale was playing with my mate Reg Bowden who was their player-coach. It was not long after I got in the Great Britain squad to play New Zealand and I think we beat them 6-0. If I remember right, John Doran, who is better known as Duffy, got the tries for us. He has a pub now in Whitehaven called The Stump on High Road. Normally, every time I got tackled I got roughed up - we all did that – but not Corky. He tackled me and as I was getting up he said: Congratulations Boxer, on getting in the Great Britain squad. I couldn't believe it. You never knew what he would come up with next. It was so typical of him.

§

There was a reporter at *The Whitehaven News* called Bruce Foster. Everyone really liked and trusted him. He was a gentle person who was loved by all the players. There was an end-of-season do at the Recre and we had a few beers and we were really enjoying ourselves. So I got some of the lads to carry him out on the field and we got some rope from somewhere and tied him to the posts at the Kells end. We left him there for a while and eventually a couple of directors freed him. He just came back into the bar laughing and started supping again.

§

Paul Grimes, an excellent back row forward, who played more than 200 games for St Helens, played with Boxer at Whitehaven. He said: "As we get older, fans' perception of how we were as players can become a little distorted. Fans often say that we were a lot faster, tougher and better than we really were. But not Boxer. He really was as good as people remember him. It was a massive coup when Whitehaven signed him and with all due respect to a club that I have great affection for, he was wanted by a number of very big clubs. Before that, I only knew Boxer from playing against him. It was a case of what a little bugger he was and that I wished he played for my team. When he signed for Haven, we got along really well. I've said many times that when Boxer was the player coach and he asked me to lead the team as the club captain, it was a great honour which I will never forget. I have very special memories of my time playing with Boxer."

§

In a First Division fixture in 1977, Boxer kicked a drop goal in Town's 1-0 victory at Wilderspool against Warrington. A 1-0 scoreline has only happened five times in the history of professional rugby league.

§

In 1978, Town won the Wigan Sevens. There was me, Ian Wright, Billy Pattinson, Corky, Paul Charlton, Ian Hartley, Bob Blackwood and Alan Banks. We beat Widnes in the first round and we slaughtered Leeds in the semi-final - John Holmes was their scrum half - I think John was too big to play scrum half. We beat St Helens in the final and it was drawn at full-time. There was sudden-death and we were on their 25 and I dropped a goal to win it. I remember when it went over, big Bobby lifted me up in the air - we were all so chuffed.

§

We were playing away at Widnes and we had to beat them to stay up in the First Division which is what the Super League was called back then. On the bus, Tom Mitchell got us all together and told us he was putting on a special bonus that he would pay out if we could win and stay up. When we got there and started getting off the bus, I said to him: 'Tom, I want your hat if we win.' He didn't answer me. It was a Texas sombrero style velvet hat that he wore all the time. After that I completely forgot about it. I think we won that game 3-2. When we got on the bus, and before we set off back to Cumbria, Tom was at the front and he was telling us: 'You were great today lads. I am chuffed to bits and proud of you all.' And Tom took off his hat and threw it down to me, towards the back of the bus where I caught it.

§

One night, not long after I had signed for Whitehaven, I got a message asking me to contact Dougie Laughton who was the coach of Widnes who had a team of internationals. He told me he wanted me to be his scrum half and that they had a young lad who wasn't quite ready – his name was Andy Gregory who turned out to be one of the greatest ever. Dougie wanted me to cause trouble at Whitehaven and to try to engineer a move. I was very flattered but I couldn't go. Haven were my home town team and all my mates were here and I was never going to do the dirty on my team.

§

Boxer Walker is the best uncapped scrum half in the country – Alex Murphy, speaking in his column in the *Daily Mirror,* Monday, November 1, 1977.

§

Jim Mills, prop forward, Widnes, Bradford Northern, Halifax, Workington Town, Wales and Great Britain said: "I loved playing with Boxer. He was very good and very competitive and he had a heart as big as a lion. He should have a played a lot more for Great Britain, and I know it is difficult to get recognised up there in Cumbria. My scrum half at Widnes was Reggie Bowden and he was a great player too. They were much the same and Boxer always gave Reggie a hard time. I don't think any scrum half enjoyed playing against Boxer.

"I think Boxer is right up there with the greatest scrum halves ever. What a tackler he was - it was like having another forward on the field. He used to upset a lot of the forwards most of the time - they didn't like getting tackled by someone so small. Boxer always had plenty to say on the field and he was a very good leader who geed everyone up. Most great scrum halves can all yap, can't they? I loved playing with him because you know he would never let you down, even if the rest of us were having an off day, he would always give 100 per cent. It was great when I played up at Workington and we got promotion, I loved it up there. Boxer was definitely one of the best scrum halves I played with or against in my career, as good as any scrum half I have ever seen."

§

In my day, if I didn't come off with blood on my shirt I didn't think I had been playing. I remember one time something happened when we were playing at Leeds and someone hit me right across the face. Nine times out of 10 if you get a facial injury, especially around your eyes, your nose will bleed so your natural instinct is to blow out of your nose to clear everything. The trouble is, air rushes up and you can black out – what a mess I was in. I ended up in hospital for four days, and the following weekend we played Widnes and doctors had told me I couldn't play but I didn't tell anybody and just played anyway.

§

The toughest scrum half I ever played against was Reggie Bowden at Widnes. How he never played for Great Britain I will never know. If you could pick 13 Reg Bowdens, you could beat any team in the world.

§

Malcolm Flynn, who was one of the nicest lads you could ever meet off the field, would get in my team any time. There was no pointing or moaning from him, never. If I was captaining Cumbria and I wanted him to take the ball in there were no questions, he was there every time and I knew he would do it over and over again and never complain at all. He would take it all day.

I was respected as a captain. To be the captain when we won two county championships, the coach might have spoken to as many as nine players to find out who they wanted as captain and apparently they all wanted me. That was great. I remember captaining Cumbria when we went to Yorkshire and beat them to win the championship - we had to get changed on the bus, and everyone was so certain that we would get hammered, the officials didn't even bother taking the trophy to present to us.

§

A few years ago I was invited to speak on a forum with Alex Murphy, and Les and Peter Gorley. It was a charity event at Wigton and we all gave our money back. Alex couldn't believe a story Les was saying about Cumbria beating Yorkshire and especially when we said that most of us had done a shift down the mine before we set off. I remember after that win in Yorkshire all the players were celebrating and the officials wanted to set off which we could understand because the match was at Hull KR, which is almost 200 miles from Cumbria. All the lads wanted to stay and because I was the captain I had to sort it out which I managed to do. In the end they had to kick us out and I even got them to stop the bus at Forton service station at Lancaster on the M6 where we had a few more drinks and a bit of a kip. We got back to Cumbria around noon the next day.

§

When I first broke into Town's first team, I wanted to do everything right. One of my first long trips was away to Hull and we were staying overnight in a hotel and I wanted to be seen as Mr Goody Goody in front of all the players, the coach Eppie Gibson and all the directors. I got to my room early in the night and just sat on the bed and watched television and I never had a drop to drink. In the morning there was a knock on my door and there were cratefuls of bottles all piled up outside my room. They had been put there by Smiler Allen and Eddie Bowman. I looked up and one of the Town directors Harry Walker was walking along the corridor as I fell over all the bottles - he thought I had drunk them all. He said he was going to make sure I would never get in the team again. Thankfully, they soon put Harry right about what had happened.

§

One time we had been playing at Widnes and all the Town players went to Jim Mills' night club. It was a great night and we didn't want to leave so me and my mate Bob Blackwood sneaked out when the directors weren't looking and tried to let the tyres down on the bus so we could stay longer but I think we had drunk that much we couldn't do it. It was a special night and Jim laid everything on for us for free. What a great man.

§

I used to love winding up players. I did that all the time. Sometimes it might mean that they are not concentrating on their game. I might tackle a player and say something like: 'Get up you soft bugger. Is that all you've got?' I had to stand back right away of course. It was just banter - there was nothing nasty in it. I would always shake hands with all the players after the match and we would have a pint together. I remember once we beat Barrow at Craven Park and Spanky McFarlane was playing for them. I was best of mates with him and he put his knees right in my back. I could hardly breathe. I tried to laugh it off because I didn't want him to know he had hurt me. Eventually I just ran it off.

§

Boxer was the eighth player to be inaugurated into Whitehaven's Hall of Fame. The club presented him with a framed document celebrating his achievements. Here is the testimony in full.

Arnold 'Boxer' Walker was born at Woodhouse, Whitehaven, in 1952 and played his junior rugby league for the Kells club. He signed professional in 1971 for Workington Town and transferred to Whitehaven in January, 1980, for a Cumbrian record transfer fee of £30,000. He played his first game for Haven on the 20th January 1980 against Dewsbury and dropped a goal on his debut.

In his first full season for Haven (1980/1981) Arnie kicked 22 drop goals, more than anyone else in the league. He captained Haven to promotion to the First Division that season gaining it with a glorious win against York on Easter Monday, 20th April, 1981. In October 1981, Arnie suffered a serious neck injury at the Recreation Ground playing against Hull KR. It was feared that he would remain paralysed but he remarkably recovered and six weeks later returned to playing for Haven. During that season he also took over the coaching reins from Phil Kitchin for a short time. He again led Haven to promotion in 1983. Sadly, a more serious neck injury in a game away to Widnes on the 28th August, 1983, ended his career.

Arnie was selected for Great Britain and played in the Third Test against New Zealand on 15th November 1980 as Great Britain won 10-2 to level the series. He made the most tackles of anyone that day (28). A few months later he represented England against France in a 1-5 defeat.

He played for Cumbria on 19 occasions (seven when with Haven) and made his county debut against the Australians at Whitehaven on the 24th October, 1973. He captained the county to the county championship and led them to a 9-3 win over the touring New Zealanders in 1980 scoring the winning try in the last minute.

Arnie played 70 games for Haven before injury cut short his career and in his combined career for Haven and Town played a total of 273 games, scoring 64 tries, 44 goals and 70 drop goals. He played in four Lancashire Cup finals being on the winning side only once but receiving the man of the match awards in two of those finals. In 1998, he was selected in the Whitehaven 'Immortals team. Arnie is the eighth player to be inducted into the Vice Presidents' Hall of Fame.

§

Eddie Bowman tells the story that Town were once packing down near the touchline in a tight game and you could hear a pin drop. This fan shouts: 'Come on Bowman, get off the field, you useless bugger.' All the players could hear it and I couldn't stop laughing. When I was putting the ball in I said to Eddie: 'Did you hear that?' And before he could answer me, the same fan shouts out: 'And Bowman, on your way off, bring that Walker with you, he's bloody hopeless too.' All the pack couldn't stop laughing.

§

Not long after Great Britain came back from Australia in 1979, Tom Mitchell telephoned me to say I had been asked to play for a Widnes Select 13 against a Great Britain team to raise funds for John Burke's testimonial. John suffered a double neck fracture when he was just 21. Dougie Laughton was our coach. I was playing with my big mate Reggie Bowden and he came up to me before the kick-off and suggested that he would play scrum half and I would play stand-off in the first half and we would change over at half-time. But in the first half there was an A teamer playing on our wing and he was mucking about, trying to tackle someone and when I came in to help, he hit me by mistake and split my eye wide open. There was only 30 minutes gone. I needed eight stitches and I had to come off. All the crowd booed me because of all the battles I had had with Reggie.

§

I really loved Tom Mitchell and I learnt so much from him. At Town, we trained on Tuesdays and Thursdays and we used to get lots of fans watching. Tom told all the players that we must always speak to the fans. They are paying your wages, Tom would tell us all. He taught us to never take them for granted and always mingle with the fans after training and matches. I loved that side of being a pro.

§

I remember playing Warrington at Wilderspool in a night match, in the 1976 Lancashire Cup semi-final and we drew 9-9. They had a really classy side including Bob Eccles and John Bevan. They had a really good full back called Derek Finnigan, who was running right at me and my stand-off Derek McMillan, who was a brilliant player. He said to me: 'You go down below and I'll go over the top and we'll both flatten him. So he's coming charging towards us and I thought to myself, to hell with this, I'm not going down below and getting this guy's size nines in my face. So I went up top, the same as Derek McMillan and Finnegan ducked. I went over the top and hit my own stand-off and broke his cheekbone. I remember Alex Murphy, who was Warrington's coach, went to hospital with him to make sure he was all right.

After the match, I got talking with Alex before Derek went to the hospital and he asked me what training we had done that day: I said: 'What do you mean training - I was down't pit at 5.15 in the morning. Aye, one o'clock up from the pit, and in the coach and straight here. He couldn't believe it.

§

We were training one night at Derwent Park in the middle of winter when the miners had been on strike for nine weeks and there were electricity cuts and we couldn't use the floodlights. Ike was the coach back then and he arranged for two cars to light up the pitch with their headlights and someone kept the engines running. The thing was the lights didn't work too well and there were a lot of shadows and dark patches. All of a sudden Ike couldn't find any of us – the whole team was hiding in one of the corners where he couldn't see us. We all loved Ike and he just laughed along with us.

§

For a long time at the start of my career I would always have raw eggs and sherry before a game. That's what all the old pros did. I have seen some of them take a tot of brandy in the dressing room saying that it would get their adrenaline going. Others would use smelling salts that we called vapours and sal volatile. When it was really cold, we would cover ourselves with stuff like Ralgex and Fiery Jack. When I played with Smiler Allen, I remember he had a lot of pain in his neck because of all the stick he got in the scrums. He would say to me in the dressing room: 'Paint it all over us.'

§

Ecky Bell coached me a lot when I first joined Workington and I was playing mainly in the A team. We always started training by jogging around the field and he might sometimes ask the players, one by one, to stop and choose what exercises we all had to do – it might be press-ups or sit-ups, something like that. When it was my turn, he asked me what I was doing and told him: Deep breathing exercises, Ecky. He just shook his head and everyone fell about.

§

When I got my back injury and I had to stop playing, I think I still had a few years left, even if it meant playing in the A team to help the youth coming up. I could have lasted a couple more years. But the plus side was that I finished at the top even though it was a bad injury.

§

Whenever we travelled away I was always messing about on the bus. I was a bit of a clown – that was my character. In the changing rooms, right up until twenty to three, I was still being daft. But one second after twenty to three I would switch on and I would be completely focused, and just thinking about the match. I would stop fooling about. When a lot of the ex-players get-together, Spanky often says: 'I didn't realise, lads, how old I was getting, until I saw this little bugger here when we were playing in the county side together. Arnold was only a little eight-year-old when I was 19. And to think, he was only our mascot, and now he's here, alongside me in the same Cumbria team.'

§

I remember being at a do recently somewhere in Lancashire and this stranger recognised me and he couldn't get over how different I was since he had seen me playing. I was with a couple of lads I had played with at Whitehaven and I told the fan: 'I had brilliant long hair when I played for Town but I lost it when I went to Haven. Every time I passed the ball to these sods they dropped it and I used to get hold of my hair and start pulling it out.

§

Alan Irving, long-standing West Cumbrian sports reporter, who covered Whitehaven and reported on Cumbria's matches for the nationals, made the following tribute to Boxer: "Some are born to be rugby players. So it was with Arnold Walker. As a little lad who was mascot to the all-conquering Kells amateur team and particularly to his idol, Paul Charlton, Arnold wanted to follow his dreams and emulate his heroes. And so he truly did. Having seen most of his games for both West Cumberland senior clubs, along with Cumbria county, I remember this Whitehaven marra, universally known as Boxer, as a player who was able to combine toughness and a never-say-die spirit with a natural ability to play the 13-a-side code at the highest level.

"I remember and admire his fearlessness, at times his bravery knew no bounds, for in an era when everything went, it took more than talent and a mastery of scrum half skills to survive and achieve the honours Arnie Walker did when rugby league was probably at its most brutal. Boxer was one of the top number sevens of the day, in my mind he did enough to earn more than the one Great Britain cap awarded him under Johnny Whiteley, but no matter, that appearance against New Zealand placed him alongside Dick Huddart, Bill Holliday, Phil Kitchin, and Vince Gribbin as Whitehaven legends to win full Test honours and that will always be a source of great pride.

"One of the most difficult rugby tasks of my journalistic career was getting together with Sam Coulter and Harry Edgar to select the Whitehaven Immortals (dream team) to help celebrate the club's 50th anniversary in 1998. Arnold deservedly took the number seven shirt, though it could easily have been the Welsh wizard Billy Banks or the Kiwi international Clayton Friend, but in the end we opted for the la'al marra alongside the brilliant Phil Kitchin, two local lads as halfback partners, who represented their country, and it would be difficult to argue against them.

"Besides that combative spirit, I shall always remember Boxer's flair for the unexpected, illustrated so superbly and dramatically in the last minute try he scored in captaining Cumbria to victory over New Zealand, and the sheer rapture that engulfed The Recre. But another more poignant memory concerns a certain game against high-flying Hull Kingston Rovers again on the Recreation Ground.

"It was a Saturday afternoon match, I was doing a 'running' report for the evening Sports Final for the *News & Star,* the sister paper of the *Whitehaven News.*

"At a critical stage of the match, Walker was suddenly felled in a clash with one of the Robins international forwards and he lay motionless for a very long time. In the Press Box we feared the worse and I was dispatched to the touchline, but it looked so bad that I actually ventured on to the pitch only to incur the wrath of the Hull KR coach, the legendary Roger (The Dodger) Millward.

"Happily, Boxer regained consciousness and after what seemed like an eternity, he was stretchered off and taken to hospital. Although I was in the wrong, Millward later apologised to me for the telling off, that was a measure of the man but our concern for the victim of that hefty clash was also a measure of the worth of Boxer Walker both as a man and to the game of rugby league.

"A few days later I was able to visit Arnold in the West Cumberland Hospital, he was sitting up, bright as a button, his only concern was how long it would take him to return to the fray. It was so typical of the man.

"Once I called him Little Big Man. As time passes, the description seems all the more fitting. His achievements for Workington Town, Whitehaven, Cumbria and Great Britain are well documented in this excellent book, which I was honoured to check for Mike - suffice to say Boxer had already entered the Hall of Cumbrian RL legends."

Acknowledgements

By Arnold 'Boxer' Walker

When Mike Gardner told me he wanted to write my life story, I wasn't too keen at first. It was all so long ago. I asked myself, who would remember me? Who would be interested? But I agreed and I am so glad I did. Now first you need to know I am not writing this. I am just sitting down with Mike and we are chatting together while his recorder is on. Later Mike will put together what I am saying. I haven't written much since I was a teenager at St Begh's 50 years ago and I am too old to start now.

The thing I was most worried about was how my life would fill a book. What would I say to him? What could I remember? I needn't have worried because it has been a great experience and not at all stressful, and just like having a crack with a friend over a few beers. He seemed to have a gift for bringing memories out of me and when we talked, the questions he asked, opened doors inside my head and all my experiences came back to me, I don't know how but that is what happened. I started thinking I would run out of things to say in half an hour and now he tells me he has more than 20 hours of interviews.

I asked only two things from him – firstly that I wouldn't come across as arrogant or big-headed and secondly that all those wonderful people who have helped me along the way would get the credit they deserved – all those great players, coaches, family and friends – without them I wouldn't have achieved anything. Mike made only one demand from me – that I should tell the truth. He asked me to trust him and he insisted that he wanted to know everything including some of the things that I have done that I am not very proud of. You should probably know that I still haven't read any of this book. He kept asking me to get involved in his ideas for what we should talk about and how he planned to tell my story - I don't know why but I kept saying no. Mike would bring me his writing all neatly printed out but I didn't want to read it. I trusted him completely and I know he won't let me down.

He would often tease me and he says that the phrase that he heard most is: here's a good story for you, Mike, but you can't print it. He tried to explain to me about something called libel and that it was important to him that we don't criticise too much or write things that might upset people, even the families of those who are no longer with us. As I have said already, I didn't want to get involved in that, I just tried to answer all his questions truthfully and I can honestly say I have done that.

When word leaked out around West Cumbria that Mike was writing this book, sometimes friends would stop me in the street and ask me how it was going and wish me all the best. I remember meeting David Lilley, who is a lifelong Haven fan and a really good friend. When I told him Mike was writing it, he was really pleased and he said he had read Mike's biography of Willie Horne and that it was the best rugby league book he had ever read, so I knew I was in good hands.

Mike told me that we would have to write a final chapter where we should thank all the people who have helped make this book possible. He said it would be better coming from me. Firstly, I want to thank some important people who helped me along the way in my rugby career starting with my father and Tom Mitchell, and, of course, my brother-in-law Les, who I love dearly and all the coaches who have inspired me going back to Billy Garratt, Ike Southward, Paul Charlton, Sol Roper, Phil Kitchin, Johnny Whiteley and so many others. As for the players, there are just too many to mention here but Mike tells me that my gratitude is fully explained in this book. I would like to say a personal thank you to all those amazing Cumbrian forwards who looked out for me for all those years – knowing I had all those big men on my side was very special.

Robert Gate is a rugby league historian who has checked Mike's writing or rather my hazy memory and put me right on so many mistakes where I got games and players mixed up. Apparently, we made more than 50 mistakes that Robert corrected, so thank you, Robert. I must thank Helen Thompson, the sports editor of the local newspapers for her support and help with photographs which reminds me to thank Joe Holliday, who also helped with pictures, as did the North West Evening Mail in Barrow, thanks to Sheila Atkinson and Heather Corner. I must also mention Alan Irving, the sports reporter at the *Whitehaven News,* who covered most of my career and who also helped with background research and more photographs. Alan, you always looked after me when I was a player and now you are still doing it after all these years - thank you and to Steve Andrews, the Barrow rugby league historian who was a big help, especially with pictures and I must give special thanks to Dave Bowden and Harry Edgar who were great supporters and advisors.

Mike tells me this book would not have been possible without the help and professionalism of Bob Fowke at YouCaxton Publications, who designed the layout and made the book look so good. The cover was designed by Matthew Jolly and I think you will all agree that it looks really good. I must not forget Paul Charlton for the Foreword and getting back to rugby, I must mention John Short, the fantastic physio who looked after us at Town.

Finally, Ian Gainford, from Kells Rugby League Club, my best friend Billy Starkey, Peter Cropper, Matt Davies, Frank Cassidy, Sheila Aldous, Gerard Richardson, Lee Robinson of Wakefield Trinity Heritage, Stewart Blair, Allen Banks, Phil Hodgson, John Spoor, Peter Hill and Margaret Crosby. So many people have helped which has been a great boost for me and words just don't seem to be enough. Thank you.

Appendix

Boxer Walker's Playing Career

Compiled by Robert Gate

WORKINGTON TOWN

Debut on 24 October, 1971 v Huyton, away, won 7-6 try, sub

Team: Thompson, McQuire (2 goals), Bell, Nicholson, Thornthwaite, Ackerley (L. Gorley), Newall (Walker), Curwen, Allen, McCourt, Bowman, Branthwaite, Shepherd.

Note – first full game was 9-13 loss at Hull Kingston Rovers on 6 November, 1971.
Note – kicked first goal on 23 April, 1973 in 8-12 loss at Huyton.

	Apps	Subs	Tries	Goals	Drop Goals	Points
1971-72	5	2	1	0	0	3
1972-73	14	1	2	1	0	8
1973-74	10	0	4	0	0	12
1974-75	26	0	4	0	0	12
1975-76	34*	0	6	0	3	21
1976-77	34	0	14	0	12	54
1977-78	25	0	11	1	7	42
1978-79	30	0	7	0	8	29
1979-80	13	1	4	0	5	17
TOTALS	191	4	53	2	35	198

*Played in every game

Final game on 8 December, 1979, Lancashire Cup Final at Salford
Workington Town 0 Widnes 11
(Walker was replaced by A. Roper three minutes before end of match).

Lancashire Cup Final 1976
Town 11 Widnes 16 at Wigan

Lancashire Cup Final 1977
Town 16 Wigan 13 at Warrington
(Scored 2 drop goals in final. Kicked drop goals in all four rounds)

Lancashire Cup Final 1978
Town 13 Widnes 15 at Wigan

Lancashire Cup Final 1979
Town 0 Widnes 11 at Salford

Promotion to Division 1 1975-76

WHITEHAVEN

Debut on 20 January, 1980 v Dewsbury, away, won 16-11 drop goal

Team: Dutton (3 goals), Hodgson, Stoddart, Stewart, McQuire, J. O'Neill,
Walker, Rea, Barwise, Fox (Try), Litt, Martin (Try), T. Thompson (Try)

	Apps	Subs	Tries	Goals	Drop Goals	Points
1979-80	11	0	2	0	5	11
1980-81	26	0	4	13	22	60
1981-82	20	1	1	9	7	28
1982-83	11	7	4	19	1	51
1983-84	2	0	0	1	0	2
TOTALS	70	8	11	42	35	152

Final game 28 August, 1983 v Widnes, away, lost 10-44, goal

Promotion to Division 1: 1980-81 and 1982-83

CUMBRIA

Date	Opponents	Venue	Result		Score
24-10-1973	Australians	Whitehaven	Lost		2-28
11-9-1974	Yorkshire	Workington	Won		10-7
18-9-1974	Lancashire	Warringon	Lost		4-29
25-9-1974	Other Nats	Whitehaven	Won	5 goals	19-12
19-11-1975	Yorkshire	Dewsbury	Lost	2 goals	7-10
6-12-1975	Lancashire	Workington	Lost	4 goals 1 try	17-22
20-12-1975	Other Nats	Barrow	Won	1 try	21-13
2-2-1977	Lancashire	Leigh	Lost		14-18
15-2-1977	Yorkshire	Whitehaven	Draw		12-12
1-10-1978	Australians	Barrow	Lost		4-47
11-10-1978	Lancashire	Whitehaven	Won	1 try	16-15
29-8-1979	Yorkshire*	Workington	Won		17-13
3-9-1980	Lancashire*	Barrow	Won		19-16
17-9-1980	Yorkshire*	Hull K.R.	Won	1 try	17-16
8-10-1980	New Zealand*	Whitehaven	Won	1 try	9-3
16-9-1981	Lancashire*	Wigan	Won	1 goal 2 tries	27-15
23-9-1981	Yorkshire*	Whitehaven	Won	1 try	20-10
23-5-1982	Yorkshire*	Castleford	Lost		7-22
30-5-1982	Lancashire*	Workington	Lost		8-46

* captain

TEST MATCH

15 November, 1980   Great Britain 10 New Zealand 2   at Leeds
Team: Burke (2 goals), Drummond (2 tries), Joyner, Evans, Atkinson, Woods, Walker, Skerrett, Elwell, Casey (captain), Adams, P. Gorley, Norton.

INTERNATIONAL MATCH

21 February, 1981   England 1 France 5   at Leeds
Team: Fairbairn (captain, drop goal), Drummond, Joyner, Smith, Fenton, Kelly (Woods), Walker, S. O'Neill, Ward, Case (W. Pattinson), Casey, Potter, Pinner